Jane Waller and Michael Vaughan-Rees are married and live in Waterloo, London, where they are active in the local community and in urban conservation. This is their third book about the Second World War, having previously published *Women in Wartime* (Macdonald Optima, 1987) and *Women in Uniform* (Papermac, 1989).

Jane Waller is a writer and ceramicist. She has also published six fashion books based on material from her large collection of women's magazines, numerous children's stories and poems, and a ceramics book.

Michael Vaughan-Rees designs specialised English language courses for overseas companies, and is also editor of a journal on the teaching of English pronunciation. He writes articles for professional journals and this is his fourth book.

Londoners stretch out on hammocks strung across the tracks at the Elephant and Castle tube station, early October 1940.

OPTIMA

BLITZ

The Civilian War 1940–45

JANE WALLER
AND
MICHAEL VAUGHAN-REES

An OPTIMA book

© Jane Waller and Michael Vaughan-Rees 1990

First published in 1990 by
Macdonald Optima, a division of
Macdonald & Co. (Publishers) Ltd

A member of Maxwell Macmillan Pergamon Publishing Corporation plc

British Library Cataloguing in Publication Data
Stories of the Blitz.
 1. England. Air raids by Germany. Luftwaffe, 1939–1945
 I. Waller, Jane, 1944– II. Vaughan-Rees, Michael
 940. 54212

 ISBN 0-356-18792-6

Macdonald & Co. (Publishers) Ltd
Orbit House
1 New Fetter Lane
London
EC4A 1AR

Typeset in Gill Sans and Parlament by
Leaper & Gard Ltd, Bristol, England

Reproduced, printed and bound in Great Britain by
BPCC Hazell Books
Aylesbury, Bucks, England
Member of BPCC Ltd.

We have made every effort to obtain permission to use the material in this book.
Please contact the Publishers if there are any queries about copyright.

DEDICATION

To all those who tried to stop the bombs
from falling; or who went into action
once they were falling.

CONTENTS

Acknowledgments   viii

Introduction   3

1 In for a hard pounding
  The start of the London blitz, 7–8 September 1940   7

2 Expectations and preparations
  Lead-up to the blitz   31

3 In the roaring centre
  London, September to mid-November 1940   55

4 Coventrated
  Coventry on the night of 15 November 1940   84

5 The provinces   112

6 Civil defence   198

7 Living with the blitz   234

8 London from mid-November 1940 to 1944   272

9 The weapons of revenge   297

Glossary and abbreviations   332

Further reading   337

ACKNOWLEDGMENTS

Our warmest thanks go to the following:

The staff of the Imperial War Museum, especially Dr Christopher Dowling, Phil Reed, Jane Carmichael and Nigel Steel, for their help in finding excellent accounts and photographs, and their support for our three books about wartime Britain.

The Women's Royal Voluntary Service, especially Megan Keeble, for providing valuable material from their archives.

The Salvation Army, especially the archivist, Major Fairbank, for valuable help.

The staff of the London Fire Brigade Museum, especially John Rodwell and Roy Still, for putting us in contact with World War II fire personnel. Thanks also to Jim Trimmer and Peggy Jacobs for providing names of former colleagues.

Harry Jones, editor of the London Ambulance Service Retirement Association *Newsletter*, and former ambulanceman Bert Purdy.

The editors of the following for helping us to contact people with memories of the blitz: *The Salvationist*, the *Journal of The Royal British Legion*, *Home and Country*, *Belfast Telegraph*, *Irish News*, *Birmingham Daily News* and *Birmingham Evening Mail*, *Bristol Evening Post*, *Western Daily Press*, *Western Evening Herald*, *Coventry Evening Telegraph*, *Glasgow Sunday Mail*, *Yorkshire Evening Post*, (Plymouth) *Evening Herald*, (Sheffield) *Star*, *Hastings and St Leonards Observer*, and *Contact* published by the Coventry City Council.

Penny Farthing, Claire Lowry and Joy Talbot; for valuable help in finding new informants, photographs, etc.

The staff of the London History Workshop, especially Doc Rowe and Rosemary Dixon, for letting us use their sound and video archives (and to Cynthia Harton for carrying out the research there on our behalf).

Michael Conway, general secretary of the 1940 Association, for providing useful contacts.

A number of city librarians and archivists, especially D. J. Rimmer, Coventry City Archivist.

John Mortimer, for generously allowing us to quote from his autobiography *Clinging to the Wreckage* (Weidenfeld & Nicolson, 1982: Penguin, 1983).

The publishers of *The Spectator*, for kind permission to quote the poem by Louis MacNeice (reprinted in *Articles of War: The Spectator Book of World War II*, Grafton Books, 1989).

Lewis Blake, for kind permission to quote from *Red Alert: South-East London 1939–1945* (Parvenu Press, Woolwich, 1982).

Les Sutton, for kind permission to quote from *Mainly about Ardwick*.

Cyril Demarne, for kind permission to quote from his book *A Fireman's Tale* (Parents' Centre Publications, no. 28, 1980).

Patrick Cockburn, for kind permission to quote from *Figure of Eight* by Patricia Cockburn (The Hogarth Press).

Collins Publishing Group for kind permission to quote from *The World is a Wedding* by Bernard Kops (Grafton Books) and from *The Harold Nicolson Diaries* (Collins).

Century Hutchinson Publishing Group Ltd for kind permission to quote from *One Family's War* edited by Patrick Mayhew.

Sidgwick & Jackson for kind permission to quote from *With Malice Towards None* by Cecil King.

Hodder & Stoughton Ltd for kind permission to quote from *The Fringes of Power* by John Colville.

George Weidenfeld and Nicolson Ltd for kind permission to quote from *Self-Portrait with Friends: Selected Diaries of Cecil Beaton* edited by Richard Buckle.

David Higham Associates Ltd for kind permission to quote from *I am my Brother* by John Lehmann (Longman) and from *With Love* by Theodora Fitzgibbon (Century).

Curtis Brown Group Ltd for *Westwood or the Gentle Powers*, Copyright 1945 Stella Gibbons, reproduced by permission of Curtis Brown, London.

Dannie Abse for kind permission to quote from *Ash on a Young Man's Sleeve*, Copyright © Dannie Abse 1954 first published by Hutchinson.

The Estate of the late Sonia Brownell Orwell and Secker & Warburg for kind permission to quote from *The Collected Essays, Journalism and Letters of George Orwell*.

George Beardmore for kind permission to quote from his *Civilians at War: Journals 1938–46* (John Murray (Publishers) Ltd).

Laurence Pollinger Ltd for kind permission to quote from *The Ministry of Fear* by Graham Greene (William Heineman Ltd and The Bodley Head Ltd).

Yale University Press for kind permission to quote from *Where Stands a Winged Sentry* by Margaret Kennedy.

Macmillan Publishing Company for kind permission to quote from *England's Hour* by Vera Brittain.

Spike Milligan Productions Ltd for kind permission to quote from *Adolf Hitler: My Part in His Downfall* (Michael Joseph).

The Hogarth Press for kind permission to quote from *The Journey not the Arrival Matters* by Leonard Woolf.

Little Brown & Company for kind permission to quote

from *The London Journals of General Raymond E. Lee, 1940–41*.

Hamish Hamilton for kind permission to quote from *Another Self* by James Lees-Milne.

Alex Mitchell, for kind permission to quote from the diaries of his aunt Gwladys Cox.

Doone Turnbull, for kind permission to quote from the written account of her godfather, Bert Snow.

Mrs Pointer Craig, for kind permission to quote from the written account of her father, Mr T.H. Pointer.

Liverpool City Council, Libraries and Arts Dept, for kind permission to quote from Norman Ellison's diaries.

'The Suspended Drawing Room' by S.N. Behrman. Copyright 1945 by S.N. Behrman. Copyright renewed, © 1972, by S.N. Behrman. Reprinted by permission of Brandt & Brandt Literary Agents, Inc. First published in the *New Yorker* magazine.

Excerpt from 'London War Notes 1939–1945' by Mollie Panter-Downes originally appeared in the *New Yorker*. Copyright © 1941, 1971 Mollie Panter-Downes. Reprinted by permission of Farrar Straus and Giroux-Inc.

Three former wardens: the Reverend Markham, who sent his invaluable and engrossing account for us to use as we wished; Laurie Latchford, whose wartime diaries bring it all back as if it were yesterday; and Vincent Wyles, who kindly invited us to talk to him at his house in Coventry.

Professor Ronald Edgerton (formerly Major Edgerton, TD, RA) for information about the role of the Royal Artillery in the blitz (and to both him and his wife Mary for their generous hospitality).

Edgar Howard, formerly of the RAF Regiment, for detailed information about the VI campaign.

The many people who gave up their time to talk about

their memories of the war, but especially the novelists Elizabeth Jane Howard and Beryl Bainbridge, and the actress and writer Siân Phillips.

And finally the many hundreds of people who have written to us. Their accounts, diaries and letters have all contributed to our building up a better picture of life in the blitz all those years ago. And whether we have quoted from them or not, they will all be given to the Imperial War Museum for use by future researchers and historians.

Our thanks also to the following for permission to use their illustrations:

The Imperial War Museum Collection; The London Fire Brigade Media Sources Section; The London History Workshop Centre; The Salvation Army International Heritage Centre; The Bristol United Press Ltd; The Birmingham City Council Public Libraries Department; South Wales Evening Post; Claire Lowry; The Clydebank District Council Libraries Department; The Belfast Telegraph Newspapers Ltd; The Hull City Council Libraries Department; The Kent Messenger Group Newspapers; Val Ranken; Mr Wilf Webb; The City of Sheffield Libraries Department.

PRIMROSE HILL

They cut the trees away:
By day the lean guns leer
Across their concrete walls;
The evening falls
On four guns tucked in bed.

The top of the hill is bare,
But the trees beneath it stretch
Through Regent's Park and reach
A rim of jewelled lights —
The music of the fair.

And the wind gets up and blows
The lamps between the trees
And all the leaves are waves
And the top of Primrose Hill
A raft on stormy seas.

Some night the raft will lift,
Upon a larger swell
And the evil sirens call
And the searchlights quest and shift,
and out of the Milky Way
the impartial bombs will fall.

\hfill Louis MacNeice, *The Spectator*, 25 August 1939

INTRODUCTION

It would sound somewhat pretentious to say that *Blitz* forms the final part of our wartime trilogy; that would imply a greater degree of premeditation than actually existed. Nevertheless, the three books we have written about Britain in World War II do form a logical sequence.

The purpose of *Women in Wartime* (Macdonald Optima 1987) was to show how the women's magazines of the war years reflected — and attempted to influence — the roles of women in real life. Its publication brought us into contact with many women who had lived through those war years, one of whom commented 'Fine book, I'm sure; but now that you've written about what we were *reading*, why don't you write about what we were *doing*?'

The result was *Women in Uniform 1939–1945* (Papermac, 1989) in which we paid tribute to the services, the nurses, the Women's Land Army and Timber Corps, the NAAFI, as well as to those working in the towns and cities: in ARP (Air-Raid Precautions), as railway porters, fire-women, clippies, ambulance drivers. We felt guilty, however, that the space devoted to this latter group of women proved inadequate to do justice to their experiences. And we were impressed by the way in which many of the servicewomen praised those who had stayed in civvy street. 'Working in ack-ack [anti-aircraft] was tough,' said one, 'but at least you were fighting back, you had your mates and you felt you were doing something. It was worse when you were back home on leave.' And one, who worked in London until joining the WRNS in 1942, said that her life as a Wren was considerably easier; no more 55-hour weeks, struggling to work through bombed out streets, queuing for food after work, nights of fitful sleep in smelly shelters when not up on the roof fire-watching.

This determined us to write a book devoted to those who stayed to face the bombs, men as well as women. As with *Women in Uniform*, we have woven a narrative around the words of those who lived through the war years. This time, however, we have included material from published sources. So, together with the accounts appearing in print for the first time, we find some more familiar names: George Orwell complaining about the problems of trying to write during the air-raids; Cecil Beaton clambering about the ruins of the City on the morning after the second Great Fire of London; a young and rather drunk John Mortimer reading Byron with bombs falling outside, and his friend in the next room being initiated into the mysteries of love.

Many of the accounts were written at the time, as letters or diary entries; some during the intervening years; others date from the last few months, often provided by people who have never written or spoken at any great length about their experiences before. It may be contended that 50-year-old memories are of little value; time will have blunted the details, confused events, exaggerated the heroism or amplified the suffering. This may well be so. Indeed, Tom Harrisson (co-founder of Mass Observation and author of the invaluable *Living Through the Blitz*) was adamant in his belief that the only useful testimonies were those noted down at the time or as soon as possible afterwards. But we are not so certain. Several of the accounts in our book are from men and women describing events that happened when they were little children; some of them, even now, we cannot read without being gripped by the power of memory to recall the tiniest details, the precise nature of the experience. And who would be so presumptuous as to claim, for example, that the Beryl Bainbridge of 1989 was unable to talk about her seven-year-old self on Merseyside in 1941.

Ah yes, but she is a professional writer; her job is to transform reality into words, we hear you say. People not used to speaking or writing about their own experiences will find words a barrier; may well just trot out those hackneyed expressions which have become part of blitz mythology. Again, that may be so. But what guarantee do we have that an account described 50 minutes after an event is by definition more 'true', more 'accurate', than one written 50 years after? Stephen Spender, in his autobiography *World Within World*, claimed that all but one of his wartime colleagues in the Auxiliary Fire Service were incapable of talking with any real accuracy about what they went through. The exception was Ned, who could neither read nor write.

Because of his illiteracy he was the only man in the station who told the truth about his fire-fighting experiences. The others had almost completely substituted descriptions which they had read in the newspapers or heard on the wireless for their own impressions. 'Cor mate, at the docks it was a bleeding inferno' or 'Just then Jerry let hell loose upon us' were the formulae into which experiences such as wading through streams of molten sugar, or being stung by a storm of sparks from burning pepper, or inundated with boiling tea at the dock fires, had been reduced.

Ned, having read no accounts of his experiences, could describe them vividly. Sir Stephen, somewhat disappointingly, gives no examples of Ned's prose style, otherwise we would have been delighted to quote some.

What we do have are accounts from as many types of source as possible, from those who were forced to sit passively, hoping the bombs would not drop on them, to those whose jobs took them out into the middle of it or who volunteered to go there, to bring help and comfort to others.

We have chosen to interpret the word 'blitz' in the widest sense: that is to say, the entire period during which bombs fell, including the time of the V weapons.

We are sorry not to have been able to devote more space to the blitz outside London. It is right, of course, that the capital should have most attention; no other place suffered such intensive bombardment, and it was the target for all but a handful of the V weapons. Furthermore, the majority of published accounts are from people who spent the blitz there. But we have tried to incorporate — in the limited space available — a representative selection of accounts from the provinces. And Chapter 4, where the people of Coventry describe that first terrible raid, can stand for the sufferings of all people everywhere, caught up in the senselessness of war.

1.
IN FOR A HARD POUNDING
The start of the London blitz, 7–8 September 1940

It seems evident to me that we are in for an era of hard pounding. The Boche has failed to knock out the RAF by attacking the airdromes, has failed to cripple industry by random and widespread bombing and has made no impression whatever on the British civil morale.

General Raymond E. Lee, US military attaché, writing to his wife from London on Sunday 8 September 1940

You did not have to be in the London area on the previous day to realise that this was, in Lee's words, 'the commencement of the real war'.

Private Spike Milligan, stationed on the coast at Bexhill, came out of the cinema on the evening of the 7th to a sky 'filled with what sounded like relays of German bombers headed inland'. And later, after finishing the evening at the Forces Corner canteen, he and his oppo Harry could still hear the bombers droning overhead.

As we approached the billets we could see a glow in the

northern sky. The sound of distant ack ack could be heard. 'Someone's copping it', said the sentry as we walked into the drive. 'Looks like it could be Redhill', said Harry. But I had my doubts. He was the only man I knew who could get lost in his own street …. We climbed into bed. 'I've never heard so many bombers before', said Harry. We lay in bed smoking for about quarter of an hour, then Smudger Smith came in. 'Cor, it looks like the sky's on fire over there.' We pulled on our trousers and climbed up on the roof. The sky was on fire. Other gunners had joined us. We watched in silence for a while. 'I fink it's London', said a cockney voice. 'Could be', said another. George Vincent went down for his prismatic compass. The bearing showed the fire dead on the line to London. Mick Haymer, a Londoner, tried to phone his family, but was told there was 'disruption' on the line and all calls to London were blocked. We looked at the blaze and it seemed to be getting bigger. I think we all knew it was London. My mother, father and brother were there. I'm not sure how I felt. Helpless, I suppose. Bombardier Edser switched on the BBC Midnight News, but there was no mention of any raid. Lots of the lads from London (we were a London regiment) found it hard to sleep that night. In the dark of our bedrooms there were attempts at reassurance.

'They've all got Anderson shelters, they're dead safe.'

'Yer, dead safe.'

'… and there's all that anti-aircraft fire … that keeps 'em up high.'

'… and there's the Underground, nuffink could break them.'

The window near my bed faced north. As I lay there, I could see the glow of the fires. The bombers were still going. Some must have been on their way back, as we heard cannon fire as night fighters got onto them. What a bloody mess. Men in bombers raining death on defenceless civilians. Still, soon we'd be doing it back to them on a scale never before imagined. For the love of me I couldn't get the feeling that I was part of this. Killing of civilians was an outrage I couldn't swallow on *any* basis, on any side. In the end there were no sides. Just living and dead.

In Chelsea, meanwhile, Theodora Fitzgibbon had just spent a pleasant afternoon with a group of friends including the young poet Dylan Thomas.

It was around five o'clock, the wine was all gone, and we began to think of going out for drinks at a pub. The air-raid siren had sounded a little earlier, but a warning about a week previously had amounted to very little, so we took no notice. It was, after all, still daylight. Out in the street, the sun was setting, and there was a faraway drone of aeroplanes and the sound of anti-aircraft guns. We decide to go to the King's Head and Eight Bells, a small pub on Chelsea Embankment, instead of the Six Bells. As we turned the corner there was in the sky a monstrous tower, looking like a giant puffball of smoke, away to the east. Even though it was too far off, the density of it made one's nostrils twitch with the imagined smell. We turned into the pub, normally empty at this hour, but the great menacing grey column in the east had brought many people out in search of news. The saloon bar of the pub had a long refectory table by the stairs, and several people sat there silently. It was old-fashioned in design, and over the bar, reaching almost to the floor, were panels of cut glass, with small windows on hinges which were swivelled open to give orders. Through these foot-wide apertures the frightened eyes of the proprietors met one's own.

We decided to play a game of shove-ha'penny, a pub game of those days. It was convenient because both Peter and Sophie were left-handed, so we didn't have to keep changing sides as we spun metal discs up the board. Men in tin hats, which we had all been issued with some time ago, came in from time to time with communiqués. When darkness came, the smoke had turned into a red bank of flames. It seemed as if they would flick out their fiery tongues and embrace the whole of London.

At about six thirty the 'all clear' sounded, and by then the sky was the colour of a blood orange, a seething, flaming mass. Donald said he would try to get home now; Dylan stayed quietly by my side. Against the now black sky, the fires shone doubly bright. After a year of the blackout it was weird to have light again, but it was an ominous brightness. It was not my night on fire-watching duty, but I thought I should report just in case. Donald walked with me to the post a few streets away. There we learned that the London docks and neighbouring boroughs had been pounded and set on fire. No, they did not want me, but would summon me if necessary. Donald brought me to the corner and went on his way.

Inside the pub, everybody was speculating as to what had happened on this sunny, Saturday, September afternoon. Jokes were made to relieve the tension; beer mugs were put down more noisily to shut out other sounds. We were glued together by dread. All our eyes were rounder, the pupils enlarged, and although we laughed, our lips twitched with alarm.

A few miles further north Stephen Melville Woodcock, an ARP warden, also looked anxiously eastwards from his post in Ladbroke Grove.

From the roof of the Lodge, we could see smoke over the whole city and dock area. After dark the red glow was a most alarming sight and one felt that East London had gone up in flames over a huge area. I came down from the roof in a very chastened mood, wondering when our own district would have similar treatment and how the fire brigade could tackle it if it happened before the present fires were dealt with at the other end of London.

In fact West London did not escape the bombing entirely that night, as Vera Brittain was to write in *England's Hour*, published the following year.

At nightfall after we have drawn the curtains, it lights up London with midday brilliance for the benefit of the Nazi raiders who fly citywards in their hundreds for the first night of the intensified Blitzkrieg. My friend and I are not aware of it; instead we are listening, startled, to the unfamiliar ringing of church bells, and wondering whether the threatened invasion has begun. But the evening siren has just sounded when the young Estonian maid peeps through the curtains of the first-floor drawing-room.

'Oh, look! Fire! How red the sky! Do come and see.'

I am just turning to look, when a blow such as I have never known even in nightmares seems to strike the house like a gigantic flail. I am swept off my feet and out of my senses; somehow, a second later, I find myself in the basement, but even before I arrive there a second terrific crash makes the whole earth rock like a ship in mountainous seas. The cook, already below, tells us later that the house appeared to gather itself up and pitch forward; for a moment she thought that we were all going to be flung into the road from above her head. The blast has blown glass from the leaded panes, though the windows were open; sulphur fumes, thick and acrid, pour through the passages; an hour or so later, from the pricking of my reddened skin, I realise that something has scorched my face. Gathering myself up from the basement, I go to the telephone with the abnormal calm that for most of us follows an escape from death before the reaction begins:

'Is that the Kensington police? Look here, when the raid's over you'd better come and take a glance at 37, Francis Square. We've either had a bomb on our roof, or it's fallen just outside. I don't know how much damage there is, but the whole house seemed to be coming on top of us.'

A few minutes later the police arrive; the raid is still on, but they know it will not be over till dawn. As they plunge ankle-deep in glass to look for damage with their shrouded torches, they tell me that seven bombs fell in three seconds within a quarter of a mile of our house. Eventually they discover that the bomb which so nearly demolished us has fallen and exploded, not upon our roof, but upon that of the house in an adjoining crescent which backs onto ours. Amazingly, a woman who was having a bath on the second floor has escaped with no more than shock.

Sitting in the basement when the police have gone, holding a cup of tea in hands now ignobly shaking, I reflect that shock is quite bad enough. Wondering whether my face is as green as the faces of the others, I contemplate with astonishment the fact that I am still alive.

But hundreds did not survive the night, most of them in and around the dock area of East London, the prime target on what became known as 'Black Saturday'. Olive Lilian McNeil was one who lived through it. She was 14 years old at the time, from a family of stevedores and dockers in Poplar.

I'll never forget that lovely warm sunny Saturday afternoon in September they set the docks alight. I was working in a small tailoring firm making uniforms and parachutes. That evening I was going to see my best friend. I was in the back yard watching my two little brothers play — although most of our yard was taken up by the Anderson [shelter] that the council workmen had put in — and I could hear this strange droning sound. Looking up I could see lots of planes very small and very high. I called the boys to look. We said how pretty they looked with the sun glinting on them, they looked like stars. But there were so many of them and they were coming over us in lines. Suddenly everything changed, the planes that were high up started to swoop down and down and the air was filled with screaming whistling sounds. The siren was blowing and mum came running out and pushed us down the shelter. But the screaming whistlings didn't stop, they got louder and louder, I could feel the thudding of the ground around me. Some of the screaming whistlings were making the earth floor in the shelter jump. I could feel the dirt and dust was coming through the cracks in the shelter. I could hardly see, it was covering my hair and was getting in our eyes. Mum told us to lie down and she lay on top of us and she kept saying her prayers and I said 'Please Jesus don't let the screaming whistlings come too close.' Mum told me to shut up and not frighten the boys. But the screaming whistlings went on and on, and one got so close that the shelter nearly got lifted out of the ground. We all screamed and we heard glass breaking and things flying around.

Suddenly everything went quiet and we clung together in the blessed silence until the all clear went and we thanked God we were all right. I was out first. By now it was getting dark. I remember standing by the shelter and looking around me, it was as though I was in a dream. The sky as far as I

Saturday 7 September 1940. 'Black Saturday' — the London docks are set ablaze.

could see all around me was orange and pink. It glowed making everything look like fairyland.

Mr T.H. Pointer, an air-raid warden, was in Royal Victoria Docks having tea when the first siren sounded at five o'clock that afternoon.

As the siren faded away the sound of airplanes was heard. Strolling to the door with a cup of tea in my hands, I looked round and up for a sight of them. Gunfire could now be heard and at last, almost overhead, I could see over 50 aircraft at rather low altitude with gunfire bursting in front and around them. They continued straight on travelling almost due west so as to pass over the Docks at an angle. With a shout to the others who were having tea, I dashed, cup in hand, for our dug-out about 40–50 yards away. As I ran I considered throwing the tea away, but finished up with about half a cup. Flinging myself into the dug-out and slamming the door behind, I heard the first of a series of bombs whistling down. Instinctively we ducked our heads and with a terrific crack the bombs burst. The rush of air whipped open the dug-out door and in came dust and pieces of rubbish. By this time the bombs were dropping all round and the door was slammed shut again by another rush of air. The aircraft had passed over us by this time and I ran up to the office for my steel helmet. As I came back the phone rang and an ambulance was requested in King George V Dock. Returning to the dining-room, I called the driver and gave him his instructions. We looked round to see what damage was done and had again to run for the dug-out. This time we could hear the whine as bombs were falling and they ripped across towards us, so I knelt down and put my head on the floor and my hands on my neck.

Waves of planes passed over the area and their dug out was rocked by bombs on several occasions, putting lights and telephone out of action.

After what seemed hours, but could only have been tens of seconds, it stopped and we staggered out of the dug-out to behold the most awful chaos possible. Burnt fragments, smoke and dust were everywhere above and it seemed that everything must be smashed. An ambulance roared up going to some casualty at the west end of the Dock. We followed in a car. As we drove along we could see the warehouse with its roof blown off and flames leaping up inside. Railway lines had been blown up and windows everywhere were smashed. The new warehouses had been hit and there were great craters at the side of the road. The Royal Mail offices were smashed to the ground, the *Illanda* was on fire and some of her crew were being treated for burns. After this we went along to help in any other cases we might meet. The next ship was not touched, but the next one had had a bomb go right through the bottom of the boat at the stern and she was settling on the bottom. The crew were throwing all their personal belongings on to the quay. The next ship was on fire and at the side a great quantity of oil which had burst from a bomb was lying. A bomb had torn its way through the quay and a balcony of the warehouses had been hit. The 'all clear' went and we hoped for the best. In the gap between two ships could be seen the flour mills blazing from top to bottom and with terrific crashes parts of the side collapsed. The next mill was just catching fire in several places and a ship lying alongside was starting. A barge was well alight and the heat from the mill could be felt across the width of the docks — about 250 yards. We started to cross the river to get back to our headquarters when we came across a great crater caused by a bomb. At this moment a delayed action bomb decided to explode in our rear and we scooted. I decided I had had enough and collected my bike and, with a number of foreign seamen, ran across the bridge from the dock.

Outside I began to feel the strain and felt full right up to top. Arriving at Leytonstone I must confess I broke down but soon felt a little better. I left for Seven Kings and just arrived home when the warning went again. I was one of the first to go to earth and didn't leave the safety of the shelter for at least three hours.

But others in civil defence had to carry on through the night, as more and more bombers — using the blazing ships, warehouses and homes as a beacon — swept in from seven-thirty that evening to four-thirty the next morning.
Pat Newman spent the night at a Woolwich fire station.

There was no time to think of what should be done, we just did it automatically. We could hear the thuds and whistles of the bombs getting nearer as the enemy planes flew up the River Thames towards Woolwich. Everyone was on stand-by and I took the first telephone call of the blitz in our sub-station, which was 'All appliances to the Light Gun Factory, Woolwich Arsenal.' The call bell was rung and the men were away — leaving the two girls and myself with the watchman in this huge school — and we had to keep the station going. We were inundated with calls for help, which we had to pass down the line to other stations in the hope that they had appliances, and that was when our topography training came into its own; we could direct appliances from other areas to any street in our district without having to refer to a map, or ask each other where so and so street existed.

It really was a baptism of fire as the noise was deafening. Our station was surrounded by the Woolwich Arsenal, Royal Artillery Barracks, gun ships on the Thames and the railway, and the ack-ack crews, bless their hearts, were firing up at the bombers continuously, which was marvellous for our morale.

At the height of the attack I took a call for help at my grandmother's house; a bomb had hit the shelter in the garden and my grandmother and several aunts were trapped. As we had no appliances I could only contact the ARP, and the first person on the scene was my mother (who was a warden) who helped to dig out her own mother and sisters who were all taken to hospital; but there was no time to feel helpless, although the situation remained at the back of my mind, there were so many other calls needing attention.

The firemen eventually returned to our station on Sunday evening after being relieved by crews from areas outside London. The men were absolutely dead tired, they had not only been sitting targets for the *Luftwaffe* in the flames created by the first wave of bombers, but had also had to deal with exploding shells from the light gun factory. Their uniforms were made of serge material (no plastic capes in those days) and the smell of the wet serge and the stench of smoke on them filled the station. There were no drying machines, washing machines, etc., and more often than not the men had to go out again in wet uniforms.

Cyril Demarne in *A Fireman's Tale* has written of the events of that night.

The high explosive and incendiary bombs had done their work. Huge fires were raging in the docks and in the factories lining the river banks. Molten tar from a Silvertown factory flowed across the North Woolwich Road, bogging down fire engines, ambulances and civil defence vehicles. Flames were

Firemen playing hoses on the fires of damaged warehouses, 7 September 1940.

roaring from timber yards, paint factories, soap works, sugar refineries, chemical works, dock warehouses and ships and the pathetic little homes of the workers. The whole of West Ham's dockland was ablaze, the flames reaching out to encompass adjoining buildings. Across the river, a huge fire raged among the timber stacks of the Surrey Commercial Docks, as hundreds of fire pumps dashed to the infernos that were consuming the East End of London.

At 7.30 the bombers were back. In West India Dock a rum wharf was lit, its buildings alight from end to end with blazing spirit gushing from the entrances. Rats fled from a burning soap works at Silvertown and flaming barges, adrift on the tideway, careered crazily along, bumping piers and craft and forcing fire boats to give way. Great blazing embers were carried aloft in the terrific heat, spreading fire over the heads of firemen. Powerful jets were turned to steam and it seemed that all the effort was in vain, the task was over-whelming. Against the glare of the flames parachutes could be seen descending, carrying a land mine resembling a small boiler and packed with a ton of high explosive, to add to the terror and devastation. When it landed there would be a blinding flash of pink light which seemed to persist for seconds, then what appeared to be a whole street of houses would go flying in the air in a great gust of smoke and dust, scattering bricks and slates, furniture and bodies. After a time the scream of the bombs and the crump of explosions became just a background to the general din, but one was always aware of the whine of the fire pumps, the dry mouth and tortured eyes, the scorching heat and the tangle of twisting snaking hose. The fearful dread of impending doom receded as time passed and the imagination became dulled. The only tangible things remaining were the surrounding fires and the brain-numbing din. Many who felt they were engaged in a hopeless task battled on, encouraged by the example of neighbouring crews slogging away at the wall of flame, crouching head down to protect faces against the heat.

The pounding high explosives fractured gas and water mains and played havoc with telephone and power cables. These were the days before the service was equipped with radio. Fire officers, unable to telephone situation reports or calls for assistance, relied upon motorcycle despatch riders or the heroic teenage messenger boys with their bicycles, to maintain communication. It was no fault of the despatch riders and messengers that controls received but a hazy appreciation of the fire situation. They rode through streets converted by incendiary bombs into passages with flaming walls, and picked themselves up after being blasted from their machines by a near miss. They skidded around unexploded bombs and piles of rubble, determined to deliver their messages, accepting the conditions as all part of the job.

George Woodhouse, a member of the AFS (Auxiliary Fire Service) was enjoying a game of snooker at sub-station 76x, in Holloway, when the warning was heard. At the sound of airplane engines and anti-aircraft guns the whole company rushed upstairs to the flat roof to see what was happening.

I turned to one of the 3 LFB [London Fire Brigade] men who were in charge of 'x' and said that I had been in the fire service for over a year but so far had not been to one fire. He turned to me and said 'You will see more than one today, George.'

Very soon after this the bells went down and there was a mad scramble to get back below and get our equipment on. I had to make sure my machine was ready to go; we were a four-man crew, Nick Fowler in charge, myself as driver/pump operator and two others. We were ordered out, our destination the London Docks. As we neared the Dockland area, we passed a large furniture factory whose whole timber yard was ablaze, also one or two nearby houses. People were frantically waving their arms at us begging us to stop but of course we were not allowed to (I have often wondered what those people thought of us). Arriving at the docks I drove through a large pair of gates to find the whole dockside area was jammed solid with fire appliances literally nose to tail. Nick Fowler left to report our arrival, the rest of us dismounted and stood watching barges alight from end to end just drifting down the river; across the river were two larger ships tied up at a wharf, one of these ships was also on fire. The whole scene was one of devastation, not one of the pumps was being used, people just stood and stared. I began to wonder what would happen if the bombers returned, and of course that did happen. We were immediately told to evacuate the docks. You can imagine the confusion as each driver tried to turn his vehicle around. I was fortunate to be close to the entrance gates so was able to make a quick getaway. We then reported to Shoreditch Fire Station and were re-directed to West Ferry Road on the Isle of Dogs.

On turning into West Ferry Road I was shocked to see lines of people walking along the road, some pushing prams with their belongings in, some with bundles over their shoulders, just like the refugees we had seen on the newsreels. It was with great difficulty I was able to drive down the road because of the debris, two buildings on either side of the road were alight, causing me to raise the door window because of the heat as I drove past. We finally stopped lower down the road and manhandled our trailer pump into an entrance beside a large building. Our idea was to join our suction hoses together and drop them over the dockside so I could lift water from the river ... we then found that the tide was out, so we had to abandon that idea. We eventually found a fire hydrant that had about enough water to give us a jet about 7 to 8 feet, so we finished in another yard facing a building that was well alight; also in this yard were two petrol pumps and a 50-gallon storage tank containing diesel, so to prevent either catching fire from the burning embers dropping all around us we spent our time playing our small jet of water over the pumps and diesel tanks ... we finally had to abandon even this small effort because of the danger of the buildings collapsing. We were also being overcome by some chemical vapour which was affecting our breathing ... in fact it turned our chrome buttons on our tunics green. We were very glad when we were relieved the following morning. I often wondered who the mastermind was who ordered all those fire service appliances into the docks, left us there as sitting ducks and then ordered us out again without one drop of water being used!

But Jim Goldsmith, an LFB regular stationed in the City, saw considerably more action that night.

You didn't need any lights or maps to find the way, you just headed for the glow in the sky. It was real chaos, buildings ablaze all round and the worst of all seeing houses flattened by the bombs. If anyone said they could not feel fear that night they must be lying through their teeth. It was here I had my first view of violent death — I had seen a couple of bodies in my peacetime duties, but this was nothing like it. In great American war films they show buildings being blown up and bodies flying through the air; this all looks rather thrilling from a comfortable chair, but totally different when you are in the middle of it.

There were sad and funny moments mixed though. We found a woman crying her eyes out as her house had been damaged by the bombing, it seemed her doors and windows had blown out. As we were trying to pacify her, another elderly lady came along and said 'What's up love.' The first lady was telling her all about the damage when the second one said 'Never mind love, let's go in and try and make a cup of tea, perhaps we can give these poor so and so's a cup.' We then asked if her house had been hit. 'Yes,' said she, 'it's over there.' All we could see was a pile of rubble, and she was worrying about someone else. With people like her how could Adolf win?

We spent most of the night in this area trying to do what we could. The fact that you were soaking wet wasn't noticed until you moved away from a building and could feel the cold going through you. If you were lucky you could find a canteen van, or the drinks were provided by people living in the Docks — heaven knows how they managed it. When things had gone quiet we were ordered back to our stations and the relief took over. The first thing was to find dry clothes, get something to eat, clean your equipment and try to get some rest ... That night it started again — I did not realize how much was left to burn.

So if anyone tells you how wonderful war is, let them have a go at putting bodies together, and try and explain to someone who has lost a relative. The smell of burning wood and the stench of burning flesh is a thing you will never forget.

Even closer to the realities of death and injury were the ambulance drivers, such as Bert Purdy, on duty in Moorgate that afternoon.

Frank Spackman and I had actually laid the table for tea, cups and saucers, and had opened a tin of salmon on the table ... All of a sudden we heard ringing and banging on the garage doors. We went outside the station ... Our attention was drawn to the actions of the people and we looked up and saw hundreds of planes flying towards us from the east over Kent. Within seconds we actually saw the bombs dropping in the area of Blackwall Tunnel and the Dock Area, Naval Row. We contacted HQ, direct line, explained the situation and departed. By this time we were actually being bombed, but we carried on to Naval Row. AM 13 was the first to arrive. It was chaos, buildings, houses all in a collapsed condition. At times my driving was erratic, I was driving up and down the bomb craters. We saw several mutilated bodies lying in the road. At one point we stopped and moved several limbs and two bodies to a point off the road, covered them with sheets of corrugated iron, intending to remove them later.

Well, it was terrible — people trapped, severely injured. People were lying about everywhere. We began to collect the people, render first aid if and when possible; take them to Poplar Hospital. Private cars were waiting outside the hospital for attention. We saw patients with severe head injuries lying on the roof of the cars, blood running down the back window. By this time, all the East End of London was involved, especially the dock areas. We worked hours; removed patients to Poplar, Mile End and London Hospitals.

It was terrible, I shall never forget that weekend. It was so unexpected and tragic. We returned to the station on Sunday morning, our tea, etc., covered in dust, but the station itself, which we had earlier covered in sandbags, was still standing. We washed up and went home, grateful that we was alive and uninjured.

As these ambulance men came off duty the majority of Londoners were emerging from homes or shelters to see what the night had brought. General Lee strolled that afternoon through the relatively undamaged West End.

After a little while I took a walk over toward Victoria; the station is closed but one can see that a bomb came through the roof all right and knocked things about badly. The sign said, with true British restraint, 'Closed on account of obstructions.' The Germans were evidently aiming at the railroads, for no fewer than 19 stations were hit, and the Rotherhithe tunnel blocked.

I walked across [St James's] Park, stopping to admire the lovely view both ways from the little bridge and down alongside the lagoon to the Horse Guards Parade, where I had sat so many times through the long ceremony of the Trooping of the Colour ... There is barbed wire all round the place now and a big flabby-looking gray balloon resting uneasily at its moorings. While [I stood] looking at its sides wrinkling and gasping like the gills of a fish, the sirens began wailing like banshees and everyone in sight, without haste but without dawdling, began to move toward shelter.

At this time John Lehmann (the writer, and director of the Hogarth Press) was travelling into London from Salisbury.

About 5.30 pm the train ran plumb into an air-raid. Blinds down, we went slowly on, then stopped; overhead a battle was going on, with sudden zooms and the rattle of machine-gun fire distinctly audible. People rushed to the windows in spite of all the warnings, shouted that they could see the battling machines — but against the dazzling blue I certainly couldn't. Then the all-clear went, and the girl next to me sighed with relief and giggled. We went slowly on, then stopped at a signal outside Clapham Junction. Time dragged on, still we waited there, light began to fade. Passengers began to think of their lost appointments — the soldier of his date in a pub at Gravesend — the little fuzzy man of his work at 9 pm — but also of darkness and raids and being caught there. The fuzzy man's fat wife began to show signs of hysteria, the girl of pathetic agitation. Then soldiers began to jump off the train and slip through people's backyards into the road for buses: the old, very irate guard tried to stop them — nothing like it had been known in his 50 years' service with the company — but they went on, and civilians with their luggage began to follow them. At eight o'clock the signal light was still at red against us, though electric trains for London Bridge were still roaring by. I decided to make a dash for London. Luckily a 77 bus stopped only a few yards away, and I packed into it with a young RNVR [Royal Navy Volunteer Reserve] officer. Only a few minutes later the inevitable sirens went again — but the bus sped on through the moonlit streets. Over the Thames and up into Kingsway it raced, and still there was no gunfire to be heard: I had an eerie, tense feeling after the weekend reports, eerier still when I jumped off the bus to get to my flat and saw the glow of fires in

Holborn. But I got home, and dined off half a bottle of wine and an apple and had some chocolate biscuits in my shuttered bedroom. Then I lay down, full dressed on my bed, and began to read *Le Pere Goriot*.

I didn't get far. Gunfire began to rumble in the distance, and now it seemed to be getting nearer, with the persistent, maddening sound of aircraft overhead. Then I could distinguish bombs dropping. Then suddenly three whistling, ripping noises in the air, as if directly overhead, getting closer, and each time violent concussions followed by the sound of tinkling glass ... When the noise of the aeroplanes seemed to be getting fainter again, I went to the window and looked out on the Square: I found — underneath the black curtains — that some of my panes had been smashed, incendiary bombs were burning merrily in the garden, and an enormous blaze was developing beyond the Balloon station in the Foundling grounds. My first feeling was: how curious and almost incredible it was that this should have happened so near me. There was no searchlight. when I went downstairs the man from No. 46, who was just getting out of his car, said he thought the searchlight had had it. Then I went to shout to my landlord in the basement shelter, but he only answered sleepily and I left him. I hung about the ground floor for some time, a little dazed, went to the door again and heard the shouts of the AFS men as they tackled the blaze beyond the Balloon site: suddenly it struck me that it looked alarmingly close to Stephen's [Stephen Spender's] flat over on the other side. 'Well, poor old Stephen's the first to go' — was the odd, sad, resigned thought that went through my mind. A little later, as I was standing by the stairs, there was another tremendous explosion, the house seemed to clench itself like a fist for a moment, then silence. It struck me as strange that I had heard no whizz of a descending bomb, and I went to the door again and peered out: the sight that met my eye was an enormous bellying cloud of grey dust advancing down the road towards me like a living thing, and a man in pyjamas curiously walking across it to his flat. There was dead silence; but it struck me that it might be as well now to go to a shelter. Hardly had I got myself ready when I heard a crowd of people moving out of the garden: I opened the door, and met the man from No. 46 again, now in a tin helmet, who said there was an unexploded bomb in the garden and they were evacuating the shelter there, and also that the houses on our side had rocked badly — he advised me to go. When I turned round I thought that parts of Byron Court looked rather odd: it was only a few seconds later that I realized I was looking at a tree beyond — Byron Court had simply been blown to bits . . .

As I passed it on the way to the shelter, the presence of death and murder seemed very vivid to me, to fill the atmosphere, as a thing now at last *perceived* in this war behind 'the furious words' and all the stories I had heard. The Guildford Street fire was still very violent, but seemed to be more under control, there was a red haze away in the direction of the City — but our searchlight sword was striking across the sky again.

And in the shelter: the hours passed by and one longed for the dawn, knowing the Nazis would retreat from it and our ascending daylight fighters. I sat on a step, scarcely under shelter, and talked to an ATS [Auxiliary Territorial Service] girl in uniform, on and on. Girls lay sleeping clasped by their young husbands, women and children were down below, someone produced a Dostoevsky novel, a group of young women huddled in an angle of the stairs with what looked like powdered hair — but they had just been rescued from the ruins of Byron Court and it was rubble dust. Then more bombs whistled by — and the banging of the lavatory door sounded like bombs too — incendiaries were dropped outside — a warden came and whispered to us that a flare had been dropped . . . At last, in the grey light of morning, the all-clear went.

Many had not stayed to see what that second night of destruction would bring. Mary Price says that she and her neighbours in the East End were simply petrified.

We didn't know where to go and what to do. The only thing we could think of was to get to Kent to the hop fields, at least we'd be safe getting out of London. Some cousins of mine came round, they'd borrowed a lorry and they said 'Come on, we're going', and I just took two bags of clothes with my five-months-old baby and we made our way to Kent. Now it was just like a convoy of refugees going out. Everything on wheels, old cars, old lorries, anything that moved. It was one steady stream going towards the coast. And we got to Rootham Hill and there was an alarm that some Germans were machine gunning the convoy and we had to get out of the lorry and get into the ditch ... Got back on and we finally got to the hop fields and there's this wonderful sense of peace.

Another East Ender not prepared to wait around was the mother of Olive McNeil. Olive recalls the sight that awaited them as they came out of their shelter on the Sunday morning.

Escorted by a warden, refugees flee from the East End to safety outside London during the first days of the blitz.

Two streets from us there was a big warehouse called the Buttersmackers. Butter was brought here in bulk from the dock by barge and the girls packed it ready to be sold. You could see that fire for miles because the Buttersmackers got a direct hit. Nearby was a warehouse where skins and pelts were kept for the fur trade; that was blazing good and proper and the stench from it was sickening. Everywhere bits of paper and lumps of soot were blowing and mum's line post was alight at the top. It looked like a Roman torch. Every bit of greenery was scorched and there was glass everywhere.

We didn't have any windows and soot had covered everything when the chimneys came down. There was no water or gas so we didn't have any tea. All the china was broken and the shelves on the dresser were all hanging down. Mum took her housekeeping and her rent money from out of the toffee tin that was on the mantel, put a few bits of our clothing in a bag, put the kids in the pram and we walked all the way to the coach station through water, glass, broken bricks, hose pipes and lots of things I like to forget. She asked the man where the next coach was going. He said Oxford, so she bought us all a ticket; she said it didn't matter where we went, but she had to get us to safety.

But many had neither the initiative nor the means to escape under their own steam. Instead, understandably enough, they relied on the authorities to do something for them. And, as the journalist Ritchie Calder discovered, the authorities were found wanting.

That Sunday he visited the East End to see the Reverend W. Paton, a much-loved local vicar, known in the area as 'the Guv'nor'.

His pulpit still stood, but the roof and the front wall had gone. The streets all around were wrecked. They were poor 'dead end' streets, running down to the dock wall, but these heaps of rubble had once been homes which sheltered the families of the East London dockers — tough, decent folk who had deserved better conditions than they'd ever had in peacetime and who were having the worst in war. Some of these battered wrecks of bricks and rubble, with shabby furniture now reduced to kindling, had been the only homes which old pensioners had ever known. They had 'married into them'; they had brought up their families in them; they had seen their children married out of them; and were eking out an ill-cared for old age in them — when the bombers came.

I found 'The Guv'nor' at last, he was ashen grey with the anguish of the night. He had been out in the raids, helping his people throughout the night. His lips trembled and his eyes filled with tears when he spoke of those of his friends who were dead, injured, or missing. But his main concern was with the living. He was dashing round the streets seeking out the survivors whose homes had been wrecked.

I went with him. We found many hundreds of them sheltering in a school in the heart of the bombed area. I took a good look at this school. From the first glance it seemed to me ominous of disaster. In the passages and classrooms were mothers nursing their babies. There were blind, crippled and aged people ... Whole families were sitting in queues, perched on their pitiful baggage, waiting desperately for coaches to take them away from the terror of the bombs which had been raining down on them for two nights. Yes, for two nights! For the *Blitzkrieg* had started in that fore-doomed corner on the Friday night before London had felt the full weight of it. The bombers had come over the Docks, searching for their objectives. They had done a 'trial run', missing the Docks, but hitting roads and houses. They had set fire to a gas-main and the resultant pillar of fire had lit up the whole neighbourhood, giving their pilots their reconnaissance for the following night.

The crowded people in the school included many families who had been bombed out already, on that first night. These unfortunate homeless people had been told to be ready for the coaches at three o'clock. Hours later the coaches had not arrived. 'The Guv'nor' and I heard women, the mothers of young children, protesting with violence and with tears about the delay. Men were cursing the helpless local officials who knew only that the coaches were expected. 'Where are we going?' 'Can't we walk there?' 'We'll take a bus!' 'There's a lorry we can borrow!' The crowd clamoured for help, for information, for reassurance. But the harassed officials knew no answer other than the offer of a cup of tea.

One mother complained that her children had been forbidden to play in the playground. The official could only say he was sorry and evade her questions. But he showed me the answer. In the playground behind the school was a crater. The school was, in fact, a bulging, dangerous ruin. The bombs which had rendered these people homeless had also struck the school selected by the authorities as their 'Rest Centre'. Note that the school had already been bombed at the same time as the 'Guv'nor's' church had been bombed. So had the parish church . . . So had other buildings and streets in a direct line with it. And then I knew, on that Sunday afternoon, that, as sure as night would follow day, the bombers would come again with the darkness, and that school would be bombed . . .

Filled with this foreboding, I hastened back to Central London. Three times I warned the Whitehall authorities during that evening that the people must be got away before more bombs dropped and certain disaster overtook them. Local folk back at the school were making equally frantic efforts to force the local authorities to act.

But all these hundreds of people spent another night inside the shelterless school. Some were taken to another school — providentially — although it was only the breadth of a street away! This was done to make room for a new flood of home- less victims of the Sunday night raids. During yet another night of raids and terror, the fourth in that school for some of the shelterers, the inevitable bomb hit the crowded building.

The next morning I saw the crater. I saw the rescue men descending perilously into it, with ropes around them, saw them pause, every now and then, in a hushed painful silence, listening for sounds of the living; saw the tomb of whole families. By then, two days after the coaches had been due, the survivors, mainly from that second school, were boarding buses. They were struggling for places as crowds clamber aboard at the rush-hour. I spoke to men, fathers of families, who had been cursing on the Sunday. They were speechless and numbed by the horror of it all.

By this time the war had been in progress for just over a year, a war in which the mass bombing of civilian areas had been foreseen as inevitable from the start. Why, then, were the arrangements for dealing with the problems of the bombed out clearly so inadequate? To understand this we have to consider the preparations that had been made for modern, total war in the light of the assumptions about what form such a war would take.

2.
EXPECTATIONS AND PREPARATIONS
Lead-up to the blitz

When that first siren went, we thought we'd had it, we thought we were about to be wiped out. Our family struggled into our gas masks in the living room — there was a comic dreadfulness about it, it seemed so unreal. They are terribly difficult to put on when you are trembling. Mine landed on my chest, my mother's at the back of her head, and my sister's ended up on her left ear. We began to laugh, close to hysteria, and my mother who was terrified of death burst into tears. We just sat there waiting for the end of the world.

Odette Lesley, then a member of the ATS

South-East England had been bombed during the first war, a mere generation back. The first raids had been made by lumbering Zeppelins, easy targets for fighter aircraft or ground fire. But a 15-minute raid on East London in June 1917 was carried out by light aircraft, leaving over 100 dead and 400 injured.

Over the next 20 years planes were developed with greater range and speed, capable of carrying increasingly large payloads. The bombs, too, had become more deadly: incendiaries to set off multiple small fires, so that subsequent waves of night bombers could find their targets easily; high explosive (HE) bombs for massive destruction through contact or blast; delayed action bombs to hamper the efforts of those battling the flames or attempting to save the injured.

Opportunities to test the new weapons had not been lacking, either. All three of the future Axis powers gained experience in their use in the 30s, the Italians in Abyssinia, the Japanese in China; and it was German Heinkel 111s and Junker 52s which destroyed Guernica during the Spanish Civil War, that dress rehearsal for the forthcoming world conflict.

Just as disturbing was the use of poison gas by the Italians — despite its total ban under the 1925 Geneva Convention. Too many shattered ex-soldiers still roamed the streets of Britain, constant reminders of what gas had done on the Western Front during the Great War.

No major European city had yet been subjected to the full might of intensive bombing. But it was generally assumed that such an attack would be swift and devastating. The 1936 film version of *Things to Come* depicted a single air-raid on London — to take place in 1940 — which left the city in ruins and the population reduced to a disorganised remnant. (The images of this film proved so haunting that one fireman to whom we spoke said he thought of it the moment he saw the approaching bombers on the afternoon of 7 September 1940.)

In view of all this, it is not surprising that a system of ARP (air-raid precautions) was already in place by the time war arrived, an Air Raid Wardens' service having been created in April 1937. And the tensions arising in the autumn of 1938 from Hitler's plans to occupy Czechoslovakia led to the mobilisation of the ARP services and a flood of new volunteers. One of these was the Rev. John G. Markham, recently appointed Rector of St Peter's in Walworth, a densely populated working-class district of South London.

As the Munich crisis developed, my wife and I decided to go to Southwark Town Hall and find out what preparations for war and air raids were being made for my parish. We explained to the young deputy town clerk who was the air raid precautions officer for the borough that we thought war would break out in ten days. 'Ah yes', he replied, 'I will put you in touch with the air raid wardens in your area.' A list was procured which comprised a man and his wife, shopkeepers in the Walworth Road, and two girl typists who lived with their parents in Trafalgar St nearby ... We were not reassured by this list, which seemed slightly inadequate for 11,000 souls. I asked about air-raid shelters. There were none. I asked about gas-masks — they were not assembled ... I offered the basement of the Rectory as a warden's post and the crypt of the church as a public shelter. Before we parted, I asked whether it would be in order to recruit wardens by an appeal that coming weekend in church. 'Yes, that would be a great help', was the reply, and a clerk was sent for some enrolment forms for the recruitment drive. Back came the clerk to announce that they had run out of forms. So I asked whether I could have some drawn up myself, and that was agreed. This was the rather disquieting start to my association with the civil defence, which was to occupy so much of my time and energy for the next five years.

But not all ARP officers were as dilatory as that of Southwark. As Angus Calder points out in *The People's War*, the days leading up to Chamberlain's meeting with Hitler at Munich

saw a hectic spate of activity. Cellars and basements were requisitioned for air-raid shelters. Trenches were dug, by day and night, in the parks of the big towns, for the same purpose. Some two score 'blimps', barrage balloons, appeared in the sky over London. On the 29th [of September] the Government published hastily concocted plans for the evacuation of two million people from the capital.

The Prime Minister's return from Munich with his famous piece of paper the following day, however shameful a sell-out of the Czechoslovak people it may have represented, did give the authorities a year of grace in which, if not to perfect, at least to improve the protection of the civilian population of Britain.

Some 38 million gas masks were issued to men, women and children. Mr John H. Smith of Bristol remembers being trained in their use.

We entered a gas-filled chamber wearing our gas masks and decontamination protective clothing. The plan was that we should dig a trench using picks and shovels and then rescue a dummy who represented a casualty from the building. We had all had a strict medical test before this. We had not been in the building for a few minutes when some of our group found difficulty in breathing, several collapsed and had to be taken out. The trouble was that they failed to adjust the speed of their efforts to the speed of their breathing. The service masks restricted the speed of their breathing. Also the decontamination protective clothing prevented any ventilation of the body and soon one became short of breath and overheated and perspiring heavily.

While Margaret Lazarides recalls that

pretty coloured gas detectors resembling bird-tables appeared in the streets and these and the flat domes of letter boxes were painted with chemical pigments which would change colour in the presence of poisonous gases — rather, as those of us with scientific pretensions told each other, like litmus paper. The issue of gas masks had been accepted dutifully by the adults, and children were delighted. In Cornwall a small boy who had disappeared for several hours was asked where he had been. 'In with the pigs', he replied stolidly, 'testing me mask.'

By the time that Britain actually went to war, on 3 September 1939, everyone — including babies — had a gas-mask, over a million and a half Anderson shelters had been distributed to householders with gardens, and people were familiar with the various sirens and other signals indicating the approach of bombers or gas attacks. So when the first sirens were heard, on that bright Sunday morning, the average British family feared the worst. As Margaret Lazarides explains:

We all, I think, half expected Chamberlain's announcement to be followed almost immediately by waves of German bombers blackening the skies above us. Months before the war, rumour had warned us that up to 700 tons of bombs might fall daily during the first fortnight, and we had already listened to the warning sirens and learned to recognise the moaning wail of 'Alert' and the steady relief of 'All Clear'. Now, with war a reality, we waited anxiously for what might happen.

That evening Gwladys Cox sat down in the flat she shared with husband Ralph and cat Bob in West Hampstead and wrote up the events of the day in her diary.

Britain has declared war on G this morning soon after break-fast. Realising that war was imminent we went down to the basement cellar below this block, which the tobacconist in West End Lane has given us permission to use as a shelter ... and placed there deck chairs, rug, candles and matches. And after that, being so fine and sunny, after a storm in the night, we took a stroll along Lymington Road and watched the barrage balloons in the cricket field. On returning home, we turned on the wireless and heard there was to be 'an important announcement' by the PM at 11.15 am — so with bated breath — the whole world was on tiptoe of expectancy this morning — we settled ourselves in the sitting-room and listened ... I shall never forget the thrill of his closing words 'Now, may God bless you all. May he defend the night. It is the evil things we shall be fighting against — brute force, bad faith, injustice, oppression and persecution. And against them I am certain that right will prevail.' Mr C's speech was followed by the playing of 'God Save the King', for which I rose and remained standing until it was finished.

Then, almost immediately, to our unspeakable astonishment, the air-raid siren sounded. Quickly turning off the gas at the main, catching Bob and shutting him in his basket, grabbing our gas-masks, we struggled down the several flights of stairs to the street, some yards along the pavement, down the area steps, along winding passages, to our shelter.

My knees were knocking together with weakness while I stifled a strong desire to be sick. I was not exactly afraid, but nervous that I should be afraid, startled and bewildered, glimpsing dimly that, already, all my known world was toppling about my ears, and behind all these mixed feelings was one of unreality because the circumstances of this first alert held such an artificially dramatic element — as if the curtain having run down on PEACE, war-planes which had been awaiting their cue in the wings suddenly swooped into view before the footlights.

Such a theatrical metaphor might have been appropriate for our next witness of that day, Noel Coward, who was driving out of London with David Strahallan.

We got as far as Lord's cricket ground when the air-raid sirens started wailing. It was a curious sensation, because although we had heard that particularly dismal sound before when the sirens had been tried out for practice purposes, now it was the real thing and for the first time I experienced that sudden coldness in the heart, that automatic tensing of the muscles that later on was to become so habitual that one hardly noticed it. A zealous ARP warden appeared from nowhere and waved us to take cover immediately. We were ushered into a large apartment building and led down into the basement, which was rapidly becoming overcrowded. Everyone was calm, but one lady carrying a baby was in tears. I remember wondering whether this was going to be a real knock-out blow, a carefully prepared surprise attack by Hitler within the first hour of war being declared. It was an unpleasant thought and well within the bounds of possibility. More and more people came hurrying down, and I decided that if I had to die I would rather die in the open and not suffocate slowly with a lot of strangers at the bottom of a lift shaft. I hissed this to David who agreed, and so we forced our way up the stairs and into the hall. Here, to my surprise, we found Morris Angel, the famous theatrical costumier, who said, ignoring the disapproval of the ARP gentleman who was trying to force him down the stairs: 'I think this calls for a bottle of Bubbly!' He then led us up to his flat on the third floor, introduced us to his wife, who was very cross because the electricity had been cut off and her Sunday joint was ruined, and opened a bottle of excellent champagne. With this we toasted the king, each other, and a speedy victory for the Allies.

As for the air-raid wardens themselves, it must have seemed — on that day at least — that they had finally come into their own. The Reverend Markham writes that, it being a Sunday, they had had their usual service

and then prepared for our Sung Eucharist. Most of the choir had been evacuated, leaving a few young ladies, one of whom had to be pressed into service at the last moment to play the organ for the first time in her life, as our regular organist had been evacuated with his firm. In due course we started, with a congregation of a few old ladies and soldiers — 50 Royal Irish Riflemen in full battle kit who had been allocated to the area as an anti-paratroop force, and who clattered into their pews with their rifles and tin hats, which they had apologised for beforehand ... I got into the pulpit for the sermon, started to preach on the Good Samaritan, when the air-raid warning sirens wailed. I looked at the congregation for a second or two, none of us daring to imagine what was about to happen. We had all been indoctrinated with the idea that it would all start with massive bombing of London. I said 'Ladies and gentlemen. I do not know what you will do; you can stay here, go down to the crypt shelter or home, but I must go to the warden's post without delay.' With these words, I dashed into my vestry, tore off my vestments, and, in my shirts-leeves, shot into the basement room of my house, to find a covey of 14 lady telephonist volunteers, hurriedly, and in some panic, being fitted with their gas masks by one or two of the men. I seized a tin hat and my wife's Red Cross army-type respirator, and dashed off into the street to see what was happening at the half-finished shelter in the recreation ground. Already the streets were manned by War Reserve policemen in full gas clothing, consisting of oilskin coats and trousers, rubber boots, helmets and respirators, warning rattles in their hands.

When I arrived at the recreation ground, I was confronted by a dense crowd of people from the East Street market, which had been at its usual Sunday morning height of activity. Prominent in front of this crowd were several youths, who had outrun the rest, and before I could do anything, they piled down the builders' ladders into the half-finished shelter. I had visions of broken limbs and panic. Angrily I tore down the Air Raid Shelter notice which the borough engineer had displayed.

There was another air-raid warning as darkness fell ... great excitement in the Walworth road, as people living in one of the flats above a shop had fled from London, leaving all their lights on and the windows without blinds. No one could get in from the street: I was summoned. How could we attract the attention of anyone who might be on the premises? My wardens wanted to break in, but I said 'Let's try once more to attract their attention; I'll get my air-pistol.' With that I ran to the Rectory, got the pistol and fired a couple of slugs at the top window at the rear of the flat. There were no signs of life, so up swarmed one of my wardens (at such speed to the third floor that I strongly suspected that he was a cat-burglar) and climbed into a window. I followed more slowly, and found myself looking into the window of the kitchen, and a sink full of unwashed dishes. So ended this brief adventure, only to be recalled by the local newspapers with large headlines 'RECTOR FIRES AT WINDOW'.

But the excitement was not to last. The sirens had sounded for a solitary, friendly plane, and Britain settled down to months of what the Americans later called 'the phoney war'. As with the period between Munich and the declaration of war, this gave those involved with Civil Defence a period of calm in which to train for what lay ahead. The Reverend Markham explains how

we wardens received blue boiler suits with 'ARP' in red on the breast pocket and chromium-plated buttons. We also got a slightly superior form of gas-mask, carried in a canvas bag instead of the cardboard box. Equipment, such as rubber boots, tin hats and six small axes appeared sporadically. At one time the crypt housed a dump of cardboard boxes, which proved to contain a large number of left-foot boots, but no right ones. Sandbags replaced our orange boxes as protection. A start was made in issuing gas masks for children and unwieldy respirators for babies, whose air-supply was maintained by the mother pumping bellows ... School children began to drift back ... When we saw them off just before the war, we had no idea where they were going, other than the fact that they left Waterloo Station ... Eventually a telegram came, telling us that they had settled in Parkstone, near Poole. Apparently, their train from London had landed them at Wareham, where coaches were waiting to take them to a variety of small Dorset villages. However, a train-load of Southampton children, carefully destined by their borough

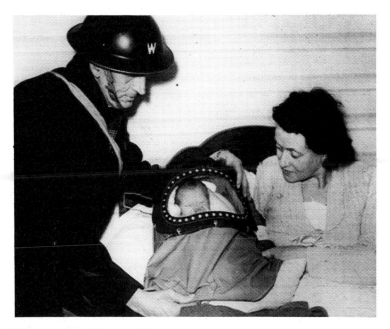

Nine-months-old baby inside a respirator.

for the wealthy billets in Parkstone, were loaded onto coaches meant for our Walworthians. The final result was that our children from the poorer district of South London were housed with the rich, while the Southampton children found themselves scattered in the more primitive villages ... It was not long before the richer families tired of their London children, and they were re-billeted with working-class families.

Besides church matters, I was faced with the task of organising the ARP post area, and the band of wardens. We embarked on an intensive series of exercises at all hours. We had to make sure that we knew what we were doing, if bombs did fall. We drilled ourselves so that in the time of crisis it would be automatic. At the time, the wardens used to grumble a great deal about this training, which often necessitated long waits in the cold and dark, without anything very tangible to keep their interest. The story runs that one, acting as a casualty, got fed up with a long wait, and went home, leaving a note 'Casualty dead. gone home' Another chore which was unpopular, and which occupied a great deal of their time, was a census of everybody in the area, indicating how many people were likely to be in the house and where, by day and also by night. This was to prove of vital importance later on ... In one of the heaviest raids, 16-17 April 1941, a large bomb hit a block of flats in my area ... After much cross-checking, which took several hours, I decided that after all the rescuing, there were still two possible casualties unaccounted for in the rubble of one of the buildings. By this time it was a warm, sunny morning. One rescue party was standing by in case of emergency: all the other services had left the site. We called and listened, by the heap of bricks and mortar. Then we heard what sounded like the faint mewing of a cat. I told the rescue squad to dig, and very soon we found two girls, one dead under the remains of a kitchen table, where she had sheltered, the other still alive, sitting in the remains of an armchair close by. She was the source of that faint sound, which was all she could make when she regained consciousness six hours later. Her throat and lungs were choked with the white mortar dust.

While the Battle of Britain began, we hastened our organisation of the wardens. By this time we had about 40 part-time and a few full-timers, who had to work 12-hour shifts. The latter were not the pick of the volunteers, but men and women who were ineligible for the armed forces, including one or two conscientious objectors. They found the long hours of duty very often boring during this pre-blitz era.

Stephen Melville Woodcock describes one way to keep the wardens busy, a practice 'incident' at an empty house in Landsmere Crescent.

It was good fun and proved instructive. Fourteen 'casualties' of various sorts were distributed about the house, with myself labelled 'unwounded'. The idea was that if the warden who was dealing with the incident had any sense he would use me as an assistant. Longman was put in charge. A determined friend of ours, Miss Smythe, was labelled 'hysterical' and others were labelled with more or less serious injuries, one being supposed to have swallowed her false teeth. 'Trapped casualties' were arranged in the basement amid a mix-up of old stones, fenders, etc.

When the fun began the 'hysterical' Miss Smythe made such a hullaballoo at a window that passers-by enquired anxiously what was wrong and Gwen [his wife], who was passing, was considerably startled. The attentions of the warden-in-charge only made for more shrieks and I wondered what Longman would do about it.

However, he dealt with her eventually and also her companion, Miss Orpen, who was supposed to have swallowed her false teeth and got them stuck in her throat. His treatment for this was to lay her on her face and shake her head about, which made her feel so sick that she had to be taken into the garden and attended to. Longman, a quiet (unless roused) publisher, flitted about in a cloak, bending over recumbent forms rather like a stage tenor searching for his true love in an opera scene. I kept passing him hints that there were three people in a bad way upstairs and three more trapped in the basement, but he seemed attached to the hall and ground-floor rooms. I felt that I had saved his reputation by fetching walking cases from upstairs, including the aged General Adair who, with a pseudo-cut-hand, was holding it over an old bucket 'to avoid damaging the carpet'. It was all very instructive and showed up our faults, but all the wounded were out of the house within half an hour and on the way to the first aid post or hospital, notwithstanding the 'bomb crater' at the front door.

Such preparations were not confined to London, of course. John H. Smith, a general purpose lorry driver working for Bristol Corporation at this time, was ordered to report for work on air-raid precautions.

Our first job after training was to go to the old coal pit tips and sandhills with slag, ashes, or any suitable ballast for filling sandbags. I was part of a convoy of lorries so engaged. Then all place names, direction signs, boundary stones, milestones, advertisement signs giving place names or information useful to invading troops had to be removed or erased. Barriers of sandbags were placed across roads and junctions, air raid shelters erected on streets. Underground shelters dug in public parks and squares. Wardens' posts established. Street lights dimmed and masked. White lines painted on roads and kerbs and posts painted white. Anderson shelters put into gardens. Concrete and brick shelters in the streets. Reserve supplies of gas and water pipes and also drums of electric cable placed at strategic points to be used to bridge the main services if they became damaged in air raids. A list made of all known wells and springs and the water tested in case of damage to water mains ...

Men who had never used a pick and shovel before worked at the digging. There were many aching backs and blistered hands. It was a colossal job and a race against time. Shifts were worked around the clock. Oil hurricane lamps lit the scene at night — these to be extinguished if an air raid occurred.

But those working for the various emergency services at this period received little thanks from the public they were engaged to protect. In fact there is ample evidence that until the blitz actually arrived they were considered to have found themselves a pretty cushy number, with members of the AFS (Auxiliary Fire Service) notably singled out for accusations of draft dodging. In his novel *Caught*, Henry Green, himself an auxiliary fireman, describes how

an elderly gent walked right into the station, cried out in a loud voice, 'You won't be getting my money much longer.' Boys, riding bikes on errands, called out to them, 'Why don't you join the army?'

And Patrick Mayhew (in *One Family's War*) confirms that

within a matter of weeks from the start of the war, and in the absence of the expected air raids, there was a reaction against all the defence forces, with a newspaper headline about 'Patriotism at £3 a week', and Judge Metcalfe sending a man to prison with the remark that 'there are too many Auxiliary Firemen anyway'.

Maurice Richardson, for one, in his book *London's Burning*, was quite frank about having joined the Service 'to dodge the army'. And he welcomed the idea of having 24 hours off every two days so that he could carry on writing his regular weekly reviews. But whatever the motives of the volunteers — and there is no reason to believe that those of the majority were anything but honourable — any ill-will towards them was soon forgotten when the bombs actually began to fall.

While those involved in Civil Defence were keeping up their training, meetings were being held up and down the country for members of the general public to find out how to defend themselves in case of attack. During one such meeting Gwladys Cox

learned that ... stirrup pumps are each manned by three

volunteers, one to fetch buckets of water, another to work the pump and a third to direct the spray. An incendiary bomb must not be tackled by a jet of water, but by a fine spray, in order to prevent the fragments scalding.

Those in country districts perhaps took matters somewhat less seriously, if one can judge from the account Margaret Kennedy gives of an ARP lecture in Cornwall in July 1940.

Mr Trelawney, the chemist, spoke first. He told us, in his mild, hesitating voice, that he believed the official air-raid advice is that resentment is a good antidote to fear. 'If you find yourself frightened in a raid,' he said, 'you should try to feel resentment.' So we all wrote down in our books: (1) Keep away from windows. (2) Corner of room better than middle. (3) Feel resentment.

In order to protect the eardrums, he said, the mouth should be lightly closed and the teeth left open. Everybody made the most peculiar faces when they practised this. I'm sure I should never remember.

Colonel Farraday, looking very cheerful, showed us how to work a stirrup pump and advised us all to get one, adding that there are none to be had anywhere just now. He also explained how to put up an Anderson shelter and said that none were being issued in that part of the country. He then showed us how to put out an incendiary bomb with sand and a long-handled shovel. He told us how he had been gassed in the last war, and that cheered us all up considerably, for it had not occurred to us that anyone could be gassed and live to tell the tale, much less tell it as zestfully as Colonel Farraday. Finally he invited us to become wardens and said anyone could become one — 'men, or women, or clergymen', which provoked us to unseemly giggles.

Both these public meetings took place in the summer of 1940, by which time many parts of Britain had suffered sporadic attacks from enemy aircraft. But in the first few weeks it was difficult to believe that the country was indeed at war. On 10 September, one week after that first false alert, John

Colville (then Private Secretary to the Prime Minister) noted in his diary that

from the point of view of the civilian this war has hardly begun in earnest, and only the black-out at night, and the barrage balloons by day, remind one that Europe has finally toppled over the brink of the precipice upon which it has been balancing precariously for the last 12 months. Doubtless there is much in store for us that will dispel our cherished illusions of peace; but for the moment the war seems very unreal.

Ever since war was declared the sun has shone with unremitting splendour, and there is nothing about the gaily dressed, smiling crowds in the streets to remind us of this great catastrophe — except perhaps for the gas-masks slung across their backs and the number of men in uniform.

A few extracts from the diary of Gwladys Cox help to convey what life was like in London as they waited for the bombs to fall, a period during which the principal peril was that of negotiating the blacked-out streets at night, shuffling along with a tiny masked torch, or driving with just one headlight on, and that covered with cardboard pierced with two-inch holes.

Sep 20 — There has been a perfect holocaust of cats in London, and, as a result, some districts according to the papers, are threatened with a plague of vermin. So, now, the authorities are begging people to keep their pets if poss.

Oct 9   In Bond Street, Ralph noticed that the sandbags, owing to the rain, were beginning to burst. Those on the pavements are being sprayed over with concrete now; some are painted bright colours, others, chiefly before flower shops, have imitation grass spread over them.

Oct 16 — My friend, Jane, told me that she had heard that [the trenches] in Hyde Park were really constructed so that they could be used as burial places after the air raids. She also told me that in Willesden, there was a factory making cardboard coffins!

Our blackout casualties are heavy. In Sept., the 1st blackout month, 1,130 persons died as a result of road accidents, as against 554 in the same month last year.

Oct 21 — It seemed that our missing barrage balloon (in cricket field) was destroyed by fire last Sunday evening at the time when we heard the fire-engines late that very wet night. It broke loose in the storm and came down on a house in Greencroft Gdns. Frightened by the scraping noise of the cables on the roof and the sound of escaping gas, the occupants looked out and saw flames outside the windows. Thinking it was an air raid, they rushed for gas masks and, then, found a room on fire. A barrage balloon had fallen partly over the house and partly on the garden. Jane says that the flames were seen in Maida Vale and people thought it was an incendiary bomb.

Nov 13 — The first bombs to fall on British soil in this war crashed on the Shetlands. Two raids this morning. One empty house was damaged, some windows broken, deep craters made on open land and one rabbit killed.

No less than 564 persons were killed during the hours of darkness in Oct, due to blackout in the majority of cases. Light bulbs have been blackened, but the heat flakes off the paint and they have to be constantly re-painted.

Nov 19 — The cricket field is becoming a bog and the balloon men squelch about in high gum boots.

Nov 22 — The price of kittens is 10/6 [52½p] each. Ordinary kittens! Now the place is overrun with vermin there is an outcry for kittens.

Jan — Casualties the worst ever, 1,155 killed on the roads in December.

Eros statue is now stored away for safety, its base boarded up with a gay frieze of Pearly Queen flower sellers and 'bobbies' gives a cheerful touch.

At home we are trying to live as normally and cheerfully as possible, but there is little social life, as so many of our friends have left town. There are no food queues as yet. The paper shortage is becoming a real hardship, not only for newspapers, but wrapping-paper, paper serviettes, etc. ... It's wonderful, however, what you find you can do without.

August 7 — So many Londoners are away that we have the place about to ourselves. And its peace, solitude and spaciousness are unspeakably refreshing.

This was possibly the last time that anyone in South-East England would be talking about 'peace and solitude'. Five days after Gwladys wrote these words the *Luftwaffe* launched major attacks on airfields and radar stations; the following day, Tuesday 13 August, was *Adlertag*, the start of the main *Luftwaffe* thrust prior to invasion. The Battle of Britain had begun.

In other parts of Britain, however, the bombs had already been falling, as we can see from the diary of Laurie Latchford, a warden living just outside Swansea.

June 1940 — The extinguishing of the navigation lights and the Mumbles Lighthouse has claimed further victims ... the prevention seems worse than the cure ... It has been very dark recently, so dark that it has been impossible to distinguish the skyline except for a slight lightening where sky and sea meet ... The flame of a match looks like a flare.

June (28 ? no date) — We had an air raid yesterday, the first over Swansea. The distinctive throb of aeroplane engines could be heard plainly. The planes must have been flying very low. No searchlights were showing. There was no siren and no AA fire ... heard this morning that a plane had dropped six bombs. One in the docks, one in the river, and one that went through a house and buried itself in the back garden. Another three fell on Kilvery Hill, not one of all these bombs had exploded! Duds or delayed action bombs.

July 5 — The raid showed some ARP teething troubles in Swansea. The shops urged people to go to the official refuges, but these were not open, and people had to wait until a warden arrived to unlock them. Near Rutland Street Station, queues formed outside the shelters in that area, with little groups of people rushing from one to another in the hopes of finding one open. The refuges were opened each in turn by one warden! Thank you Jerry for a most valuable dress rehearsal!

July 19 — The defences in Swansea area are still growing. More soldiers have arrived and more searchlights have been installed. Iron rails are being driven into the wide sands of Swansea bay, about 100 feet apart. They are about 10 feet high. The swimmers' diving platforms are being used to help drive the stake. Special twisted iron stakes to take barbed wire have been set up along the shoreline, and are being clothed rapidly.

July 21 — Our balloon barrage now has 'pups'. Another two balloons have been added. Across the bay, Port Talbot has its first balloons, five, sailing against a background of fields and cloud-shadowed moons sloping up to the mountains.

Aug 1 — So much defence is being done that I wonder if Swansea Bay is being considered by the authorities as a possible secondary or diversionary invasion point.

Aug 12 — Landore had a tragic Saturday Night [the 10th]. Many bombs were dropped. Reports of 16 people killed, and many injured. [It] is a working class district full of independent, if not truculent people. They would not take cover. Nineteen bombs were dropped roughly in a straight line ... A woman and her children standing at their house door, who a moment before had been asked to take cover (she had replied that she would do as she liked in her own home), was badly cut with flying glass. A family of five in an Anderson shelter had a bomb explode underneath them. Not one survived. A wardrobe in their house fell, and knocked on the electric light switch. With neighbours frantically yelling to them in front of the home to 'put out that light', the family were all dead in the remains of their Anderson shelter in the back garden.

Sep 1 — In the evening at about 9 o'clock the sirens went. Very soon the air was full of the throb of aeroplane engines punctuated by bomb explosions. The raid developed into the most savage attack. Wave after wave of planes came in from the west ... The raid showed a distinct pattern, one wave of bombers dropped high explosives and turned away, then the next wave showered down a great mass of incendiary bombs, the following wave dropped high explosives, and so on. I could see the white flashes of the incendiaries as they hit the ground and the casing began to burn. There were hundreds of these intense white flaring lights. Some suddenly ceased to show as wardens and others put them out, others burnt themselves out, but with others, the white light turned to an angry red glow where the fires had started. When fires within the town were well alight, the devils began to power dive the bigger buildings, the engines screeching to a frightening crescendo. At one point the roar of bomb explosions became almost continuous. All the while, fresh waves of bombers followed up ... incendiaries, high explosives, incendiaries ... As I patrolled under the continual throb and roar of incoming aircraft, a red glow began to spread across the fires from the direction of south west ... The eastern sky was now a deep orange glow. I then went to the village vantage point by the steps. As the view opened up I stopped in sheer shock and horror. I found my mouth open, and my eyes staring. All Swansea Bay was lit by a deep red light ... above rolled slowly a dense mass of orange smoke miles high. Throb of the German planes was still continuous, growing in volume then fading to be replaced by the throb of another wave of aircraft ... The inner suburbs were suffering badly. The windows of the houses on the hill slopes, reflected the fires and made a red, seemingly flaming frame for the fearsome picture of the burning town. Finally at about 4 am the 'All clear' went. Slowly I went to the port and then home. All around was silence. Smoke from burning buildings drifted westwards in the still night across the gardens, fields and parks like an autumn mist, bringing with it the smell of burnt wood. The red stain from Swansea filled the whole sky.

His diary over the next few days refers to a 'slowly-twisting column of black smoke several miles high' rising from some

nearby oil refineries on Wednesday 4 September, and air raids 'at almost hourly intervals' during the night of the 6th, with soldiers taking up street guard duties and the Home Guard 'mounting anti-looting patrols at night'.

Even remote country districts were within the range of bombers, and Margaret Kennedy reported an attack on the little Cornish village where she was living with her children that August.

Just as the news bulletin finished we heard a whistle. The village is too small to have a siren, so the local warden, who keeps the general shop, gives the warnings on a whistle. If he has on a tin hat it means 'Alert' and if he has a cap it means 'All clear'. When the whistle goes everyone rushes out to look at him and see which it is.

We thought we had better get home, as we had most of us left children unattended at the boarding house. But Viola said there was no hurry, at which everybody smiled. I expect her refusal to have traffic with the war is a bit of a joke with them. We started down the lane and heard the zoomzazoom-zazoomzazoomza of a German bomber. (I don't care what anybody says: it has got a different note from our planes, which go zoomzoomzoom.) Searchlights pencilled the sky, AA guns began firing from the surrounding hills and shells burst overhead. There was a sudden flare of incendiaries in the direction of the Objective, and a crump which sounded like heavy explosive.

We ought by rights to have taken cover or lain down flat under a hedge, but we were worried about our children and hurried on as best we could ... We found all the children hanging excitedly out of the boarding-house windows watching the raid. I began fussing and said they should keep away from the windows. Viola had just begun a crushing 'My dear Margaret. It's quite unnecessary ...' when there came a loud CRUMP a good deal nearer than previous crumps and she hastily seized Dinah and thrust her under the nearest bed. After that the raid seemed to die down for a while and we all went to bed.

By this time London was subject to constant alerts. Vera Brittain noted that during one fortnight in August the capital had 30 raids,

and her citizens visit department stores in thousands to purchase mattresses and campbeds for their inadequate shelters. Gradually they become accustomed to nightly descents into the basement, and dawn trips back to their bedrooms after the sound of the all-clear. We believe we are discovering how well we can manage with a few hours' sleep — or none.

At present, since only a few districts have suffered, there is no rushing to shelters when the sirens begin, though one morning the sight of an old man dropping dead in front of Kensington Cinema at the first banshee note makes me realise the secret terror with which it is awaited by the elderly and the helpless.

'Don't hurry, dearie!' urges a woman walking quietly towards a shelter to an agitated old lady on a Sunday afternoon. 'It's not the raid, it's the hurrying that upsets you.'

After a few days, most people continue their occupations when the siren sounds; often, writing my book or dictating letters, I become so oblivious of the raid that when the all-clear goes, I imagine it to be another warning. In some of the big stores, 'roof-spotters' now relay a running commentary to the customers taking shelter below. 'There's a puff of smoke to the north-west ... Now there's nothing, so I'll put on a record.'

The only persons who suffer from London's half-amused indifference to raiders are the air-raid wardens, who cannot take cover until others have done so. But even the sang-froid of the capital's workers will not continue for many more days.

By the 23rd Londoners were beginning to be seriously annoyed by the raids. George Orwell noted in his diary that there had been a warning at three o'clock that morning, so he

got up, looked at the time, then felt unable to do anything and promptly went to sleep again. They are talking of rearranging the alarm system, and they will have to do so if they are to prevent every alarm from costing thousands of pounds in wasted time, lost sleep etc. The fact that at present the alarm sounds all over a wide area when the German planes are only operating in one part of it, means not only that people are unnecessarily woken up or taken away from work, but that an impression is spread that an air-raid alarm will *always* be false, which is obviously dangerous.

He added, on 31 August, that

air-raid warnings, of which there are now half a dozen or thereabouts every 24 hours, [are] becoming a great bore. Opinion spreading rapidly that one ought simply to disregard the raids except when they are known to be big-scale ones and in one's own area. Of the people strolling in Regent's Park, I should say at least half pay no attention to a raid warning.

The authorities were apparently of the same opinion, since, in September, they stopped sounding the sirens for every single raider. The 'Warning' became the 'Alert', with work stopped only when an enemy plane was reported by roof-spotters as being practically overhead.

By this time the raids were becoming so frequent that on 7 September Orwell could write:

Air-raid alarms now frequent enough, and lasting long enough, for people habitually to forget whether the alarm is on at the moment or whether the All-Clear has sounded. Noise of bombs and gunfire, except when very close (which probably means within two miles) now accepted as a normal background to sleep or conversation.

But that was the day, remember, when the relatively minor raids gave way to the full-scale blitz, and the bombers came to London for 65 nights running (with one exception because of atrocious weather). Few people now would forget if there was a raid on.

What some people were wondering during the period leading up to the all-out blitz was the extent to which the time of preparation had been well spent. Margaret Kennedy had received a rather worrying letter in June from a friend of hers in Liverpool.

She is rather perturbed lest the people don't even now realise the ordeal that is in front of them. She knows what she is talking about, for she is in the thick of the Merseyside ARP. She trained to be a warden ... in May 1938, after Hitler went into Austria, and when ARP was first started. Now she is working in a slum district and comes into contact with all sorts of people.

She says they are brave enough for anything, and will stand any amount of horrors if only they know what to expect. But she fears the first awful shock when the raids start. She thinks there may be a dangerous interval of sheer, numb stupefaction, before they pull themselves together and adapt themselves. Because neither the masses of people nor the majority of the officials have the least idea what it will be like. They are prepared for deaths and injuries, but they seem to think that if a bomb doesn't kill you or maim you life will go on quite normally. They don't envisage whole streets of homes wiped out, and huge fires, gas, water, and electric light cut off, traffic dislocation, and telephones out of order ...

I get the same account from Claire's parents in London. They say all the preparations there seem to be made in the expectation that everyone will shortly be dead. In the hospital where they are living there are 30,000 cardboard coffins all folded flat, stacked up, and waiting for occupants. And there are acres of trench graves already dug.

A dead Londoner will be wonderfully catered for. So will an injured Londoner. The medical services are well organised, the ambulances and first-aid posts are all ready, there is plenty of hospital accommodation, and supplies of blood are kept ready for transfusion. But a homeless Londoner is going to be out of luck, though there will surely be more of them than of dead or wounded.

Anna says the same thing. She says there should be emergency feeding centres, hostels and clothing depots, but hardly any preparations of that kind are being made. She talked to an official in an East End district and he actually said: 'People from a bombed house can go into a neighbour's'. Anna pointed out that one bomb can demolish a street. There might be no neighbours. Want of imagination is the curse of this country. Everything that has been foreseen has been very efficiently provided for, but our preparations seem to be a mixture of superb organisation and purblind muddle.

Far too much, Anna says, is being left to local authorities. They are often genial woolly-headed old duffers, elected because they are popular in the district and quite capable of fixing a water-rate or deciding where the new recreation ground is to be, but they hardly know the difference between a high explosive and an incendiary bomb and will be about as useful in Armageddon as a popgun.

And these were the type of people whose incompetence was to cause the needless deaths of the bombed-out East Enders referred to in Chapter 1. Ritchie Calder, in the book from which that account was taken, confirmed that the authorities had entirely misjudged the effect of intensive bombing.

For years before the war CD experts had been estimating the possible effects of the *Blitzkrieg*. They made abundant, and in the light of what happened, extravagant provision for the dead. Their predictions of the number of injured were fantastically greater than the actual numbers. We were told to expect 100,000 casualties a week, or 3,000 killed and 12,000 injured each night ... Actually the figures for September were: killed 6,954; injured 10,615; those for October were: killed 6,334; injured 8,695. Those were for the whole country, but four-fifths were in London ...

The number of homeless, however, which on any estimate would obviously be greater than either the dead or the wounded, or both, was ludicrously underestimated. The provision for them was niggardly and inadequate. A cup of tea and a bully beef sandwich at a bare, cheerless Rest Centre was all the care the country had to offer its Front Line civilians bombed out of their homes. Twenty-four hours of crowded lodging-house conditions and then — scram!

3.
IN THE ROARING CENTRE
London, September to mid-November 1940

This, then, is a wonderful moment for us who are here in London, now in the roaring centre of the battlefield, the strangest army the world has ever seen, an army in drab civilian clothes, doing quite ordinary things, an army of all shapes and sizes of folk, but nevertheless a real army, upon whose continuing high and defiant spirit the world's future depends.

> J.B. Priestley, ending his BBC 'Postscript' of Sunday 15
> September 1940

Another temporary Londoner, like Priestley, was 22-year-old Nancy Bosanquet who sent her parents a series of letters describing life in London during the weeks she was waiting to be posted to Cardiff as an ambulance driver. The first was written from Kensington on the night of 12 September.

My dear Mummy,
I am writing this in the shelter at about 9.00 and when I have got the first news over I may make it into a diary. At present guns are going off loudly all round. Coming into London

there was scant sign of damage except two large buildings apparently without a single window to their name and a hole in a church roof. They say there are two houses down in Palace Gardens Terrace or Vicarage Gate, one in Bedford Gdns, two in Sheffield Terrace, no windows left in Blenheim Crescent and a mere shambles left of Madame Tussauds. They say the Victoria and Albert has been hit and we are waiting for one in Pembridge Rd which has not yet exploded, so the roadway all round is positioned off and all nearby houses are evacuated. I got to Paddington at about 2.30, and at 3.15 sped off to get my passport and photographs done — for identity I suppose. By the time the bus had got to the Bedford Dairy a warning went, but nobody got off the bus so neither did I, but went on to Victoria, got the photographs taken, and came back. Still the warning was on, so I went to the garden where Mary and Mrs G were standing by the shelter ready to pop in. As I emerged from the back door I heard a plane, so I belted up the steps, tripping slightly as I went, and we all went under cover. The plane came near, and there was a beastly swish as it dropped a bomb, which only exploded faintly, and then it sounded as if the plane was hit and falling, but it may have been diving over something. I must say I hated that. We got in after 5.0 and made tea. The kettle was just boiling when another warning went so we took it outside with us and had it in peace. After tea was taken mostly in preparing for the night. The shelter is crammed with rugs and cushions — May and Mrs G and two chairs and me opposite them on a rug on the steps. Any sort of bed or bunk would be utterly impossible, and so would sleep.

My! that gun is near — an extraordinary hollow sound. Like a terrific tympani — and then after it the comfortable sound of a train putting out at Paddington ... I rang my ambulance station (here comes a plane) and offered myself at night for the next ten days (what an Irish remark) and they replied that they would be delighted to see me and that they have been SO busy. It will mean 24 hours work a day and something like 168 per week — no that's wrong because I shall only be training for five days and I can stand it for five days — but continual warnings during the day are going to be a trial. Anyway I feel frightfully pleased that they want me and it will be a case of training during the day and priceless experience by night. (Here comes another plane in a great hurry and such a welcome of guns for him — the same old throbbing noise.) The more I see of Londoners the more I admire their amazing calmness. True they all look a trifle white and tired, but not drawn and most cheerful and ordinary.

10.30 My God! This is hellish! Over went a plane just now and dropped about six bombs, each one swishing as it dropped. I just crouch terror-stricken with an eiderdown up round my ears, but it has gone away now, and here comes another. Oddly enough I didn't hear the bang of the bombs, so they must really have been miles away.

11.30 Well — we're still alive anyway and honestly I don't find it so alarming except when bombs fall. That sounds just like those fireworks which send up stars with a sudden swish, and IS beastly. The guns I am already fond of as old friends. They have all very distinctive voices, there is one very near that sounds like a thunder clap straight overhead, and the one that sounds like a giant tympani, and what is so nice is that they mask, with their shouting, and their YELLING and BAWLING, the drone of planes, which is frankly horrible … the guns are still booming away. I should like to go and pat them on the head. It is marvellous too how safe one feels in here — a nice safe little nutshell, half-buried in the ground, and so infinitely small when you think of the size of London.

Lord! How we shall want to dance for joy when the all-clear sounds. I must roll over and rest for a bit — with my tail on a cushion half way down the steps and my head on a pillow on the kitchen stool, and the position only kept by having my knees pressed against the side of the shelter.

1.30 Fancy that. I think I now consider myself quite case-hardened. A bomb came whooshing down and then exploded about as far away as the bottom of Church Street, and I didn't bother to cover my ears for it. The detonation of the guns is a queer process — a big bang as they go off, and a gentle pop as they presumably explode in the air, rather like the bob to a jump. I have decided now that the noise is something like an enormous carpet-beating.

2.00 From the sound of it, that whoosh was near my ambulance station.

3.30 One gets beastly cold at this time of the morning, and I think I must be getting very tired too because that last series of whooshes set me palpitating with alarm. I don't think the last was an incendiary. The clap of thunder hasn't spoken lately. I do hope it has not been silenced. At rare intervals I hear a car going by which may be an ambulance. Apparently Mitchell was very upset yesterday after helping to rescue some people buried under their home — I shall find it pretty beastly at first if I go out tomorrow night on duty. (Did you realise how safe this shelter was? It will be almost impossible for it to be hit as it is so surrounded by buildings.)

4.00 The voice of the thunder has spoken again, and shaken the air with his speaking. Also a bomb or two came whistling over our heads just then and exploded somewhere VERY near. Portobello or Chepstow Villas, though I shall probably find it was Arthur's (?) Corner.

5.50 The all clear has gone and I am going to bed. We crawled out of the shelter as darkness began to fade — tousled and giddy with exhaustion. Of course it doesn't seem possible now that it ever happened, so it doesn't feel so very bad — my though, it was a LONG, LONG night, and beastly uncomfortable. May and Mrs G seemed unperturbed on the whole ... I feel myself that having survived last night I can survive anything ... I may find doing day and night work too exhausting, in which case of course the night work will have to be abandoned.

Yours with v. much love, N.

  Please would you send me two thick vests from my room and a small quantity of the eyebright lotion from the corner cupboard.

The next day she took the 31 bus to sign on for her ambulance work and for the first time was able to see the effects of the bombing.

Dear Daddy,
... The damage done to the East End and the Docks seems to be unimaginably awful. They say the fire put the Great Fire of London to shame, and that in the mews of my station you could have read by the light of it and every window reflected the red glow. They brought fire appliances from every district of London and round London — thousands of them — and at the height of the fire-fighting, back came the raiders and bombed and machine-gunned them as they worked and a great no. of men were lost. Part of the docks at any rate are utterly destroyed and whole streets laid waste.

West End ... everywhere are roads blocked by 'No Entry' or 'No Entry, Unexploded Bomb': so the 31 bus now curls about in all sorts of back streets, and meeting it going east and west, you don't know which corresponds to the south-bound and what the northbound. Eventually I got one.

An ambulance man came in while I was at 'Western' and said that a public shelter holding 500 at Becton or Merton or some such place had been hit by high explosive bomb and everyone believed killed. That is the sort of affair that gives the demolition squad their ghastly job of digging out the bits. They were considered the scum of the earth before all this happened, but now no praise is too high ...

22 Sept 1940.
Dear Daddy,
Walking up Oxford Street wasn't quite so easy as you might think. Large portions of it were roped off and one had to go by roundabout routes to the back of Portman Square. There I saw the usual sights — houses reduced to heaps of rubble — broken windows with the frames hanging out — and everything powdered with dust. I stood at the top of the stairs outside your bedroom and tried to imagine this house in the same state. It isn't possible to do so — so I hope it won't happen. Selfridges seems very little damaged, though near

Fire in Piccadilly caused by an incendiary bomb, 14 November 1940.

the back of Orchard Street was a crater, and over it the twisted skeleton of what might have been a bus or a large delivery van. But John Lewis's was a different story. I have never before — except for that church (the Church of Our Lady, by Earls Court Road) — seen the result of a big fire. This was still smoking in places and the sooty smell of it hung about the air. The west end of it seems fairly intact, though of course all the windows are gone and there is a black hollow look about it, but the Oxford Circus end is reduced to four corners and strips of stone between, the stonework shattered and the ground floor filled with charcoal, wet wood. What a good thing that Peter Jones is untouched so far, but what a crash of glass there would be if it WAS touched ...

Continued on Wednesday night ... I came home via Church Street this evening and as I passed the tube station at 6.0 I saw London going to ground — a crowd four deep waiting to shelter there for the night — of a size normally only found where there is Royalty or a first class accident. Another very notable thing now is the way private cars seem to stop as a matter of course at bus stops to pick up all they can. I saw two people, a man and woman, going home on the back of a car sitting on the luggage boot with their feet sticking out and chatting together most composedly. Of course, when I come home just before 6 one meets plenty of people going off to the shelter with their rugs and refreshments. Half London is going underground already and the other half is hurrying home to snatch a hasty meal before it follows suit ...

Nancy's mother also received a letter from a Mrs Slade, dated 26 September and referring to a raid on the 23rd.

40 Albert Square,
Stratford, E15

Dear Mrs Bosanquet,

As you can see, we are still at the same address. It is really most depressing as we have been, and are still having a really rough time. Monday night was THE night though. The guns started firing before the siren had gone at 7.10 pm and the din went on throughout the night until 5.45 am. The first few bombs set a timber yard ablaze, which could be seen from miles around ... Three roads away from us was struck either by an aerial torpedo, or a land mine, which are being dropped around these parts. Seven steel shelters were taken right out of the ground; the casualties so far are unknown. Of course this sort of thing can't go on indefinitely. It is heartbreaking to see the queues of homeless people standing about waiting for buses to take them a little further out, or outside the town hall or municipal offices waiting for help or advice. But it is still amazing at all the places still standing, and the number of people still carrying on in their usual manner ... I am afraid my husband's work will suffer very shortly, as a result of Air Raids; they start a few minutes EARLIER each evening, consequently he finishes a little earlier so as to get home in time for his evening meal. By the time winter really sets in, he will not be able to get in any hours at ALL. He is a builder and decorator, and all their work just now, consists of boarding up windows or covering roofs and pulling down dangerous structures. But we must hope for the best.
H. Slade

Not everyone in London shared Mrs Slade's feelings of resigned fatalism or just stood around waiting for the authorities to help them out. Many, as we have seen, fled the capital altogether. Others left the hard hit East End for less affected areas. As early as 10 September George Orwell was noting in his diary that

all over South London, little groups of disconsolate looking people [were] wandering about with suitcases and bundles, either people who have been rendered homeless or, in more cases, who have been turned out by the authorities because of an unexploded bomb ...

One of the East Enders whose house was badly damaged on the very first day was Emily Golder.

We couldn't get in the Rest Centre as that was full so we finally settled down in a brick surface shelter. During the day we would just wander around because there was nowhere, no toilets in fact, so we would find different cafes or places open to get something to eat and even to wash. At night we stayed in the surface shelter. We sat around on forms for several nights. We couldn't wash in there, there was nowhere, no running water. In fact all the gas and electricity were cut off. After several days in this shelter, then the council decide to lay on some coaches and get as many people away from that area that they could. Well, we finally finished up in the Majestic Cinema in Woodford — My God what a big building ... And all we could do was to sit in seats, once more there was no cooking facilities, we did manage to wash in the toilets there, so we'd go out during the day and find somewhere to eat.

After several days in the Majestic, then they decided to move us to Walthamstow, and by this time we were all beginning to feel like refugees, we never knew from one day to another where we were going to be and as for our jobs, it was impossible for us to get to Silvertown because actually there wasn't much transport, we could never have walked there and also if we had of gone, when we came home we never knew if any of the rest of the family had been moved on to somewhere else. We just wanted to be together and keep together as a family.

Some of these refugees ended up in West London, as Stephen Melville Woodcock noted on 13 September.

East Enders evacuated to Kensington, filled up our two basement shelters and the trench shelter for the night. I had 15 aliens and 20 East Enders in my basement at 2a Stanley Crescent. All went well until a worn out girl asleep on a bench dropped her baby on the floor and pandemonium ensued, with the baby's screams and all evacuees complaining of the lack of comfort. All they had been issued with was one small thin blanket. Added to the trouble, one girl was very, very sick. The Kensington food had not agreed with her. After calming the evacuees and assuring them that things would be improved tomorrow, I opened the box of emergency food comforts which the wardens have subscribed for and kept in a locked box for such occasions as this. Tea and Bovril made on an oil stove made everyone happier and the trouble was shelved ... the next day I sent [the girl] a parcel (at Gwen's suggestion) containing a blanket, large towel and two bits of soap. We hoped the mother would not think the soap an insult, but it was badly needed. The evacuees can't be blamed for being dirty ... one can forgive their outbursts of wrath, as the Borough of Kensington has shown up badly and was obviously caught unprepared, at any rate for the 100 evacuees sent to our part.

The East Enders are really quite nice; rather smelly after days without proper washing facilities and very grateful when they realise that someone is seeing to them ... it is a touching sight seeing them huddled together in all sorts of attitudes, with the children close together like sardines on the floor — and I suppose they may have to sleep in shelters for a long time to come.

The lucky ones, as Mrs Trixie Duke explains, were those with families to go to.

My parents lived in Manor House and I in Ilford — 2 miles away and we had an arrangement that which ever of us was bombed, moved in. In my parents' street there was a direct hit by a 100 lb bomb which killed many neighbours. My mum's house was severely damaged, she was unable to stay so they came to me. They were so upset, they had seen families pushing prams with their bits of home to outer London — Grange End, Chigwell etc to get away. Dad was at the Arsenal making munitions, so once the house had first aid repairs, her and Dad went back. Then a week later we had a land mine dropped 100 yards away — but the house was terribly damaged. For many months I had black paper ceilings and glass windows you couldn't see out of — I went to mum's for a couple of weeks. The water tank in the loft was blasted and with water pouring through our home we lost much of our furniture and all our wedding presents — and now when people show me what they had, I feel sorry we lost it all. I have one piece of furniture, scratched and dented left. An assessor from the bomb damage dept came to see me over my claim and he said if I was nice to him he would see I was well reimbursed. Needless to say I told him to get lost and got little for a lost home. This is what happened to women on their own — my husband was in the army. Then at Mum's an unexploded bomb dropped on a cycle shop at the corner of the road and the army was called in to defuse it — but unfortunately it went off and five young lives went — again Mum was back with me. The next time it was a terrible raid. We had the Polish Airforce at Fairlop Airfield and they were after that and through the night it was one thump after another. I was scared for me and my little lad. In the morning I got up, looked out on the garden and thought 'That looks funny' and went out to investigate, and there in the vegetable garden was this huge crater — so I put on our coats and went to the air raid warden and reported it. Within 15 minutes the army had arrived and I was told I had to go while they defused it — everyone in the street had to go. By now I was getting streetwise and I first went back to the air raid warden for my Lord Mayor's £10 for bomb victims, then to the Town Hall for coupons for food and clothes and then to the Red

Cross for clothes and we had enough to have a clean change
— then — yet again to Mum's.

**You needed to become streetwise, as Trixie puts it, very
quickly. Ritchie Calder explained in the late autumn of 1940
how the complex network of bureaucracy, at local and
national level, exacerbated the problems of the homeless.**

To try to maintain the patchwork of Metropolitan Boroughs,
with boundaries invisible in the built-up jigsaw of streets,
became a farce. The system of local councils proved itself
inadequate to the task imposed by the bombardment. Some
were better than others, but even the best of them were
heavily 'under the weather' as disaster piled upon disaster; in
some instances the administrative offices were themselves in
ruins. Local administrators and officials, with certain exceptions for whom no praise is adequate, were futile and
incompetent. Let that be stated frankly, for it is one of the
lessons of London which, having been learned, must not be
forgotten ...

Yet the blame for the breakdown belonged far more to the
Government than to the local authorities. Dealing with the
human problems of the air-raids were the Ministry for Home
Security, the Ministry of Health, the Ministry of Labour, the
Ministry of Transport, the Ministry of Food, the Ministry of
Pensions, the Regional Commissioner, the London County
Council and the borough councils. And the confusion of functions, the overlapping, the indecisions and, to quote a Cabinet
minister, 'the buck-passing' meant increased suffering for
thousands of unhappy raid-victims through the desperate
days of the Blitzkrieg ...

In the second week of the bombing, fourteen hours after a
high-explosive had wrecked five streets in another district of
one of the worst-bombed areas, I found hundreds of people
wandering desolately among the ruins of their houses. No
one was doing anything for them. No one had been near
them. They had no food. We hastened to find the nearest Rest
Centre, which was only a few streets away. The officials there
were most indignant when we remonstrated with them and

demanded to know why they had not collected the homeless and brought them in. 'They've no excuse,' they said, 'there is a notice outside the library telling them where to go and what to do.'

I saw that notice. It was a long series of instructions which read more like a manual of military manoeuvres than a comforting message to the homeless, and it finished up with this piece of official 'helpfulness' — 'If you have become separated from some of your family and do not know where to find them, apply to the Citizens' Advice Bureau. The officer in charge of the Rest Centre will tell you where to find this.' Imagine the effect of 'advice' of that kind to a mother whose family are missing after a raid!

But that was only a tail-piece to directions about: going to the Rest Centre; applying to the Public Assistance Officer for help-in-kind; seeking billets through the Town Hall; reporting to the Engineer's Department in respects of damage; getting compensation for lost household effects through the Assistance Board; getting in touch, if injured, with the chief Regional Officer of the Ministry of Pensions, 'whose address can be obtained at any Post Office'; recovering another food card through the National Registration Officer; and writing for a National Health Insurance card to the Ministry of Health's department in Blackpool.

I personally visited, in that Borough, all the different offices at which it was suggested the homeless should call in order to get immediate and essential needs. It meant walking three and a half miles. In a neighbouring Borough it meant eight miles. In a third Borough, five miles.

One effect of such official incompetence, Calder went on to say, was that servicemen who had been given compassionate leave to visit their bombed out families could, during the first three weeks of the blitz, be seen

wandering among the ruins or trailing round offices and Rest Centres trying to trace them. One soldier had already been to four different districts in the Greater London area trying to find his parents.

Another who, a fortnight afterwards, had found his parents in a school Rest Centre, miserable and broken, said: 'When I came through Dunkirk, I didn't think Mum and Dad would have to go through Dunkirk too.'

Calder added that

what the Government had to worry about in East London was not lack of morale among the people, but an excess of morale; not panic, but a rising flood of indignation.

Such mutterings of discontent were not, of course, mentioned in the papers or on the radio, subject as the media were to quite strict censorship. But contemporary diaries are full of examples. John Colville (still the prime minister's private secretary, but now with a new master) accompanied Mrs Churchill to her husband's constituency on Friday 4 October where they

toured the place with the Mayor and some of the councillors and inspected the havoc wrought by bombs and parachute mines. The saddest sight was the homeless refugees in a school. One woman, wheeling a baby in a pram, told me she had twice been bombed out of her house and kept on saying disconsolately: 'A load of trouble, A load of trouble'. One woman said, 'It is all very well for them,' (looking at us!) 'who have all they want; but we have lost everything.'

Harold Nicolson, on 17 September, had already noted that

everybody is worried about the feeling in the East End, where there is much bitterness. It is said that even the King and Queen were booed the other day when they visited the destroyed areas.

And on the same day a somewhat less disconsolate George Orwell described how

the other day 50 people from the East End, headed by some of the Borough Councillors, marched into the Savoy and demanded to use the air-raid shelters. The management didn't succeed in evacuating them till the raid was over, when they went voluntarily. When you see how the wealthy are *still* behaving, in what is manifestly developing into a revolutionary war, you think of St Petersburg in 1916.

The big West End hotels were, indeed, crammed full of the rich and well-connected. Ritchie Calder, after spending a night among the homeless in the East End, visited one such hotel to see how the other half lived.

The majority of the people there were homeless. They, too, had undergone the ordeal of bombs. Their houses in the fashionable squares were in ruins. To that extent they were 'in it' with the people of East London. I spoke to some of them. There was nothing wrong with their morale, either. But there was a world of difference in the way in which their morale was being maintained, and in the treatment which money could buy for them. For instance, a wealthy merchant from one of the fashionable squares told how he and his wife were dug out of their basement by the rescue squad, how a warden got them a taxi while some warm clothes were salvaged for them. Then they drove to the hotel where they were welcomed as old clients. The hotel staff wrapped them up in blankets and took them down to the spacious, well-heated shelters in the vaults. They were given brandy and sal volatile. There were comfy settees on which to sleep, and hot water bottles. Next morning there was a lavish breakfast, and it had now been arranged that they should go to a quiet country hotel. All the technical details had been handed over to the family solicitor.

Many people simply moved into the big hotels, as Cecil King (then director of the *Daily Mirror* and *Sunday Pictorial*) discovered on 11 September when he tried to get a room for the night after dining at the Dorchester with Duff Cooper.

The hotel, to my astonishment, proved to be crammed full and I had the greatest difficulty in getting a bed. Apparently a lot of jittery people, who do not regard their own houses as very stable, have moved in there. It was amusing at 11.00 pm, when I went up to bed, to see the astonishing mixed grill of people, mostly women with knitting, assembled to spend the night in chairs, or in the shelter if bombing got too bad.

Later that month, on the 23rd, he had dinner at the Savoy with Hugh (later Lord) Cudlipp, editor of the *Sunday Pictorial*.

I made for the restaurant (the Grill Room is long since closed altogether), but found that meals were being served in the air-raid shelter, so we threaded our way through endless passages and down into a large pillared room. Apparently the pillars were inadequate as the whole ceiling was supported by steel scaffolding — vertical and diagonal supports about six feet apart. As a consequence it was very difficult to get to one's table and equally difficult for the waiters to serve the food. These difficulties did not, I am afraid, stimulate the staff to do their best. The food was indifferent in quality and scanty in quantity, and the service was careless and sulky. The only thing up to the usual Savoy standard was the violinist operating behind some sandbags.

On our way out we overshot the exit by a couple of yards and found ourselves in the residents' portion of the shelter, inhabited by one fierce elderly military man in pyjamas and dressing gown and his wife, a stout matronly woman in crepe-de-chine nightie and wrap. Besides this couple there was a younger one in evening dress, and miscellaneous domestics. We eventually stumbled out into the Strand, where the air raid warning had been on for some time.

For the great majority, who could not afford to flee to second homes in the country or seek the comparative safety of the great steel-framed hotels, there was always the option of taking the law into their own hands.
At worst this meant using the anonymity of the blackout

to loot unguarded homes and shops. This again was little written about at the time and is an aspect of wartime Britain edited out from many people's memories. Cases of looting may well have been rare, and the good neighbourliness referred to in so many accounts of the period absolutely typical of what happened; nevertheless it would be mealy-mouthed to conceal that it did occur, putting an additional burden of grief on those raid-victims who suffered from it. One such was Gwladys Cox, as her diary shows:

Oct 2, 1940 — Last night, most of our home, together with the whole floor of Lymington Mansions, was destroyed by IBs. I am so dazed, so tired, so numb, I can hardly think . . . There was a terrific crash quite close . . . making the building stagger. We sprang to our feet . . . almost immediately the plunk, plunk of IBs was heard above, on OUR OWN ROOF! The sound was different to anything in the nature of a bomb almost soft, like footfalls of some giant stepping mincingly over the tiles.

They escaped to a shelter in another road as fire swept through the Mansions.

ARP wardens kept coming to the door to the shelter, taking a roll-call shouting out the names of missing people. Firemen looked in occasionally to report the progress of the blaze . . . The all-clear sounded at 11.15 pm and, immediately, we all left the shelter, and peered about us. Above, flames from our drawing-room roof reddened the sky, while searchlights swept the heavens. And when the firemen told us, bluntly, that no one could be allowed to return to the flats, we at last realised that we were literally homeless. We had always counted on being able to shelter in the cellar in the event of being bombed, but had reckoned without the AFS flooding — the area was already inches deep in water. As Mrs Snepp had so often asked us to go to her in an emergency, and her house was nearby we determined to take up her offer.

She returned to the flat with her husband Ralph the following day:

My neat and orderly home was a scene of indescribable desolation. The dining-room was completely burnt-out, neither of our windows remained. R's beautiful outsize desk, which besides our marriage certificates, fire insurance policy, contains all the letters I had written to him from abroad ... not even the ashes remained; his loss of books, his chief hobby, collected during a lifetime, were congealed black masses of cinders, hundreds of gramophone records had vanished into air. In the dining-room ... what remained of the furniture was covered with a shining layer of molten lead from the burning roof. The carpet was inches deep in a wet mixture of ceiling-plaster and burnt rafters. Wanting my cigarette case, which I had placed the night before, in a drawer, I found that it had disappeared. Under my bed, my trinket box was lying open, its contents scattered over the wet carpet. It had been taken out of the dressing-table drawer which had been forced, and everything of the least value removed. R's room had been ransacked and most of his underclothing, as well as a gold watch taken — all this the work of LOOTERS.

Other evidence comes from the Reverend Markham, writing of the events of the 28th of the month.

We wardens were on patrol around midnight, helping the police, whom we had alerted, to seek out some looters looting the belongings of bombed-out houses. We failed to catch them ... and returned. Jenner, my messenger boy, and I mounted our blitz bikes, brakeless, lampless, and started off down the street alongside the churchyard. We heard the explosion of one or two bombs in the distance, and carried out our usual drill — falling off our bikes without stopping. As we hit the ground, five bombs exploded around us, so that we could see orange flashes ... as we sprawled in the gutter. We got up and rushed to the church ... Then I heard a dull, confused murmur from the crypt, and a dusty figure struggled among the sandbags ... crying out 'help' ... I shouted that I would get help and ran round the church into the Post, dashed off a message ... giving a rough estimate of 200 casualties guessed from the number in that part of the crypt that appeared to be hit, and then ... ran round to the school next door, shouted to the RAF balloon crew, 'get your beds ready, and plenty of boiling water, and I will send all casualties around here' ... In a remarkably short time, the Mobile Unit, with a doctor on board and a complement of nurses were able to work on the casualties ... The balloon crew worked like trojans, helping in the crypt to bring out the casualties.

Two hundred and fifty were seriously hurt, and over 70 killed, with further hundreds of lesser casualties, caused mainly by splinters from the wooden partitions dividing the various parts of the crypt. The blast had torn the match-boarding into countless needle-like splinters which ripped into people and their belongings. Later on, when we salvaged the hundreds of handbags left in the crypt, we found them filled with minute fragments of wood which had pierced the leather or cloth of the bags without tearing them noticeably. Falling from a height of perhaps 20,000 feet, the bombs literally bored their way through the successive layers of the church ... one young man was lying asleep on the floor when the blast hurled a wooden kitchen chair through the air, and a slab of stone, likewise projected by the blast, drove the leg of the chair through his hip, where it was firmly embedded. When he was found, the rescuers sensibly left the chair-leg embedded, detached the remains of the chair, and sent him off to hospital. Within three months, he was back to work in his factory ... Another strange case was that of a young woman, who was sitting in a chair by the brick pier supporting one of the arches in the crypt. One of the bombs exploded just the other side, blowing a whole family, six members of which I commended to Almighty God a few days later at a funeral service in a neighbouring church. The young woman, just a few feet away from them, was uninjured except for a burst eardrum ... The dead were laid out in one of the undamaged aisles ... their blood stained the stone flags: I was glad I was able within a week to establish our altar on that very spot, where we offered the sacrifice of our worship.

With such slaughter happening every night it is no wonder that many thousands of Londoners chose another way of flouting the law, by disregarding official objections to using the underground stations as places of refuge.

Before the war the Chamberlain Government had concentrated on providing as many houses as possible with Anderson shelters (while recommending that individual householders strengthen their own cellars or ground floor rooms). But Andersons had to be erected in the garden, which was of little help to the people living in flimsily built terraced houses, still typical of inner cities from London to Belfast.

It was not until a few days before the actual outbreak of war that orders were given to start building public shelters. But these were all relatively cheap surface structures, many of them put up in haste and with much skimping of materials. It was also decided that shelters should be fairly small and widely scattered, in order to minimise loss of life if any single one received a direct hit.

The only way to avoid such danger altogether would be to build very deep shelters. These were ruled out, however, since it was believed that, in the words of Angus Calder, 'the craven populace invented by the official imagination would contract out of the war effort and immerse itself more or less permanently in the womb-like security they would provide'.

General Lee, writing in his diary on 7 October, suggested another reason for official reluctance to provide proper deep shelters.

It is now one month since the heavy attacks on London started. For that length of time the people, particularly the poorer classes, have resorted to all kinds of improvisations for safety. Unused subways, public building basements and railroad freight warehouses are crowded every night with uncomfortable refugees, men, women and children. This was all very well for a temporary expedient in warm weather, but now that the nights are getting colder and it becomes evident that these conditions may obtain for the whole winter, the Government are being confronted with the problem of safe and sanitary accommodation for millions of people. For two years they have shied off the provision of deep, well-constructed shelters on account of the expense, but something now must be done.

Such shelters would, in fact, be built later in the war. Meanwhile vast numbers of Londoners had taken to buying a tupenny ticket to the Underground and spending the night in the deeper stations. Among the East Enders who took over the tubes the day after the first big raid was the family of 14-year-old Bernard Kops, who describes how

Thousands upon thousands the next evening pushed their way into Liverpool Street Station, demanded to be let down to shelter. At first the authorities wouldn't agree to it and they called out the soldiers to bar the way. I stood there in the thick of the crowd with my mother and father and brothers and sisters, thinking that there would be a panic and we would all be crushed to death.

It was the worst experience I had up until then and I wanted to rush out of that crowd, but I was jammed tight, I would have preferred to take my chances in the street with the bombs. Anything was preferable to that crush. I shouted my head off, went limp and was carried along by the surging masses, trying to hold on to my slipping identity. The people would not give up and would not disperse, would not take no for an answer. A great yell went up and the gates were opened and my mother threw her hands together and clutched them towards the sky, 'Thank God. He heard me.' As if she had a special line through to Him and He had intervened with the Government on behalf of the Kops family.

'It's a great victory for the working class,' a man said, 'One of our big victories.'

And though I felt ill and my heart was beating over-fast, all the family were thrilled to know that people had taken over the underground and made the Government acquiesce.

But things remained disorganised for some days after the start of the bombing, until some form of order was imposed and the shelterers began to develop their own rituals and regulations. Another East Ender, Emily Eary, recalls that in the first few days of bombing

people would rush to get to the tubes, almost knock you over to get down the escalator, because when it started, it was really going — and there were bombs coming down and people were getting panic stricken to get down there, to get out of the noise, to get out of the devastation. The porters and station staff used to say, 'clear out, you're not supposed to be

Liverpool Street underground shelter, 12 November 1940. Masses of people lie huddled together on either side of the arched tunnel in the station.

down here', so we would travel the tubes, just pretend we were travellers, travelling, just to be down there, because we knew it was illegal, but gradually it caught on, and we would just stand by the wall, and they would try and move us on if they could, but we stood there and then when somebody said, 'well, it's very heavy up there, they are dropping bombs right left and centre,' we would say 'well, right, we are here for the night', and we stood there, and gradually when the trains stopped running, we'd put down our parcels of bits and pieces, our old blankets and pillows, and we'd sit for a while against the walls, and then gradually unfold our blankets ... you didn't know who you were going to sleep against, I mean we were in our clothes we had worn all day. And we would be down there and there were sick people, bronchitis ... people coughing all night. There were dirty people and just frightened people really so you had no choice. We all caught scabies, we were all itching and scratching. But it was either the tube or putting up with the bombs.

The Government had to accept the takeover of the tubes (and of other unofficial shelters). They also took responsibility for the welfare of the nightly shelterers, though some improvements were long in coming. John Colville's diary shows that the Government could respond to pressure from interested parties, describing how on 18 September he was visited by Violet Markham, a social worker concerned about the effect of air-raids on the people.

At the moment nothing was being done to ensure their safe transport home — the buses stopped running in raids — and no steps were being taken to feed them when they came out of their shelters after long, cold and weary vigils. I rang up Sir John Reith (Minister of Transport) and arranged that she should go and see him and promised to see that further steps were taken from here if satisfactory results were not achieved. It is clearly most important that everything possible should be done to lighten the cross which the people of London have got to bear — particularly as their lot will become increasingly unpleasant as the winter draws on.

This concern led to the setting up of a system of mobile canteens and buffets known as 'blitz dives', as well as measures to improve the sanitary arrangements in official and unofficial shelters alike.

Another immediate and positive action was the increased anti-aircraft (ack ack) barrage ordered for the night of 12 September (coincidentally, Nancy Bosanquet's first night in London). Gwladys Cox was so impressed by the *Evening Standard*'s report that she copied it into her diary.

Immediately after the sirens, guns answered one another in a thunderous swelling chorus, as group after group of airplanes came in. Great streaks of blue and violet flame swept the horizon from each side. Shells burst continuously round the German airplanes, harrying them, chasing them far out of sight. At one time, several airplanes appeared in the centre of a ring of exploding steel. Then came a time when so many airplanes were overhead that their drone rose above the crash of gunfire. New guns went into action, ripping the sky with deeper and harsher reports. German tactics were entirely different from the previous nights. The airplanes turned before the flashing shells and ran, more often than not, without dropping their bombs. When they did drop them, London's reply was such a fury of sustained fire that it sounded as if bombs were hurtling to earth in their thousands.

Despite the fact that few enemy planes were downed, this was a great boost to the morale of Londoners. Orwell wrote that the noise was tremendous, but 'I don't mind it, feeling it to be on my side.' Margaret Kennedy's warden husband wrote to her to say that " 'the grand new barrage ... seems to be a great comfort to all Londoners'. He says it sounds noble, 'like a pride of lions roaring round the town'." Theodora Fitzgibbon says that it was

like a mad Wagnerian orchestra. The preliminary shock to our ears was terrifying, until we realised that we were in fact hitting back. For the first time that week, groups of people stood out of doors watching German planes caught in searchlight beams, and saw the twinkling shell-bursts like fireworks in the sky. That large, jagged, murderous-looking pieces of shrapnel fell around them did not matter. In fact they were collected like seashells and displayed on mantelpieces like trophies ... the noise was sweet music to our ears.

One of the German pilots flying over London that night is quoted in *Blitz over Britain* as saying that 'the London flak defence put up a great show; but very few of our aircraft were hit. I myself never collected so much as a shell fragment.' Indeed General Pile, head of AA Command, later referred to the barrage as 'largely wild and uncontrolled shooting'. But none of this seemed to matter to the public.

It did have one immediate effect on the enemy, however, forcing the bombers to climb higher (according to *Roof over Britain*, from 1,200 to 22,000 feet). From such a height it is clearly difficult to pinpoint targets with any great precision, and it may well have been an error on the part of the single German raider which dropped a bomb on Buckingham Palace the following morning. Whether deliberate or not, this showed the people of London that privilege could not guarantee safety. The Queen was heard to say 'I'm glad we've been bombed. It makes me feel I can look the East End in the face.'

The barrage may well have accounted for few enemy aircraft. The RAF on the other hand, was proving very successful. On 15 September, in the course of a day-long battle, the *Luftwaffe* was routed by Fighter Command. George Beardmore took the train to London the following day and found that

All on board were smiling, also the soldiers one met, the porters and the passers-by in the street, with a grand air of suppressed joy. A fair half of an invading air fleet was yesterday shot down ('littering the suburbs' as the papers say). In all we are told that 185 were destroyed with a loss to ourselves of only 25. The figures are incredible. We wonder whether superior design and workmanship, or the fact that the battle was fought over home ground, are enough to account for a seven to one victory.

The word 'incredible' was aptly chosen, in fact. It has since been estimated that German losses that day were probably in the region of 52. No matter; it was perceived as (and indeed *was*) a stunning victory. And over the next few days the *Luftwaffe* continued to lose planes at double the rate of the RAF. (And remember that a British pilot bailing out over Kent could be flying the next day, whereas a German would be in a British prison camp.) On the 17th, Hitler postponed Operation 'Sealion', the planned invasion of Britain; on the 27th only 20 out of 300 German bombers got through to the capital; on 12 October 'Sealion' was further postponed 'until the spring of 1941' — in effect abandoned.

During this period the bombs were beginning to move westwards, leaving much of the West End in ruins. On 19 September Harold Nicolson wrote in his diary

I get sleepy and go back to my room. I turn out my lights and listen to the bombardment. It is continuous, and the back of the [British] museum opposite flashes with lights the whole time. There are scudding low clouds, but above them the insistent drone of the German 'planes and the occasional crump of a bomb. Night after night, night after night, the bombardment of London continues. It is like the *Conciergerie*, since every morning one is pleased to see one's friends appearing again. I am nerveless, and yet I am conscious that when I hear a motor in the empty streets I tauten myself lest it be a bomb screaming towards me. Underneath, the fibres of one's nerve-resistance must be sapped. There is a lull now. The guns die down towards the horizon like a thunderstorm passing to the south. But they will come back again in 15 minutes. We are conscious all the time that this is a moment in history. But it is very like falling down a mountain. One is aware of death and fate, but thinks mainly of catching hold of some jutting piece of rock. I have a sense of strain and unhappiness; but none of fear.

One feels so proud.

Indeed the nightly bombardment was becoming accepted as a part of life. Queenie Stearn, then a civil servant living near the Albert Hall, tells us that

after the first bomb damage we suffered in my area of London on a late summer Saturday night in 1940, people with a ghoulish curiosity came to gawp at the damage. Later, no one came — presumably they were too busy clearing up their own rubble. I recollect that in the relentless Nazi attack on London, people began to wear lapel buttons saying: 'Please do not tell me your bomb story,' for the endless morning-after recitals were becoming tedious.

Some nights still merited the exchange of stories on the morning after. One such was that of 15 October when a full 'bomber's moon' lit up the unmistakable twists of the Thames as the Heinkels and F-Ws came in from the east, dropping over 500 tons of HE, leaving 400 dead and shutting down practically the entire rail network into London. Even the BBC was hit, as one of their staff describes in a letter written shortly afterwards.

Dear Old Thing,
I think I'd better take back my invitation to you in my last letter! What a night! They say it was the heaviest yet and I can believe them, altho' of course first thing next morning always seems hopeless. I think Margaret slept right through it: at any rate there wasn't a sound or light from her room the whole time. I went to bed about midnight, during a lull in the gunfire, and was wakened just before 2 by a terrific barrage. Then all our guns went quiet and fighters went up and there seemed to be a terrific air-battle going on just over our heads. The wretched things were dive-bombing, which made it sound much worse. Then about 2.15 a plane zoomed down close to us — I thought it sounded as if something was wrong with it — then it zoomed up again and a few minutes later there was a sickening thud and the whole world seemed to shake, followed by several explosions. It was a Heinkel down on Campden Hill, just behind Patrick's place!

B[roadcasting] H[ouse] itself is all right, but all around it caught badly. Our building structure seems to have stood firm, but the inside is just blown out. We clambered up to our offices, over blown-down walls and doors, and floors littered with glass and rubble, and have spent the morning salvaging. I got busy with brooms and duster and actually our office doesn't look so bad. The telephone had been blown right out of the window, hanging down its cord, and when I rescued it and put the receiver back on it rang — still working! It was P. to know if I was all right. The City apparently didn't get it so badly, although it was pretty widespread. They're still digging for people under a pub just opposite our windows — it's rather sickening, but how those AFS men do work!

Ah well, I didn't waste my sleepless hours. I darned all the stockings I could find, and plucked my eyebrows and made some tea! But I would have liked someone with me all the same. One thing I'm thankful for — I didn't shampoo my hair last night as I intended to — I'm covered with white dust now! It seems so heartbreaking, just as people were getting tidied up and rebuilt to have the whole lot devastated again! But I suppose that's war — or this kind of war anyway.

The stoical, indeed cheerful attitude of the people of London struck most observers, particularly those from overseas. General Lee passed on a story told him by a friend who, during a visit to the East End,

approached a worn middle-aged housewife who was wearily grubbing in the wreck of her home for such household goods as she might salvage. She expressed the utmost indignation over what had happened to her home and said: 'I don't think much of them Germans. Why, if one of 'em should land right 'ere in this street with a parachute, I don't believe I'd even offer 'im a nice cup of tea.'

Bert Snow, an Australian, was on holiday in England when war broke out. He promptly joined the ambulance service, and still remembers with amazement

that so many people could be completely orderly in such nerve-shattering experiences. With cheerful, even if fearful, resignation, they shared bleak brick and concrete public shelters, which had no more amenities than plain seats, or huddled together in the small corrugated steel shelters that were in the back yards of many houses. Some who sat and dozed nightly in such retreats had important jobs to face next day. Students and teachers went to school after disturbed nights.

And like many others he was struck by the signs stuck outside blitzed businesses,

'More open than usual', 'Blasted Well open', 'Down but not out', 'Bombed but not beaten', 'Broken glass but not broken hearts.' A sandbagged warden's post, attached to one side of the Bank of England displayed the sign, 'built with sound financial backing'

And so London adjusted, with patience, good humour and determination, to its role as the 'roaring centre of the battlefield'. The homeless and the shelterers still had some grumbles, but the coalition Government — armed as it was with powers most dictators would envy — was showing that it was prepared to act swiftly and respond sympathetically to the pleas of well-informed lobbyists.

But had the rest of the United Kingdom learned 'the lesson of London', to use the title of Ritchie Calder's book? During the autumn of 1940 he visited many of the provincial cities to judge what provisions they had made for raids on the scale of those experienced by London. Some towns had already been attacked and, as Calder wrote,

it was difficult, without seeming callous, to tell people who had had repeated raids and losses that, by comparison with London, they scarcely knew what raids meant ... Even Merseyside, which had then passed its 200th raid and, next to London, was the most heavily bombed area, was untouched by comparison.

He reported that most local leaders argued that their area would never get it as bad as London. They were too far from German airfields, the planes couldn't carry enough bombs to make the hazardous journey worthwhile, they were not worth attacking in the first place. But such arguments failed to convince him. He believed firmly that

if there was one thing which London's experience had demonstrated it was the danger of under-estimating the possibilities of being caught napping. It was necessary ... to imagine the worst and then add a margin for error.

He found, by and large, that the arrangements made for housing the homeless were encouraging (notably on Merseyside, in Manchester and Glasgow). But the provision of shelters was inadequate, especially on Clydeside which, with its crowded tenements could not, he said, afford to neglect the fullest precautions. It was the provision of shelters that he concentrated on throughout his tour. And everywhere, he said, he found room for improvement.

On the morning of 14 November the German bombers left London, ending the first continuous period of blitz. That evening Ritchie Calder turned on the radio, having just finished the chapter on the degree of blitz preparation in the provinces. He heard that a massive attack on the city of Coventry had just started.

4.
COVENTRATED
Coventry on the
night of 15 November
1940

In the event of a potential raid a 'Yellow' signal was phoned from HQ to the Post and to me. In the early stages we had a 'Yellow' almost every night, invariably when one had been in bed for about half an hour, I would put some old togs over my pyjamas and proceed to the post (at that time I think a 'Yellow' was signalled if an enemy plane had crossed the coast!) However we soon became somewhat blasé. Most of them were nuisance raids anyway.

Mr R. Vincent Wyles, head warden for central area of
Coventry

We were a typical Coventry family of the time, one of thousands of families who had recently moved there because there was work. By November 1940 we had become used to broken nights, and the schools were operating a sliding scale of opening times, depending upon the length of time the previous night's alert had lasted. We had also come to recognise that the fuller the moon the greater the risk of interrupted sleep.

On the evening of Nov 14th Dad set off for the night shift at the nearby Dunlop factory with the comment 'I reckon we'll have visitors tonight' when he saw a full hunter's moon in a clear sky as he wheeled his bike out of the yard.

Mr J. Brown, 14 years old that night

During the night ending 15 November strong bomber formations were sent to attack Coventry in order to cripple considerably this centre of the aircraft and aircraft accessories industry. The attack took place in especially favourable weather conditions.

Extract from the Luftwaffe Operations report for 1000 hrs, 15/11/40

The attack was launched by 13 pathfinder planes, Heinkel 111s from the crack KG 100 group, following the newly developed X beam direct to the target. Their task was to drop a mixture of flares and incendiary bombs to light the way for the main force of Junker 88s and Dornier 17s. It was believed that a major attack was likely that night, probably somewhere in the Midlands, but no advance warning had been given to those on the ground. The bombers flew in three separate streams, each plane some 12 miles from its nearest neighbour, which made contact very difficult. Fighter Command put up over 100 sorties, but only one enemy plane failed to reach Coventry. The transmitters intended to jam the German homing beams were set to the wrong frequency.

According to Mr Wyles,

the raid started like any other and our reaction was the same at first. After reporting, the wardens dispersed and I remained at the Post, but as things warmed up I sent my wife to a nearby underground shelter and went on the 'beat'. The phone was dead so there was no point in staying there. The first 'incident' as I recall it was when I was running down an alleyway near the Post with Willie [his messenger] following a few yards behind. An incendiary bomb was burning away harmlessly in the centre of the alley and I jumped over it. It happened to have an explosive charge (which was always 'delayed' to enable personnel to get there before it exploded) and it went off before Willie reached it. Apart from scattered burns on the back of my coat, all I felt was a blow like being hit with a wet towel when naked. Willie was less fortunate and had to go to hospital.

Things got worse, communications broke down, and I decided on a 'tour of inspection' of my area. A police motorcyclist agreed to give me a lift to the Cathedral which had its own fire-watching squad of wardens under Provost Howard, within my jurisdiction. As we were in Hertford Street, approaching Broadgate, an HE fell through an adjacent building and it must have exploded at ground level because the wall, up to the height of the ground floor windows, simply shot out almost in one piece for about 6 feet and the building collapsed within itself. The blast blew us off the bike but we suffered nothing worse than bruises and shock: the dust was cutting visibility to almost nil and I could just see the glow of fire through it. I proceeded on foot to near the Cathedral where a fireman told me they were 'working on it'.

This had brought me to the other end of Little Park Street, furthest from my home and the Post. As I went along Little Park Street several buildings were on fire and some had obviously been hit by HEs. I was surprised by the number of people who were about instead of in the shelters. They seemed more excited than afraid. Along here I ran into one of my wardens, an idiot I'm sorry to say, who ran up to me saying, 'They're dropping gas!' This was utter nonsense and with a few well chosen epithets I soon brought him to his senses. When I reached home it was well alight. The shop window had gone and people were helping themselves to the bottles which were within reach. Better than letting them be destroyed, I thought. It wasn't looting as I saw it. I then went to see if my wife was all right and we took a stupid risk, I suppose, by going to see the last of our 'honeymoon home' of only four months! It was a very old building, the internal walls being of wattle and daub. Next morning it was hard to believe that a house full of furniture had stood there. It was just a rather pathetic pile of ashes.

Pastor Victor J. Ensor, then a 19-year-old member of a rescue and demolition squad, thinks he must have attended to one of the first casualties.

I went on duty just after 6.00 pm and as I was cycling up Three Spires Avenue a stick of incendiary bombs was dropped. Two fell in the road in front of me. I extinguished one and a fellow who lived in the street went to deal with the other. Unfortunately his bomb exploded and severely wounded him. I applied bandages before managing to get him sent to hospital in Harry Plumb's car.

Later that night in Beake Avenue, Radford, it was heart-rending to see some children bare footed and in nightclothes making their uncertain way to an underground shelter. I remember carrying down one or two little tots and unceremoniously dumping them on the first willing person's knee. I was annoyed to hear someone remark 'Must be bad if a rescue squad chap has come into the shelter', especially as I'd only entered for a moment to bring the children in.

Communications were impossible that night. The phones were out and consequently events were chaotic.

Bob Paxton spent much of the night in his Austin sports car driving a doctor round the city, dealing with urgent cases.

It was not long before incendiaries, HEs and parachute bombs began dropping, and our first call was to the Green Lane district to investigate an incident involving a young woman and child. I parked my car at the entrance to Beanfield Avenue and whilst the doctor went off to attend to the casualties I asked a local warden if there was any other incident I could help in. He silently pointed to a body in a front garden and advised me to remove my car as soon as possible since I had parked it on an unexploded bomb! When the doctor returned I asked him if he would help me push the car away in case any vibration would set it off. He said that since he had survived all the London blitzes he would retire to a safe distance whilst I drove it off and if the bomb exploded he would look after me. I ran to the car, started it up and drove off like a Le Mans racing driver.

Later we were about to turn onto the Birmingham Road where a water mains had burst, sending up a large fountain. Standing in the midst of all the bombing was a lady of about 50 who asked us if we could stop the water from escaping. The doctor said that since he was a medical practitioner he could do little about it. We both raised our tin hats and carried on to our allotted incident.

As the action became more and more severe it was decided to evacuate the post since many of the casualties were severely injured, and as my friend and I were preparing to help with the stretchers a parachute bomb exploded near the playground and blew us down the corridor. I had just put on my new motoring gloves and when I picked myself up they had completely disappeared. I was then commissioned to take five bus drivers up to near the Cedars public house to collect their buses and thus started the evacuation of the casualties to Allesley.

It was a most horrendous experience and, at 71, I can still recollect every incident I was involved in, including seeing the scalp of an 18-year-old girl suspended on the jagged end of an air raid shelter where a bomb had burst immediately below it. On a mound nearby was the body of a man that appeared to be pulverised, since when I attempted to pick him up his whole body sagged into his clothing. If I close my eyes I can still see the brilliant flash of a bomb about 100 yards in front of me and five bodies pinned against a wall. When I arrived at the spot all were dead. I saw great acts of bravery by all kinds of people, and at no time did I see any panic.

Here are a few accounts from people who, happily, suffered no more than the loss of a night's sleep, the first from Jean Hughes:

My family and I, together with other inhabitants of our street, wended our way as usual to what was known as 'Neale's shelter'. Almost immediately the bombs began to fall, even before some of us had detected the dull drone of enemy aircraft.

At around 10.30 to 10.40 pm we were informed by the police that we were all to assemble at the door of the shelter for evacuation to another in Trinity Street, due to an UXB that had landed close by. Women and children were lined up against the walls of the houses and crouching down, guarded by our menfolk, we proceeded slowly and cautiously towards the other shelter which was underneath Wakes fresh fish store at the bottom of Trinity Street. What normally would have taken a couple of minutes to walk seemed to take us hours. I could see fires raging, as well as some heavily bandaged firemen being rushed to hospital. We eventually reached the other shelter and remained huddled together for the rest of the night.

Les Saunders, a 19-year-old aero-engine precision inspector, did fire-watching at his factory two or three nights a week.

At about 6.50 pm I was on my way to work when the bombs started falling. I arrived at the factory a bit before 7 pm just as the sirens started sounding and all the workers scuttled to the shelters. I was due on the roof that night, as it happens, from 7.00 to 9.00 but of course there was no point as by now the high explosives were falling all around, hitting the Humber car plant and the Armstrong Siddeley works nearby. At about 10 pm a foreman who worked on blower section in the fitting bay asked me if he could go down to his station to get his overcoat as it was cold in the shelters and he'd left his sandwiches in the coat pocket. We were not allowed to let anyone up the stairs to the shop floor, mainly because it was in total darkness. We argued for some time, and in the end I said I would go and fetch it for him. As I started to climb the stairs a voice called out, 'Les! What the bloody hell do you think you're doing?' It was a friend of mine who was a warden in our area. We spoke for some minutes and he agreed to let me go.

In normal light it would have taken only about four or five minutes to get the coat, but it was in complete darkness, as I've said, and I just had a little torch to help me find my way across the floor which was covered in boxes of components. Suddenly I was stopped in my tracks by a terrific explosion and the blast made me retreat back to the shelters, the time now being 10.18 pm. If my friend and I hadn't argued on those air raid shelter steps I would have been underneath that bomb because it was a direct hit on the blower section. By the way, the overcoat was never found and probably neither would I have been!

Eileen Jones, also 19, was working at GEC. Her fiancé, Bill, was slightly deaf and had been turned down by the RAF but was in the fire service, doing duty on top of his regular day's work.

I arrived home a few minutes before the sirens sounded. Mother had been washing and I was tackling the ironing when Bill arrived. The two families had an understanding that if I was at his house or nearby I stayed there and vice versa.

At first we were alert but relaxed. This wasn't the first raid by any means, but it soon became apparent that it was going to be a big one. Some neighbours of ours came for company. They had an Anderson shelter in the garden but still preferred to be with friends, especially as we were well prepared. Dad had put buckets of water and containers with sand at strategic points, especially upstairs and he'd made wooden shutters to all the downstairs windows which not only made excellent blackout covers but also protected the glass.

Dad as usual patrolled the garden, the street and upstairs. (He was very deaf and sailed through the war totally unaffected by guns or bombs. I really believe if it hadn't been for Mother's anxiety he would have taken a chair into the garden and, puffing away at his inevitable Woodbine, would have watched the blitz with interest and complete unconcern.) Our under-the-stairs sanctuary held four, while Bill and I took shelter under the table making ourselves comfortable and trying not to feel silly.

The idea of such a refuge was not as stupid as it seems. It would have been quite useless in a direct hit, but it had been proved that a table often held firm in a collapsed building, creating a sort of cavern in which one could survive until rescued. Ours was substantial mahogany with large bulbous legs and it gave us the illusion of safety, if nothing else.

Never before or since have I lived through such a long night. The noise of guns and bombs never stopped for more than a couple of minutes. At one point a neighbour came, greatly distressed, to get help to dig out a collapsed home-made trench shelter. About a dozen people had been buried. The men went with spades and spent frantic hours digging them out. Four were dead including a small child, a much loved little girl three years old. Her mother and two neighbours were also lost. The tragedy was harder to bear because all of them would have been quite safe in their own homes.

The night wore on, hour following dreadful hour. There was a moment which we thought our last. A stick of bombs was heard exploding first at a distance, coming nearer and nearer with each explosion until it seemed the next one *must* hit us. I remember screaming and the floor shaking as it landed. There was a thud as more ceiling came down upstairs. Suddenly there was an uproar next door. An incendiary had gone through the roof and set the bedroom alight. The woman in the house had locked herself in and the firefighters couldn't make her let them in at first. When she finally did the upstairs was ablaze. Dad helped with his already filled buckets and someone else produced a stirrup pump. Those air raid wardens were the tops, they deserved medals every one of them.

From time to time we emerged from the shelter to make a hot drink. There was no gas, but we kept the fire going in the range and the kettle was always singing. In the morning the table top was a shambles of dirty cups. We just kept taking clean ones from the Welsh dresser until it looked like the aftermath of a party, but what a party!

Lilian John spent the night nursing her 11-day-old son, Tudor, born on 3 November 1940.

The whole night was very unreal. I don't know why, but I wasn't afraid, I just nursed my baby all night. Anne, our little daughter, who had a bed under the stairs, gave me courage when she said she wasn't afraid. Thank God, we survived.

Gladys Harrison strolled with her mother to post a letter to her auntie around 6.40 pm. Not far to go. Should be received next morning, she remembers thinking.

Ten minutes later sirens sounded and bombs began falling. We called to see my dad in the local, and firemen were already in and out, blackened and sweaty. On the way home some wardens stopped us. We must go in the Morris Motors shelters. The bombs falling incessantly, people coming in their nightclothes clutching an armful of clothes each, as some had to evacuate during the night. Falling into fitful sleep sat round on very narrow benches.

Some, like Margaret Rose, found no sleep that night. Margaret, 10 years old at the time, was one of the few girls in her school preparing to take the scholarship [11+] exam, her nights mainly spent in a public shelter at the corner of Holyhead Road and Moseley Avenue, about a mile from the city centre.

It was horrible down there, damp, with fungus everywhere. We sat on wooden slats formed into benches in rows rather like passages in a supermarket. There were a few toilets round the edge with a loose piece of sacking for a door, affording very little privacy. I don't remember ever using one as they were just holes in the ground. Part of the shelter was above ground covered with earth and grass and part beneath ground. Protection from a direct hit would have been useless; they were mainly for protection from bomb blast, shrapnel and incendiary bombs. Some people went down every night armed with thermos flasks, blankets and caged birds. We never went down until the siren sounded to warn us of an impending raid. Usually we were in bed by then, Mum, Dad and me, and I used to grumble like anything at having to get out of a warm bed and go to the shelter.

My father used to get home between 5.30 and 6 pm, so our evening meal was around 6 pm. On 14 November 1940 it was pitch dark by then, although it was full moon that night. We had just finished our meal and I remember I was reading a book when the siren went. It was covered in dust by the morning. My parents decided it was too early to go to the shelter at that time, about 6.45, as it couldn't be a serious raid so early in the evening. Of course they were mistaken and the bombing started immediately and continued for many hours and we were trapped in the house. Some people had their own Anderson shelters in their gardens, but we were considered too near a large public shelter to warrant one, and we had a small garden with a garage taking up a lot of room.

We were stuck in the house with the continuous bombing. The roof was badly damaged and most of the windows were blown in. There were very few short lulls, but in the first one after several hours, Mum and Dad decided to make a break for the shelter, 200–300 yards away. As Mum and I set off down the path the next door neighbour screamed out 'Come back, there's a land mine dropping!' So we ran back to the house. It did drop about halfway between us and the shelter, making a huge crater in the middle of Holyhead Road near the Holyhead Hotel. My father was nowhere around and we were split up. At another very slight lull Mother called after him and after what seemed ages he staggered to the door with a gash in his forehead. He thinks the blast blew him and the door, and the front door knocked him out. It wasn't too serious, thank goodness, and he joined us next door.

By this time it was like broad daylight outside with the lights from all the fires. People at Warwick 10 miles away could see the flames. The water supply had run out so the hoses were useless and what guns we had seemed to be useless too.

At another short lull about 1 am Dad decided we'd got to get to the shelter somehow. He grabbed Mum and me and we started running. Again the neighbours shouted and Mum ran back. Dad told me to keep running (I was in front being the swiftest, I suppose).

About halfway between one house and the main shelter we were making for was a brick surface shelter near the bus-stop. We dodged in there to wait for Mum. We were in there again for some hours. There were a few other people in there, no children, only me. Someone offered Dad a cigarette which at first he refused but then he accepted. He had been a heavy smoker in Ypres and the Somme in World War I but had given up because of the cost when he married my mother about 12 years previously.

The noise and explosions continued, sometimes deafeningly so, all night long. I don't remember feeling cold, although it was November; must have been the excitement kept me warm. I don't remember feeling frightened, either. To me it was my life, and that's how my life was.

While we were in that shelter a load of firemen piled in from Birmingham 18 miles away. They had been sent over to help put out the fires, but as there was no water they were waiting for a van to take them back home. I don't know how this was arranged but they did go off in a van. About half an hour later someone else came in the shelter and said he had seen the van blown across the road a quarter of a mile away and they were all killed.

Another lull happened about 3 am and Dad decided to go back for Mum and told me to wait in the shelter. He just got a few steps away and she appeared at the corner. We then skirted the Holyhead Road, around the crater made by the land mine and sprinted for the underground shelter at last. The whole world was on fire, or so it seemed.

An air-raid warden, a friend's father, was standing at the shelter entrance in his tin hat. He took me on one side and told me to say nothing of what I had seen or what had happened outside. I expect he could see an eager 10 year old rushing in with all the 'news'. I remember it made me feel very important, sharing such a terrible secret.

And many lost their homes that night; especially those in the city centre, like 19-year-old Irene Ross whose parents ran a pub.

Several customers were in the pub having a drink when suddenly we heard bombs, then the air raid warning went, and by 7 o'clock fires were breaking out all round us. The top floors were ablaze and I remember an official rushing in and telling my dad to get us out. We didn't have time even to get our coats. We started to go across the road to the cathedral crypt shelters, but we couldn't make it, so we turned back and finally found shelter in another pub where we spent the night in the cellar.

Scenes of damage in Coventry in the centre of the city. The Pioneer Corps assisted in clearing the debris.

The noise was awful, and by 9 o'clock the electricity had gone. The strange thing was I never felt frightened and certainly never realised how serious things were. When the all clear sounded and we emerged we couldn't believe the sight that we beheld. We struggled through the debris and finally reached our home but it had been bombed to the ground. There was nothing left.

Brenda Cleveland never managed to make it to her first aid post.

I was late home from work and when the sirens sounded was just starting my tea. I hurriedly got ready to go to the FAP and was in the sitting room having just put my helmet on when a puppy dog we had taken in, as his owners had just fled to the country, started to whimper. I bent down to speak to him when there was a 'crump' and the house disintegrated around us. I was thrown into a corner of the room by the fire-place with the dog in my arms, and when I eventually managed to extricate myself I realised that I had lost my helmet — this was found at the bottom of the garden, and I am convinced that if it hadn't been for the puppy I would have lost my life. We lost everything that night (a land mine had dropped in our front garden). We never found a stick of my parents' furniture, it just disappeared. My parents and I later made our way to a friend's house and stayed there until the all clear. My mother wouldn't let go of me and her hair turned grey practically overnight.

One 14-year-old lad, J. Brown, took responsibility for several other people that night.

My mother's friend, who had a baby a few months old, dropped in for a chat about 6.30; her husband was also on nights. She lived about 200 yards away, but when the sirens went decided to stop with us rather than rush home to an empty house.

As our shelter was flooded (not an unusual occurrence) my mother with my two-year-old brother together with friend and baby took shelter in the pantry under the stairs. My brother and I opted for the kitchen table as a fairly substantial 'shelter', and as we scrambled under it my brother pulled a fireside stool to the front of the table to act as a 'sandbag'.

We soon heard the noise of the approaching bombers, and then the shoosh-shoosh-shoosh of falling incendiary bombs, but then behind the noise of the incendiaries I heard another sound I did not recognise and instinctively bunched into a ball beneath the table. Surprisingly I have never been able to recall any noise of explosion but saw a brilliant flash as the door and window sailed into the room. The window frame hit the stool 'sandbag' and stopped without injuring either of us, and as the room was now filled with light (which the bombers must see) I pushed younger brother out from under the table and into the pantry, switching off the light as I did so, and joining the pack in the pantry.

The pantry was one yard square and it now contained two well-built adults and four children between six months and 14 years. Within minutes I, as the eldest male, was out of it and back in the kitchen to dowse the fire that had started when blackout material from the shattered window landed in the open grate. All this happened within a few minutes of the start of the raid when a land mine demolished St Francis's

Church in Links Road, Radford, and the blast severely damaged the adjoining row of houses in Treherne Road, including ours at no. 146.

We spent the next 10 hours in that pantry, treading and sitting in a mixture of flour, jam, sauce and all kinds of food-stuff blown from the pantry shelves onto the floor. Those 10 hours passed in a kind of daze from which there are few clear recollections, other than the whistle of the bombs, the dwindling anti-aircraft flak and the increasing glare of the fires penetrating even into our pantry haven. It was a long night.

As the dawn broke and the all clear finally sounded we looked round the house in sheer amazement. The two fire-places were standing out six inches away from the walls against which they had been aligned, all the ceiling plaster-board was corrugated and every light fitting in the house was smashed, besides the major damage to the roof, windows and doors. It was obvious that the entire house had been compressed by the blast and had sprung back to its original size.

It was not hard to believe that we were the only survivors, but people began to appear from wherever they had taken shelter and you realised that you were not alone. Dad arrived a few minutes later pushing the bike he did not dare to ride over the broken glass lying everywhere, and we were soon swapping experiences, for he had not had an easy night in a factory that had attracted its fair share of bombs. The house was too badly damaged to be habitable, but after a few days spent in a friend's house we were able to find another house only slightly damaged, where my parents lived until 1982.

Some, like Mrs W. Riding, were lucky to survive.

My house was demolished in the big raid. We spent the night in a brick-built surface shelter and my husband and I were the only two alive next morning. Eleven were dead, eight adults and three children. We were on the injured list for two years.

97

But the all-clear did not guarantee an end to danger, as Miss J. Harris discovered, then living with her mother in a two up, two down in Henrietta Street, backing onto the Ordnance Works.

Mother and I didn't like the public shelter nor the Anderson in any of our neighbours' gardens, so we cleared out the bogey hole under the stairs. We put in two stools and a ready packed suitcase for a quick flit.

A few hours had gone by when we heard the whistle of the bomb coming down. The whole house shook, the back door flew off when the bomb buried itself in the back garden and exploded and the soil from the crater was halfway up the stairs.

When the all-clear went we walked up to my sister's but the streets were sealed off because of UXBs, so we came back home. I cleared the ashes from the grate and made a fire to boil water for a cup of tea. The kettle was nearly on the boil when I felt the floor moving and yelled 'Come quick, Mother! Under the stairs!' when the bomb went off and blew the chimney pot down. All the rubbish came down and put the fire out and upset the kettle.

After all that bombing there were eggs in the pantry not even cracked.

The people of Coventry were by then familiar enough with the nuisance raids to go out for the evening; to the cinema for instance, like young L. Wilkins and his brother, who rather fancied the double bill at the Scala, *Dr Cyclops* and *Table for Two*.

We got to the theatre at 4.30 pm, then at 7.00 pm a message on the screen said the warning has been sounded but the film will go on; but at 7.20 pm it said on the screen 'Activity in the Vicinity' and the film was stopped.

We was told to go under the balcony for protection. At 2.30 am one 500 lb bomb landed between the screen and the balcony, another one landed towards the front of the theatre. Seconds later I went to take my glasses off but the blast and excitement had removed them from my face and I was help-less without them. The manager told us about 50 people was killed being in the balcony; he told us to go to Gosford Green shelters, about four minutes' walk. At 8.30 am my brother went back to see if he could find my glasses but it was hopeless. We left the shelter at about 9.30 and went to a public house called the Ivy Cottage where the landlady bathed a cut on my brother's forehead.

Elsie Towersey was also at the Scala, having a night out to celebrate her husband's birthday. They'd gone there on their tandem, leaving it at the rear of the cinema.

Just before the feature film came on, the sirens sounded and we were advised to stay in the cinema. We moved to the back of the stalls and the bombs started falling. Two hit the Scala, people started panicking and screaming, but we had to stay there. We were there until 6.30 next morning and those of us that could walk went to the Gosford Green shelter until the all clear. We left people in the foyer and took the name of one injured boy so that we could let his parents know.

We walked through the streets past some houses on fire and when we arrived home found our doors open with the blast. We were covered with plaster and very shaken. We had no water and my husband said he didn't want to risk another night in Coventry, so we decided to go to my parents in Birmingham and the only way we could go was on the tandem which was still (we hoped) at the back of the cinema. We walked to Gosford Green and found the area was roped off due to UXBs, the warden said my husband could go through at his own risk, I stood waiting and was amazed when he rode towards me. A beam had fallen across the bike and had protected it, leaving only scratches on the seats. We went home and started off for B'ham, with our cat on the front of the tandem in a basket with a curtain net over it (halfway down the road she escaped, but we were able to recapture her). We had to cross craters and debris but eventu-ally arrived in Erdington, on the outskirts of Birmingham, a ride of 18 miles. Just when we got to my parents' home the sirens went, and that was the night of the Birmingham blitz!

Most people, as we can see from the accounts, can only talk of their own small part of the city that night; a cubby hole under the stairs, perhaps; the four walls of a shelter; a frightening dash to another place offering a greater chance of safety. Even those out on the streets were often pinned down to their own confined area as 56 tons of incendiaries, 400 tons of HE and 130 aerial mines rained down over the 10 hours of the raid. But one person has described what it was like to see the whole of Coventry ablaze: Guenther Unger, aboard one of the bombers which set off from northern France in the early hours of the morning.

We started from Abbeville, already on the coast, and as we were flying over the Channel we could already see Coventry burning.

I attacked at about half past two at night and there was no defence. The flight up to then had been relatively calm. There was very little flak and no night fighters, and when we reached the target there was a huge sea of flame.

I have never come across such a concentration of fire during a raid, not even on London. Usually in our target cities the areas of fires were dispersed, but not this time, and so there was no chance of missing the target.

With such an easy target it is perhaps surprising that there were no more than 500 or so dead. Thousands more were injured though, including Mr J. Pfleger, then safety and ARP officer at Courtaulds.

As a member of a textile works fire service, I was directed to one of many fires within the factory. A small explosion nearby, something penetrated my leg, bringing my fire-fighting to an end, and I was a stretcher case. I was loaded into a small van and two very brave men started a nerve-racking journey to the city hospital. Normally this took 5–6 minutes, but that night it seemed endless, with diversions caused by bomb craters, houses on fire and building debris blocking the streets. As I was being carried into the hospital I thought it was a case of being 'dumped out of the frying pan into the fire'; directly overhead was a perfect square of marker flares, with the city hospital within that square.

The Coventry and Warwickshire hospital was, indeed, right in the thick of things. During the night some 20 HEs fell within its walls, five making direct hits. By the next morning fewer than 100 of its 1,600 windows were still intact. Dr Harry Winter, the resident surgical officer that night, has described what it was like, starting with the yellow alert, when all patients were placed under their beds, with their mattresses over the top of them.

Nurses were wheeling other beds down from the top floors and lining them along the ground floor corridors, away from flying glass ... I went on up three flights of stairs and stepped out on to the flat roof of the building. I could hardly believe my eyes. All around the hospital grounds glowed literally hundreds of incendiary bombs, like lights twinkling on a mammoth Christmas tree.

Shortly after this he went down to check the reception building, where casualties would soon be arriving. They were more or less organised for heavy raids (in fact Dr Winter was surprised that they hadn't started earlier); St John's Ambulance Corps volunteers were standing by wooden trestles, ready to take the stretchers. It was then that, in Dr Winter's words, 'the real fun started'; the first incendiary fell on the nurses' home and the building had to be evacuated. The last nurse had just left the home when the first HE hit.

About 8.30 another shower of incendiaries started fires on top of the Men's Medical Ward, the Women's Medical Ward, and the Eye Ward. With the other surgeons, the orderlies, and nurses, and even some of the able male patients, I ran across the open space between the main building and these wards and began transferring the patients. The nurses wheeled the beds outside while the rest of us hoisted patients on our shoulders and carried them pick-a-back across to the main hall ... As I reached the door of the main building with the last patient on my back a bomb screamed down and plunged into the Men's Ward. As I instinctively turned round after the explosion I saw the whole wall of the building fall slowly outward and crash across the open ground where we'd been a few seconds before.

Shortly after this the casualties started arriving from the outside. Mr Pfleger, who was brought in later that night, describes the casualty hall as being

full of people who had walked in for attention or who, like myself, had been assisted there. After receiving an injection I was carried to join dozens more stretcher cases on the floor of a long corridor. The early hours brought some respite, with an easing off in the intensity of bombing. Finally the drone of the bombers was replaced by a sequence of dive bombing planes. Each plane carried two bombs which, on release, made a screaming noise on the way down. One heard each plane start a dive and the two bombs falling. The dive-bombing continued until 7.00 am and was the worst part of the blitz.

Throughout the long night we were watched over by a very young nurse who must have been extremely frightened but showed no signs. Our corridor section remained intact, but without the connecting building at the far end.

The in-patients, one of whom was Mrs A. Zebrzuski, were equally impressed by the dedication and sang-froid of the hospital staff.

I had an operation on 7 November and was still quite poorly and on bed rest by the night of the 14 November. I awoke as the sirens sounded to see the wall opposite my bed disappear. A doctor and nurse were lying on top of me to protect me from flying glass and debris. The ward sister, who should have been off-duty by then, began to organise evacuation of her ward. I was carried down the large curving staircase in my bed by soldiers to the basement, being the first patient to arrive there. As they left me a bomb screamed down and I screamed with it. One soldier ran back, folded me in his arms and rocked me. Other patients then joined me, and all night the noise of screaming bombs was terrible. I saw an incendiary stuck in the wall just like a torch. At dawn came the all clear and it became eerily silent except for the crying of a baby, some said newly-born.

Our ward sister, who had stayed with us all night, went off duty for an hour. She came back in a clean veil and apron saying, 'Good morning everyone', just like an ordinary morning! She was tall, slim, blonde and very pretty and to my weary gaze looked like an angel.

Evacuation of the hospital began. My father turned up looking haggard and afraid. Where my bed had stood in the ward was a huge hole, so he thought the worst. My family had watched from the village, fearing for me, their eldest, helpless in the hell that was Coventry that night. My father helped to carry me out to a waiting ambulance pulling the blanket over my face because he said it was cold, but really so that I should not see the rows of bodies lying there.

It was the discovery of a delayed action bomb just outside the ground floor operating theatre which caused the hospital to be evacuated, meaning that, for the hospital staff, the coming of dawn brought no respite. For most of Coventry, however, it was a time to crawl out of hiding and find out what had been going on in the outside world. Eileen Jones says that at 6 o'clock in the morning

we were all too tired to care if we were bombed or not and left our shelter and flopped into chairs. When it got light and the all clear had sounded Bill went home. He found the car intact except for a great dent in the door where an incendiary had struck.

It's strange how the mind works after such an experience. Our friends went home. None of us in our house went to bed. Mother went off somewhere, so did Dad. It was Friday, but no one thought of going to work. I remember cleaning the house and actually polishing the furniture. My mind was quite empty, no feeling, no emotion, tired but not wanting sleep. Dad kept bringing complete strangers in, people quite unhurt but disoriented, looking for relatives, looking for goodness knows what. We fed them and gave them hot drinks and they just went away again and others took their place.

Then the detonations started. The floor lifted under our feet with the shock-waves. Someone said the army were having to dynamite some of the buildings in town because they were unsafe. Some said it was delayed action bombs going off. I was very reluctant to go out into the street but I made myself go. It was very quiet, almost deserted. Every house was damaged. One was gone completely and the next to it half down. I walked round the block and came upon a crater big enough to bury a double decker bus. The wall of the church was split from top to bottom. I remember wondering how it would be repaired, if the whole wall would have to be rebuilt. I returned home.

The rest of that day was very strange. We had our evening meal by candle light and the glow from the fire. We had tinned salmon — how odd that I should remember that. Bill came in the evening to say their house was damaged but all were safe. His family were in the Anderson and although a bomb had fallen nearby and riddled the house and his father's car with shrapnel, they were all safe. We had a radio which ran on a battery and so were able to hear the news. For once the city was named and a great wave of anger and sympathy was transmitted. Bombs due to be dropped on Germany had 'For Coventry' chalked on the side and the word 'coventrated' was coined to mean great destruction.

For those separated from their loved ones the dawn was a time of apprehension. Joe Keogh had spent the night in an Anderson only 25 feet from where a 500 lb bomb landed, demolishing a block of five houses, theirs being the middle one.

I was digging in the rubble for £30 my mother had saved in a money box, that being a lot of money in those days, when I sensed somebody looking at me. There stood my father, he had been on nights at Humber Works Ltd, his face was all ashen, he said are you all that's left. I had a mother and four brothers in that shelter. For a moment I could not speak, then I cried out no they are all safe, they are having breakfast in a neighbour's house opposite. Not one of our neighbours died that night. My father has been dead these 20 years and I was but a lad of 15 years that night. By the way, I found the money.

And 17-year-old Peggy Morris, a riveter working on Bristol Beaufighters and Mosquitos, emerged from the shelter and set off to meet her father, coming off night shift at Courtaulds.

I knew which way he walked home. I went over the bridge in Spon End into Spon Street. What a sight! The little shops were either flattened or on fire. Heartbreaking. I turned into Barras Lane, you had to be careful where you walked, there was rubble everywhere. When I got to the top of the road I turned into Holyhead Road and there he was, tears in his eyes and in mine.

Jean Mitchell had spent the night in two different shelters belonging to her employers, the GPO.

I thought I would be able to cycle home to Green Lane, but because of roads covered with broken glass I had to carry it most of the way. By this time it was about 7 in the morning. My husband, who had been on Home Guard duty all night, met me at the junction of Kenilworth Road and Renpas Highway. He was very dirty, having been helping to dig out people who had been bombed out of their homes. When he told me that we would not be able to live in our house because all the windows were broken, the roof badly damaged and all gas and water mains broken, I wept, although I am not a weepy person normally. Never will I

Salvation Army mobile canteen in the Coventry blitz, 1940.

forget his comment to me then. 'The house is not habitable, dear, but we still have each other and that is all that matters'.

For most there was no source of power or heat and, as Jean Hughes recalls, the water supply was contaminated due to pipes fractured in the bombing.

Yet one wondered where the water came from to make the endless cups of cocoa always on hand supplied by the good ladies of the WVS [Women's Voluntary Service]. How grateful we were to Pearl Hyde, one-time Lord Mayor of Coventry, and her co-workers. These resolute ladies, always in the thick of it and without thought for their own safety, produced words of encouragement and cheer along with their cups of cocoa and soup, the memory of which I shall cherish as long as I live.

But it was a time of mutual help, too. One Coventry woman, then 10 years old, remembers

going to the Co-op on the corner of Villa Road and Chereral Avenue and seeing this queue stretching from the Co-op right along Bulwer Road, the people having buckets and bottles to fill from the tap in the street, as they had no water in their own homes. On the way back after getting what Mum wanted from the shops I stopped at the end of the queue and I asked if they would like to come along to my home to get their water. Six or seven people went back with me. I explained to my mother and she helped to fill all the buckets and we found some bottles and filled them, then we took my doll out of her pram, putting in all the containers we could filled with water and helped the people back to their homes. I remember the warmth of people in those days, you don't get it now.

But many, bombed out or not, could not stand it and just got out of the city. Mrs E. Brown, eight months' pregnant at the time of the raid, had spent the night in the Anderson shelter next door.

There were houses ablaze all round us, our windows were all blown out and we had lumps of earth all over the rooms. We didn't hear the all clear. Someone came at 7 am to tell us it was all over and made us some tea with rainwater. I decided to go up North, we walked four miles to try and get a train. No trains or buses were running and many houses were still burning. We walked back home to see if we could get a lift to Birmingham, which we did and I went on to Sunderland, my home town.

'There were no services at all', adds Margaret Rose, 'and everywhere was a terrible mess.'

Dad managed to get his head stitched and dressed at the doctor's. Fortunately, a few days earlier, he had met a man who offered us his home at Tamworth for some nights to sleep, but Dad hadn't decided what to do as it was about 10 miles away northwards. But that morning, 15 November, he turned up and repeated his offer, which was marvellous, and we took him in our car and stayed there until after Xmas. We had a job to find roads that were passable and had to make many detours.

People were glad to take anything going. Brenda Cleveland's boyfriend (now husband)

had his house damaged and his boss, who lived in the country about six miles away, opened his house to us. He already had about a dozen relatives from London living there but he cleaned out some empty chicken roosts, laid some mattresses on the floor and we slept on them for about a fortnight until we found rooms in a nearby farmhouse.

And some left the city without knowing the fate of members of their family. Gladys Harrison's brother had been left with his 10-day-old baby while her sister-in-law

had been evacuated to hospital in the nightmare. So we took the little one to the country to my Auntie's and when we walked in after a journey of 40 miles and five vehicles she just broke down and wept. Couldn't believe we had survived. It was four days before my brother found out where his wife Dorothy was. You see the hospital where she was had been bombed and she had to be moved again. She told us later that the bed next to hers had been on fire.

It is not surprising that so many left. The entire centre was a mess of rubble, broken glass and charred timber; 21 major factories, the official targets, had been hit, but so had many of the historic buildings of this ancient city, most distressingly the great Cathedral. The Provost himself had been one of four fire-watchers on the nave roof when the bombers arrived. The first incendiary hit the chancel roof at 8 pm. No professional help arrived until a single fire-engine battled its way in from neighbouring Solihull at 9.30. But the

water soon ran out and, at 11 pm, the Cathedral was left to burn.

Coventry Cathedral devastated – photographed in the spring of 1944.

Many of those left in the City were sorely affected by the experiences of the night. Mass Observers — in Tom Harrisson's words, 'fresh from long London blitz experience' — were there from the Friday afternoon. They reported that

there were more open signs of hysteria, terror, neurosis, observed than during the whole of the previous two months together in all areas. Women were seen to cry, to scream, to tremble all over, to faint in the street, to attack a fireman and so on.

The overwhelmingly dominant feeling on Friday was the feeling of utter *helplessness*. The tremendous impact of the previous night had left people practically speechless in many cases. And it made them feel impotent. *There was no role for the ordinary civilian. Ordinary people had no idea what they should do.*

But people soon pulled themselves together and tried to get things back to normal as quickly as possible. Mr Wyles remembers that

it was surprising how quickly people adapted to the changed living conditions. That is, those who stayed put. Many moved out of the city altogether, leaving undamaged homes very often, while others used to go into the country to sleep. Gradually they all filtered back, some, it must be said, a little shamefaced.

'None of us had had any sleep or rest,' writes Mrs Walsh, then a teenager working for GEC, 'but we washed, dressed and got ready for work.'

When I arrived at work I and all my workmates had a terrible shock when we saw the damage that had been done. The machine shop was still smouldering and the offices were in a state. Such a lot of invoices, paper work and furniture had been destroyed. The management called us to a meeting and explained the position, so we all helped where it was possible and after a week things began to get back to normal.

And out of all the chaos arose a feeling of great pride. Nowhere, not even London, had received such a concentrated attack on the historic centre. Why, the Germans even used the name of their city to coin the verb *coventrieren*, meaning 'to obliterate by massive bombing'. And though observers had heard people on that Friday afternoon muttering 'Coventry is finished' and 'Coventry is dead', such defeatism was soon replaced by a determination to get on with things, symbolised by Provost Howard's declaration, standing in the ruins of the Cathedral, 'it will be rebuilt to the glory of God'.

The factories of Coventry, the destruction of which had been the sole reason for the raid, were all back in production within a matter of days. And when General Lee visited the city a fortnight later, on 1 December, he found that 'there was no evidence whatever that anyone was shaken in his determination to keep on with the war'.

Such determination was going to be needed, however, and not just in Coventry. For the 14 November raid was just the first of many that would affect the people of the United Kingdom in the years ahead.

5.
THE PROVINCES

In one after another of the target cities, the whole centre was wiped out, either in one night or by the accumulation of bombs and fire spread over several raids. True, in Southampton, though whirlwinds flung away the shops of the long High Street, the Bargate still stood, defying bombs as it had defied the centuries. But in Portsmouth, the bright shopping centre of Southsea was gone. In Liverpool the great homes of the shipping companies were hollow shells. In Manchester one side of Piccadilly stood like the ruins of Ypres. In Swansea, Bristol and Plymouth, a large part of the centre of the town is now a levelled expanse of soil pitted with broken brick ... Though these cities may have had one or two raids, half a dozen or a dozen, against London's tale of scores of attacks, there are few indeed where minds and memories, like the physical fabric of the streets, are not deeply marked by the white heat of intense experience.

From *Front Line 1940–1941*, published in 1942

THE ARMS TOWNS

Birmingham

Birmingham was the most obvious of targets, turning out everything from Spitfires, Hurricanes and Lancasters to small arms and shells of every shape and size. But the people of the Birmingham area, like those of Coventry, had never really believed that bombers would penetrate so far inland, and were caught unawares by the first bombs to hit the West Midlands on the night of 25–26 June 1940. These fell on West Bromwich, but during the August there were frequent small raids on Birmingham itself. The first real blitz took place on 19 November, when 350 bombers hit the city, only 50 fewer than had devastated Coventry five days earlier.

The destruction was usually aggravated, as in so many cities, by water mains being hit. Leslie Brown, then working in a wholesale textile warehouse, recalls that 'In one of the first raids in August 1940 when the Market Hall was burned down, I saw firemen helplessly standing by, unable to get water as the mains had been fractured.' The 22 November blitz was Birmingham's most serious raid, and concentrated on the heart of the city. Rhoda Evans, a nurse

went down Macdonald Street, stood on the bridge and counted 60 fires. The whole town looked alight, gaunt shells of buildings black against the flames — smoke hung down everywhere. Firemen with their hoses stood in the river in a vain attempt to get enough water.

The following morning, only one-fifth of the city still had a supply of water, 'If the *Luftwaffe* comes tonight', said the Earl of Dudley, the Regional Commissioner at Civic House, 'Birmingham will burn down.' The next raid was not until 3 December and the longest (a 13-hour raid) on 11 December. On 9 and 10 April 1941 there was a particularly devastating blitz with 250 killed. There were again raids in May, June, July and August 1941, with the two final raids in June and July 1942.

Tom Gillen, then in the army, reached Birmingham just in time for the main November raid. He and his friend John, a local man, had decided to hitch north during their 48-hour leave and stay with John's parents.

It was about 10 pm when we arrived at Spring Pools, now the beginning of the M5. We pulled in. Quite a number of cars were parked. We soon found the reason for this. Looking towards the city we could see flares floating down. The exploding of ack-ack shells and the crump of bombs could be heard even at that distance. By then the whole sky was red.

I suggested to John that we wait until the all clear, but he

The Prince of Wales Theatre, Broad Street, Birmingham, victim of a direct hit on 9 April 1941.

had come to see if his parents were safe and down to Aston he intended to go. I had no relations in Brum but agreed to go in with him.

We started to walk down the Bristol Road into the city and had only walked about a mile when we were offered a lift in a small Austin P/V. The driver turned out to be a woman in uniform, something to do with Civil Defence. She told us the raid had started early, at about 6 pm, and had been very concentrated, mainly on the city centre. Lots of HEs had been dropped and there were incendiaries all over the place. To make matters worse they had hit water mains, leaving the AFS short of water to fight the fires. We now could hear the bombers overhead and the ack-ack fire intensified. We were not far from the city when she stopped the P/V. We could go no farther by car, the road was blocked by bomb debris. We thanked that brave woman and started to walk towards the centre, the time now being about 1.30 am.

It was time to put on our steel helmets, there was no let up in the bombing, the droning of the planes. We passed lots of burning buildings, though we didn't see many fire tenders, due to the lack of water. One AFS group told us how to get to Aston. More and more incendiaries were now dropping and there was very little we could do about them, so we decided to seek shelter. But this was easier said than done.

We settled down to rest for a while in the doorway of a garage, but shrapnel started to come through the glass roof, so we decided to move. We could hear a strange sound which we learned later was made by incendiary 'bread baskets' coming down, but our main danger was from shrapnel, it just came raining down.

It was now about 3.30 am, still no letup in the bombing, but luck was with us and we found a YMCA building with a very dim green light displaying an 'Open' sign. The door was locked, but we started knocking and kicking it until it was opened up by a man who looked very surprised to see us. But he let us in and took us down to the cellars to join the people already there. The time was 4.30 am. It was nearly 7 am when we left our refuge to head towards Aston; the guns were still firing as the all clear sounded. The people who had been trapped in the city were leaving shelters and cellars to head for home and work. The fires were still burning and the desolation of the raid could still be seen.

We finally arrived at my friend's home. His parents were safe, but a land-mine had dropped in the vicinity and their home had been badly damaged. We had a brief reunion but decided we must make our way back to the south coast. After a meal and a beer with friends we were back on the road again.

Mrs E. Lamping was in Aston that night. Her husband worked at Atkinson's Brewery and they lived, together with their one-year-old daughter, in a company house in Queen's Road.

We heard the sirens go off then, having shut the dog and cat in the house, we went in the shelter which we shared with a young widow and her small son. I will never forget what happened next. There was a huge explosion out of the silence, we didn't hear the bomb coming because it was a land mine on a parachute. We managed to make our way in a state of severe shock to the beer cellars under the brewery which were filled to overflowing every night. The next morning was a sight to behold. There were over 200 houses damaged beyond repair, we didn't see the cat for days, he stayed up the chimney, the dog found us in the brewery shelter. We couldn't go for help from our neighbours, we were all in the same trouble. We managed to stay with a friend during the day and in the brewery cellar at night. The people salvaged what they could from their ruined homes. But a lot of stuff was stolen.

During the 13-hour raid on 11 December Derek Harrison's parents, publicans of the White Swan in Navigation Street, decided to remain open despite the lack of customers.

Later on in the evening the railway carter came running into the pub shouting 'the stables in Suffolk Street are all alight, the horses are trapped, we need help!' Father left the pub to help, my mother remained behind the bar.

On reaching the now well-blazing stables the men could hear the horses stamping about in fright. These were not light animals, but heavy shires and there was only one way to lead them through the flames, put sacks over their eyes. There were plenty of those about, so in a steady stream the horses

Collapse of a three-storey house in Birmingham.

were led away from the blazing buildings. A good sharp smack on the backside sent them trotting down Suffolk Street, still with the sacks over their heads. Some drifted into Navigation Street to collide with the tramcars parked there during the raid. Some of the horses were stunned, a couple even lay on the cobbles too dazed to move. In the confusion, the men, Father included, had forgotten to remove the sacks.

Fire brigades from many outlying towns came in to help B'm that night. In some cases their standpipes and hoses were of different patterns, unable to fit B'm hydrants. Those that did were on duty up to 18, even 36 hours at a stretch. The fire chief asked Mother at 1 am on the morning of 12 December 'Any chance of tea and coffee, sandwiches too, if possible?' Luckily, as Mother did catering at the Swan, she had a fair supply of bread, butter, margarine, cheese; some pork and ham too! The fire chiefs sent the exhausted men into the White Swan in relays. Payment was promised but never came, but Mother wouldn't have taken a penny. It was her contribution to the war. Next day when the fire chiefs came to say a big thank you to Mum and Dad one started measuring the hallway saying, 'Just a precaution if the raiders come back tonight — we want to know where to start digging you out.'

The Bristol area

Of the 77 occasions on which bombs were dropped on Bristol, six were officially classed as major raids — those of 24 November, 2 and 6 December 1940 and 3 January, 16 March and 11 April 1941 (Good Friday). The November attack took place on a Sunday (like so many during this period) and some 5,000 incendiaries rained down, reducing much of the heart of the city to ashes. 'Bristol', declared the German official news agency, 'has been wiped out.'

The strangest of all was the January raid. It lasted 12 hours, in weather so cold that frost formed on the uniforms of firemen fighting the blaze, and while flames poured from blazing buildings, coats of ice from the firemen's hoses covered the nearby houses.

Water tower coated with ice after a terrible winter night's blitz in Bristol on 3 January 1941, when the clothes froze on the bodies of firemen and ARP workers.

Less severe attacks came on 4 January, 29 March and 3 and 4 April. But the worst single incident was that of 28 August 1943, when a single bomb dropped on Broad Weir without warning from a very high altitude, exploded next to three buses, and left 28 dead and 26 seriously injured.

Mary Palmer (then Firewoman Matthews) explains that

it was inevitable that Bristol would be a blitz target because we had huge aircraft factories and engineering works, together with the docks. Our first raids were daytime. Two days following, raids were carried out on the Bristol Aircraft Co., which was on the edge of town. They missed, and bombs fell on the air-raid shelters killing a lot of people. At this time there was virtually no air defence.

We lived on the outskirts of Bristol near the aircraft factories. On the first night of the big 24 Nov blitz, we spent looking out of our windows to see the action in the distance ... aircraft turned above us and then dived back over the town dropping hundreds of high explosives and incendiary bombs. They hit the water hydrants and the firemen had to pump water from the docks where it was possible. We listened to the whine of enemy planes and saw them caught up in our searchlights like moths drawn to the light. It was exciting to us and we never thought of taking cover.

The 'Wells Road squad' was on day that same Sunday. At about 7.45 pm the phone rang. It was Bristol Fire HQ asking for a major pump crew to report to Bridewell, Bristol. Clifford Latchem, another fireman, describes the journey there.

We did not talk very much going in, but to be honest I did not feel very brave myself — also, in the open-backed lorry, we were very cold ... We went on down Brislington Hill until we got to the Arnos Vale cemetery, where in the road were stones, shrubs, branches of trees, and earth, which made driving very difficult (we were told later that a bomb had fallen into the cemetery and the stones were from graves). Even the debris, the dirt, and the road looked red with the glow. As we went past Temple Meads approach entrance, we noticed how rough the wind was. Then we entered Victoria Street ... Raging fires in the buildings, debris all over the road, it was like going through a tunnel of fires, belching out of windows and doors, from the top to the bottom of the buildings, and the WIND was like a tornado! The flames were hundreds of feet high, the heat was terrific, even the shop window glass was melting. We four who were sat in the back of the lorry certainly had a magnificent view, but very frightening. We did not see anyone about, and I should think that we were the last to go up Victoria Street that night, I think it was about 9 pm, the buildings were still up then, but all afire.

We got through all right but were told we had to go back to Temple Meads approach road and attend to the fires in the Templegate area. A bomb had dropped and blocked the Pithay, so the only alternative was to turn the lorry and the pump around and go out the way we came in. As we moved off, I saw a fantastic sight, a fireman on the top of a turntable ladder using the monitor jet on a blazing building, and the backcloth of this marvellous sight was nothing but fire — a very brave man.

By going around the back of the Old Market and Midland Road, eventually we got back to Temple Meads, and put the pump beside the two static water tanks on the approach road to the station. We started to dowse the fires that were burning — mostly on the roofs and caused by incendiary bombs. But there was NO WATER IN THE HYDRANTS; most of the mains had been fractured by the bombing, so I used the water in the tanks until by 11 pm they were dry. The River Avon was nearby, but when we looked at it the tide was out, so we could do no more.

At midnight the all clear sounded and in no time at all people came from everywhere, including wardens, police, firemen and ambulance personnel. As we had no refreshments, I asked if I could find some. I went to a pub on the corner, where Temple Meads garage is now, and shouted through the open door 'Is anybody there?' Eventually a man came up. I told him the all clear had sounded and would he sell me some beer or lemonade as we were parched ... and he said he could not let me have any as it was gone closing time. I will not write as to what I thought of the man, because I told him it was for us firemen who had been on duty near his pub. I took another mate with me and we went into a big hotel nearby. There was quite a crowd inside making merry, and the landlord saw us and asked where we had been during the raid. I told him and he said, 'Right!, all your drinks on the house, and thanks for what you have done tonight ... Send down your mates and they will be treated the same.'

This raid found a lot of faults in the organisation — going to the centre of Bristol to report. This was altered by the next raid, you had to report to fire officers on the outskirts of the city. That night there were 839 casualties including 200 killed.

Mrs Anne Chalmers set off for her shop the next morning.

I managed to board a bus, but it only went as far as Old Market, and I had to walk the rest of the way to Bond Street, where firemen were still hosing the buildings remaining near the Haymarket. There were cinders flying all over the place (and one of them went into my eye and that evening I had to go to my doctor to get it taken out). There seemed to be no one around except police and firemen, and they didn't want to let me through, but I told them I lived there and saw that our shop, and house above, were still standing. I unlocked the front door. It was very quiet — like going into the *Marie Celeste*. I went up into the attics and looked out. It was devastation — masses and masses of rubble. Gone were Spencers, who made and sold billiard balls next door, gone the Health Food stores, and indeed the whole of the Upper Arcade with the incorporated shops and houses. Gone the Barton Warehouse which sold drapery, the Queen's Head pub, the sweetshop and at least one side of Barr Street had been gutted. I stood there utterly horrified.

That night I made my way back through streets where not a glimmer of light showed. The whole city was blacked out except for small lights on the buses (some of which had taken the place of trams). We soon found out that the whole of Wine Street, Castle Street, Peter Street, part of the High Street, including the Dutch House, had gone, and so had the historical Mary-le-Port Street, with its eighteenth century church.

When the raid started, my family were safe, they had all gone into the cellar and, although there were sounds from above, they had no idea what was going on up there. No one had bargained for incendiary bombs, fires had been started all round, and they could hear buildings crashing down around them.

John H. Smith, a heavy rescue lorry driver, remembers in particular the Good Friday blitz, which lasted from 6 pm to 7.30 am on the Saturday morning.

Avonmouth escaped a lot of damage as the ground was so boggy that the bombs sank far into the ground before exploding. In Sea Mills and Stoke Bishop the rocky nature of the ground caused the bombs to explode on the surface and the resulting surface blast caused greater damage to

The 17th century timbered Dutch House at the corner of Wine Street in Bristol was reduced to such a charred skeleton that it had to be pulled down for safety; 24 November 1941.

surrounding property. Driving a lorry at these times was a hazardous task. The roads were dark and strewn with debris, blocks of masonry from blitzed buildings, craters, fallen trees and many other obstacles. Concrete bollards called 'Dragon's teeth' had been built across many main roads to obstruct the passage of enemy tanks, etc., and the narrow openings between these had to be negotiated in a zigzag pattern — a difficult feat in the blackout.

Another night there was a terrible thunder and lightning storm. Many barrage balloons were in the sky at the time and one did not know whether it was the sound of bombs exploding or claps of heavy thunder as there was an alert on at the time. The rain was very heavy. Then one by one the balloons caught fire and slowly fell to the ground. Many landed on the houses and their anchor cables hung from the roofs over the roads. Many roofs were damaged, there were miles of cable. We first had to haul these in. It was a messy job as they were coated in a black grease and in the pouring rain and darkness it was a far from enviable job. There was danger too that in falling they had come into contact with some high powered electric cables. We were lucky to complete the task without any casualties.

Regent Street, Clifton, was the scene of one bombing. A large crater in the road caused a broken gas and water main. The gas had seeped up through the water in the crater and caught alight on the surface of the water lighting the whole scene. The gas filled the cellars of the shops, it had travelled up the water downpipes from the roof gutters then caught alight making flame torches about six feet high. Several people, we were told, were trapped in the shop cellars. We tried to get down to them but were driven back by a sheet of flame. Huge gusts of air were drawing everything into the flames and one's clothes flapped around one.

One time a bomb formed a crater in the West Town Depot amongst a pile of kerb and paving stones. The depot cat had chosen the spot as a home for a family of kittens. We thought that they had been killed by the bomb but were surprised to see the cat carrying the kittens back to the crater the next day.

A mobile gun traversed the Avonmouth railway line between the tunnel at Bridge Valley road and Avonmouth, firing random shots at the enemy planes and then shunting to a new position. This caused many bombs to be dropped on or near the Portway. A large gun, nicknamed Purdown Percy by Bristolians, was sited on Purdown; there was also Big Bertha near Ham Green Hospital. Around Avonmouth Docks, trailer vehicles called Smoke Stacks were parked at intervals. These were set alight during raids and sent billowing smoke over the dock area, forming a smoke screen if the wind was in the right direction.

Mary Palmer again.

One night the enemy managed to get below the barrage balloon cables and bombed the huge oil storage tanks at Avonmouth docks. This was an incredible sight and many miles away it was so light that you could read a book at midnight out in the street. It was an almost impossible task to get these fires under control. They burned and burned for days, making it an even more vulnerable target.

Sometimes the enemy just jettisoned their bombs onto the nearest back garden and headed off for home. Late one night

Bombed out in Bristol, 1941.

Dad came back from Home Guard duty very late. Over a stretch of open land called the Downs he found that he was surrounded by hundreds of incendiaries. He stayed and helped to try with other local people to put them out. He said it was a picture, just like fairyland.

On one occasion we had some firemen from Luton to give them a rest from intensive action in London blitz but as soon as they got to us they were called out to a blitz on nearby Bath!

Sheffield

The great steel city, another inevitable target, was next on the list. For nine and a quarter hours on the night of 12 December and again for three hours on Sunday the 15th, Sheffield was attacked by a total of 300 German bombers. The steel works, ironically, were not badly damaged; but the city centre was ravaged, with 668 civilians and 25 servicemen killed and thousands injured. Nearly 3,000 homes were totally demolished, with a further 3,000 badly damaged.

125

On the first night, Geoffrey White, then 15 years old, was working at the Dorma Drill, Napier Street.

We were due to finish at 8 pm. Suddenly the sirens sounded. Everyone carried on working and at 7.30 a red alert sounded and we were told to switch off our machines and go to the shelter and we stopped there till 9.30 pm. My friend Cliff suggested we came out of the shelter. The first thing we saw was an ambulance in the crater, also a shop front blown out. We walked on to Pomona Street and saw a man throwing water on an incendiary bomb which flared up more — he should have put sand on it.

Next a man asked us to help him put a fire out in his loft, and as there was already no water on tap I got a ladder and got water from the river running at the back of his house. We then went on to Ecclesall Road where we helped another man put a fire out. This person gave us a large bottle of whisky, which we drank as we were scared. Next we saw a garage on fire on Arrow Street and pushed five cars out onto the road. We went up the main road and saw a jeweller's shop bombed and diamonds, rings, watches and other jewellery all over the pavement. Later that night a direct hit on a shop killed a student who was passing ... We then walked on to London Road just as a bomb dropped on the Hermitage Inn, killing all in the pub. We wandered around and at 6.30 decided to go home. Lots of roads had unexploded bombs on them and it took ages. Arnold Laver's wood yard was ablaze and we were lucky not to have gone in the centre of town as it was very badly bombed. In the High Street, Marples, a public house had a direct hit, 70 people lost their lives. At the bottom of Carver Street a bank had a direct hit and a crater filled with water and thousands of pound notes floating in the water, but also a ring of soldiers guarding the money.

We arrived home to find everyone in the family safe. My sister spent the night in the basement of the Abbeydale picture house. My great grandma had a lucky escape as an unexploded bomb dropped on her house in Abbeydale Road. They were on the cellar head and escaped. It blew up one hour later destroying the house.

The next day we realised how bad the raid was. On street corners there were stretchers with bodies on them covered with tarpaulin waiting to be moved. We had 87 HE bombs on our district called Netheridge. About 500 yards from where we lived was a crater in the middle of the main road with a tram 20 feet from it.

For weeks water wagons had to supply people, also no toilets or electricity. A boy of 14 was killed on Woodseats Road when an incendiary bomb hit him on the head. A body in its coffin was blown out of a bedroom window on Woodseats Road.

One amusing thing happened. My auntie was baking in her shop when they were told to leave (unexploded bomb). When she came back three days later the flour had risen all over the floor, as there was 16 stone of flour in the pan!

On that same evening, 18-year-old Wilfred Surplice, of Combined Naval Operations, set off for the city centre to go to a dance at the Majestic Ballroom.

The bus conductor warned us that there was a red alert and Sheffield was rumoured to be the target. My first call was Marples pub where I had a glass of beer, and it was demolished, but I had moved on to the dance. All the time I kept wondering where all the dancing people were, but obviously they had never left home.

I finished my runaround at 8.30 pm in the cellar of the Royal Oak in King Street. Later a warden came and asked for people to help at the Sheffield Cathedral where people were trapped in a shelter with debris on the escape routes. We duly cleared the debris and headed back to the Royal Oak cellar. The entrance to this shelter was blown up so we decided to evacuate and I was elected to go up the loading cellar steps and find another shelter.

I found one across the road with a number of exits if we needed to get out. The strange thing was that most of the people in the Royal Oak shelter were blind and the problem was to get everyone across the road, which was a mass of debris and buildings blazing all around. So we decided I would go first and everyone should hold each other's coat or hand and we weaved our way across like a lot of people doing the conga — and such bravery for those blind people to face unseen dangers. Made me feel so proud of them. No one complained and they all survived this terrible night. I often wonder where these blind people had been to before the bombs fell.

Other pub shelterers were less lucky, as Len Doherty reported in the *Sheffield Star*.

The customers spent the evening singing in the cellars of the Marples Hotel, knowing this would be safe. At 11.44 it had a direct hit. Its seven floors of offices, concert rooms and bars and lounges, orchestra dais and heavy furniture, its massive walls had come crashing down on the cellars where 70 people were buried under the ruins. Sheffield's most famous pub had become a tomb. Seven survivors were rescued from the smouldering ruins next day, but of the others only 14 bodies could be properly identified. This was the worst single incident of the blitz in terms of human life.

One of the trapped victims being rescued from a shelter under the Marples Hotel, Allen Square, Sheffield, which was destroyed in 12 December blitz.

Harry Sellors, a voluntary ambulance driver, remembers that

things were getting a little warm, guns were going in the
distance when we heard a very loud bang 100 yards away
from our house. I went into the garden, the flames from a gas
main were 100 feet into the air in front of our houses. I
thought 'Oh my God! Walt and Beat, they have had it!' I ran
to their door, called out, but no answer. I went in over broken
furniture. I moved broken bits here and there, but I saw
something burning on the fire back. I thought 'No it cannot
be, but here goes' and I pulled at it and it was Walter up the
chimney, feet first, every bone in his body broke. I managed
to get him out into the back yard then went in the house
again and I heard a moan under a turned-over table, there
were Beat in a terrible state. I carried her out into the shelter. I
said 'Arrest all the bleedings with a torn sheet, I have to get
back there. All three houses are going up in flames if I don't
do something to stop it.'

So I went back in our house — as luck would have it the
water was still on. I took the sink-bowl full and threw that on
the fire in the fire-place. Same in each house. Then back into
the shelter to see what I could do for Beat. I did all I could,
then I was getting calls from all over the place ... 'There is
one dead on my back door, his wife is in a very bad condition
...' Then I got old Mrs Turner out of the house and walking
her down the road when thump something hit her on her
back and down she went dead as a door nail. I was left with
two dead. Then our team came and our captain Hardy said
'Why did you not turn in tonight, we are one driver missing?'
I said 'Look, I have two dead and one in a very bad way,
come I will show you.'

I had been married four months, all new furniture, the lot,
gone, all but a glass dome with Our Blessed Virgin Mary
inside it, that was still intact.

**Mrs C.M. Smith had learned the morning before that her
grandmother had died.**

So we went to Heeley, and there she was laid out in the front room. At about 8 pm we were told by wardens to keep in the shelters as they said Sheffield was the target. As we sat and nothing happened, my Uncle said 'I'm going in the house.' As it was fairly cold, we followed — we didn't like the idea of Grandma lying there alone, as the undertaker could not fetch her. We made my baby and small sister comfortable and went into the kitchen all in darkness.

At between 11 and 12 we heard a train coming from Sheffield and the next thing from nowhere bombers appeared in the sky, just dark objects. We stood with the kitchen door open looking down into the valley; then from the bombers came bombs with parachutes on them, just white objects. Then came the terrible explosions blowing houses sky high one after the other about so many yards away from us ...

As soon as it became daylight I had to go to see to my little dog who I had left at home. As I got to the top of my mother's road, I looked towards Sheffield and it was just a red blaze. I was very frightened but carried on because of my little dog. I had not gone far when I had to climb over beds and furniture as about four houses had gone up. I will never forget that journey, about a mile, with roads up, houses just gone, wardens trying to stop me, telling me I was walking over unexploded bombs. When I reached my home at 6.30 I wasn't allowed in at first as we had got unexploded bombs all around. I took my little dog to my friends (and if you were to look on the cellar door, at the bottom were the clawing marks my little dog did in terror on my cellar head). We then all had to go in Ann's Road to school to live as we couldn't go back home. We slept on makeshift beds, and the soldiers cooked in the school yard for us. My poor grandma was in the house for a week before the undertaker came.

Joan Farmer, a nurse.

Next door to us lived old lass Brownhill and Billy her husband. She was frightened to death of the raids ... After the blitz finally ended, we could not see sight or hear sound of them in their house. Calling their names we heard a faint sound coming from the cellar head (this was like a pantry at the top of the steps which led to the cellar where the coal was kept in a tin bath). Poor old lass, there she sat, all her fat wobbling with fright, no head visible because of the tin washing up bowl covering it, whilst Billy sat between her outstretched knees with a saucepan on his head. What a sight and what a job we had persuading them to come out as it was all over. They had never heard the all clear, being shut away in the dark with their improvised tin hats!

It was a strange experience going the rounds after the bombings. Everyone was checking that family and friends were all right and never considered the burning timbers, or the unexploded bombs which were to shatter the peace for many hours to come ... Dad tried to retrieve the contents of a neighbour's house which was going up in flames. He staggered out with a mattress which burst and he was covered in feathers — they were like snowflakes everywhere.

All the gas, electricity and water services were disrupted for many days to come. Gardens were churned up with the shafts of unexploded bombs sticking out of the soil and the mangled service pipes decorated the roads and pavements for ages. How thankful we were to have a coal fire as the only means of boiling water for the cup that cheers and for Mum to prepare a hot meal which was mainly hash — meat and veg, thrown into an earthenware casserole dish to steadily cook before dumplings were added. Eventually a water cart, provided by the army, came round at regular intervals during the day and we queued up with buckets ... Mrs Brownhill had to have hers fetched as she never felt safe to go out again.

Although Mrs Barden's husband was a tram driver, he put in lots of hours in his spare time as an auxiliary fireman.

He helped many people to move things — even a piano he had on the platform of his tram, and lifted bags of coke from the gas works on his route. He said he could hardly drive for stuff he carried for people.

The night of the blitz he had left his tram — which was a good thing, as it was burnt out in the city centre ... When he came back next morning from fire-fighting, he was smoke filled and heaving and worn out, but he had been learnt to go up the turnstile ladders.

Reg O'Donnell drove a coal lorry, and the morning after the 12 December blitz he went to work as usual.

I had to walk, and I finally got to the garage, but the police stopped us because of the mess, and told us to go home, so we went walking round the city, what a shock. Tram cars was everywhere, either smashed up or burnt out, buildings all over the place was still burning, just shells, people was being dug out, unexploded bombs was cordoned off, lots of people was killed, some bombs was delayed action. A friend of mine, her mother went across the yard to the toilet, and an unexploded bomb went off, she has not been seen since. My friend was heartbroken.

Mrs N.J. Cocker, then only ten years old, was excited at the idea of taking part in the pantomime put on by the Elles-mere Road Methodist Church.

I had my white fairy dress which the musical teacher bought me and ballet shoes and headdress which my mother bought me. The show had just started when the sirens went. Of course that stopped everything. Mother said 'Get all your clothes, we have to go down in the church cellars.' It was rather dark and forbidding down there with all the pipes around us. We all huddled together, Mrs Charles, and Margaret, my friend, were with us. Mrs Charles was so nervous, and wanted to go home to her husband. She kept begging my mother to go home. She kept on and on, and by ten o'clock my mother said we would risk it.

We came out, but as we got to the doors, the guns went. Then silence, so my mother put her arm round me. I rubbed up to her coat, and she said we were going to hurry across the road, which was very wide, and make for the entry between the terraced houses opposite Ellesmere Rd. I can remember my heart thumping and the guns starting again. We seemed to stand in this entry ages until the guns stopped. Mrs Charles and Margaret went further. We went into the cellar to my father. When the bombs dropped I remember crying. I could hear the falling bricks, and my mother holding me close to her. We stayed like this until the all clear went. Going upstairs we didn't know what it would be like. The windows had been blown out, everything was covered in soot and dirt, no lights, but we were all all right, only very dirty ... Later we found that a bomb had dropped on the entry where we had sheltered, and all the people had been killed, many more who had come out of the church to shelter in the entry had also been killed. My mother kept saying 'It could have been us.'

Manchester

The last of the great arms towns to be blitzed was Manchester. Alerts had been sounding regularly since 20 June 1940, but it was not until the nights of 22 and 23 December that the city went up in flames. On the first night over 200 HE bombs were dropped on the city and on the second over 50, preceded as usual by thousands of incendiaries. The two nights left 363 dead, with 455 seriously injured.

On the 22nd (another Sunday) Les Sutton was on his first army leave, with a small group of his friends heading by train towards Manchester.

Our chatter was of Manchester pubs and other places of interest. After a very slow journey the train stopped outside Warrington. We stumbled through the dark to the station platform and were told no more trains would be going to Manchester as there was a raid on, so we hitched. A lorry picked us up, and perched atop the load we hung on to the lashings, the icy wind whipping our faces, each of us thinking Manchester might be no more by the time we got there ... As we neared the burning city the frightening glow reached high into the heavens and lit up the countryside. We could hear the dull impact of bombs and the barrage set up by the big guns. Passing through Irlam we could plainly see the fires of Salford, and in the open fields on both sides of the road scores of incendiaries were burning away. Reaching Victoria Bridge, at Woolleys the lorry had to turn back because of the mass of fire hoses covering the road like giant spaghetti. The firefighters, though busy and intent on their job, yet had a curious air of detachment and unconcern, and from them we learned of the city's ordeal.

We dispersed anxious and apprehensive. I took the shortest route to Ardwick, pausing only to look down Oldham Street at the conflagration that was Piccadilly. Our street was deserted and a Warden directed me to St Silas Church shelter where I found Mam and Dad with neighbours, all looking rather the worse for wear.

Years later, when researching his book about the Ardwick area during the blitz, Les was sent the following letter from a neighbour describing the events of the same night.

We were finishing tea around 6.15 when the sirens sounded and we went out into the brick communal shelter. There was plenty of activity overhead but no bombs to be heard just then, so around 8.30 to 9 pm we went out along Pink Street where we saw quite a lot of incendiary bombs being dealt with. The wardens warned us to go back into the shelter, which we did after making a flask of tea. About 11 pm we heard bombs dropping, then at 11.45 three almost consecutive explosions which rocked the shelter. A blast of terrific heat shot through it, singeing our hair and eyebrows ... a young woman who had only that week come to live next door to us rushed into the shelter in a very understandable hysteria. She had heard the noise and was diving under the table with her baby when the blast hurled them both against the wall. Neither she nor the baby had any clothes on except a few strips of what had been a coat, although they had been dressed ... We lost many neighbours in just our little radius caused by these three landmines which had been dropped.

ATTACKS ON THE PORTS

Just as important to the war effort as the arms towns were the great ports. None — even Belfast — proved to be beyond the range of the bombers. But the most vulnerable were those on the south coast, a mere few minutes' flying distance from occupied France.

Portsmouth

During the main blitz period Portsmouth had two air raid warnings a day on average. The city experienced 50 attacks altogether, the heaviest being those of 10 January, 10 March and 17 April 1941. The most demoralising of these was the January raid, when 450 bombs were dropped and the Civic Centre gutted. Further notable raids occurred on 15 August 1942 and in March and May 1944, with the navy and the Free French sailors always being quick to volunteer help.

Jessie Plumb, who had joined the ARP together with her mother (a trained nurse), recalls the first time they were called out, on 11 July 1940, a beautiful bright sunny day.

The sirens went and we hurried to our depot. Heard a swooshing sound, looked up, and saw three black things coming down against the very blue sky. We lay flat on the pavement, and there was this most awful crunch and bang. Glass breaking, debris falling. Then the all clear was wailing. Mother and I got up and were horrified to find our depot had been hit. The very first bombs on Portsmouth and our first aid post got a direct hit. The building and neighbourhood was a mess. Nearly 30 people died in our post — people we had to know and work with all those months. It was a sad, shocking job we had that afternoon, some bodies were mutilated beyond recognition. If my mother had not taken a few extra minutes to change her shoes before we came, we would have been inside. Two days later nearly all those who died were buried in a mass grave with a public funeral, the city's tribute of honour. Those of us left moved into the new infants' school just up the road.

135

On 1 October 1941, the Hippodrome, Portsmouth, where top variety shows and touring musicals appeared, was one of the casualties of the blitz.

During the 10 January raid, 1941, hundreds of incendiaries were dropped on Portsmouth and Southsea during the night; then HE bombs and parachute mines (called land mines at the time). The beautiful Guildhall was burned out and lovely shopping centres devastated in Southsea. They broke the mains so there was no water for the firemen — they could not even get any from the sea as it was a very low tide. Firemen came with their engines and water from as far away as Guildford. Our old cat warned us that an incendiary had landed in our bathroom so not much damage was done. Two first aid parties were sent from our depot to Southsea to give help; but there wasn't much we could do in all that heat and burning buildings.

In the 17 April blitz, the Royal Hospital was bombed and Audrey Scarlett writes of the bravery of her sister Brenda, sister-in-charge of the first aid station.

Her post was in the basement next to the pharmacy. There were no lights and the basement was flooded — many of the chemicals from the pharmacy mixed with the water. Firemen arrived to extricate survivors from the ragged hole in the ground, and Brenda, who was the last to leave, heard a voice saying 'Sister — don't leave me!' In the darkness, Brenda and a fireman crawled back into the dark flooded basement and found Barty, a VAD, trapped under a door. They managed to prise the door off her and carry her outside. She seemed unable to walk and Brenda said in her brisk fashion, 'Come on Barty, walk.' 'I can't' said Barty, and they found that her surgical scissors, which were in her pocket, had penetrated four inches into her thigh. She also had multiple fractures — but eventually made a good recovery. Six of Brenda's staff were killed that night.

Claire Lowry, a Portsmouth Wren, explains that

as well as night raids, spasmodic daytime air-raids still went on. Sometimes a lone enemy plane would dive-bomb a crowded shopping centre, and strafe the shoppers. Once,

Auntie and Grandmother were on a bus when a plane dived out of the sky and machine-gunned it. They all immediately lay flat on the floor and, although the windows were shattered, no one was hurt.

As my grandmother was terrified of the air-raids, my auntie and uncle would stay with her overnight. There was an air-raid shelter at the end of the road, so when a raid was on they would rush to the shelter, whilst Uncle would rush to his bank to fire-watch. Grandmother could not walk very fast, so eventually they stayed in the house during raids. One night a bomb dropped on a house nearby. Auntie thought the roof had blown off, so they tried to open the front door, but it was jammed, so they struggled in the dark to the front room to get out of the window, but Grandmother said 'Look, the whole of the front is blown out' and they calmly walked out. The next day Auntie returned to see that the whole front of Grandmother's house was devastated, and she was amazed to see that the glass blown from the large bay windows had splintered into hundreds of pieces, firmly embedded into the walls. In the sunlight the glass flashed like chandeliers, and tinkled like Chinese chimes.

Jessie Plumb again

After a bit of a breather from Hitler, high explosives were dropped quite near our depot on 1 April, and my team went out. We were all searching in the rubble when the siren went again. A lone plane passed over. I turned to look and saw this box thing coming down on a parachute. Everyone started to get away from it. I was with my team, half in the crater, lay down, crossed my arms and put my head on them. An almighty BANG. There was I seeing my body floating up to heaven and I heard myself praying. I seemed to be shouting 'Please God don't let me die.' Next thing is I am coming to and am kneeling, a fractured gas pipe with a fierce flame ... must get away from that, fell over several times before getting on my feet ... tripped over something, a woman with just her head and one arm showing. She had a big hole in her head so I put a field dressing in, when someone kneeled beside me, I could see it was one of the special constables, I asked him if he had seen the first aiders and ambulances. Said they must be behind that wall of rubble. The lady unfortunately was dead.

The policeman and I then went looking for people, found no more. Went through all the damaged houses. Found some dead in their front gardens, others were in their air-raid shelters, those with cuts I attended to. We ended up at a pub, damaged but it was handing out tea to the crowd of people seeking shelter. The policeman then disappeared, so I decided to go back to my depot. I do not remember much about getting there, I do remember how dark and quiet it was, and I never met another living soul. Just as I was thinking the depot must be over there, have to cross road, it must be round the corner, crossing the road, found an elderly man lying there, no bones broken but in a mess. Managed to get him up. Well, I do not know how long it took us to shuffle our way, but eventually got to the depot.

I surprised everyone by appearing. How I came out of that almost unscathed I do not know, the rest of my gang were dead, lots badly injured, all I had was something had hit the bridge of my nose (my tin hat perhaps, though I was wearing it when I was floating up there in the sky). My eyes and my nose were all swelled up, and was black and blue. Right side of my hair and face was all scorched, left side was ingrained with dirt. Some weeks later was able to pull the skin off, dirt and all . . . I did, some weeks later, suffer from delayed shock, cried for a week, and got over it. Now I know how the casualties felt.

Wonderful people we British. A woman who only had her head showing among all the debris of her house was asking me to look for her new hat. Told me which cupboard it was in. Others always had a joke or two, always false teeth to look for! The worst was going through damaged houses, and finding children hiding behind doors or in cupboards.

There was one night an unexploded bomb landed in the front garden of some terraced houses, we were sent to evacuate the people. Two old dears in the house with the unexploded bomb ticking away in their front garden were sitting in their room drinking cocoa, one playing patience, the other knitting, with a cat on her lap. What a job to get them to move ... must take our money (hidden in priceless old teapots, a box under the flagboards, and favourite chair over it. I found so many elderly people hid their money rather than trust the banks). Eventually got them out.

The 17 April raid would have been the most serious of all, since 249 aircraft came over, more than double that of any previous raid. They were successfully lured away, however, by a decoy starfish site on Hayling Island. These were masses of highly inflammable material, set alight at the start of a raid to simulate the effect of attack by incendiaries. On this occasion, while only eight bombs hit Portsmouth, some 170 HE, 32 parachute bombs and thousands of incendiaries rained down on empty fields or in the sea. (Sadly, an AA site received several direct hits, but there were far fewer casualties than if the real target had been attacked.)

Southampton

The relatively small port of Southampton received far more than its fair share of bombs. Starting with a small attack on 13 August 1940, Southampton had 51 bombing raids, including three daylight raids during September, a Sunday raid on 17 November and three heavy night attacks on 23 and 30 November and 1 December. Significant raids followed on 19 January 1941, and June 1942, with 631 people killed and over 40,000 properties damaged. Some people killed and over 40,000 properties damaged. Some 2,200 bombs fell on 1 December alone, leaving nothing, as local historian Bernard Knowles put it, 'that was not wilting, wasting or warped'.

Wendy Steele, a FANY NCO who drove a staff-car and ambulance, writes:

We slept for many, many weeks in full uniform with gas-masks and tin hats at the ready, driving through the black-outs and continual raids, while our ATS companions all around us manned all the gun-sites under terribly dangerous and frightening conditions amid all the chaos and din and terror which none of us seemed to notice.

On Saturday 30 November, 14-year-old Brenda Pritchett (née Logie) was looking forward to her first grown-up dance. She and her friends

had just got into the foyer of the Guildhall when the first bombs landed. There was no warning at all. All the glass in the windows of the foyer broke and showered over us. The management decided that the hall must be closed immediately and we were all put outside. There were not enough shelters to go round and we just did not know what to do. By this time the bombs were falling everywhere and the first of the fires were breaking out. We were joined by some soldiers. Two of them gave us girls their tin hats and we decided to go down the High Street to see if we could find shelter. We were dodging falling masonry as best we could, when we got to the corner of Ogle Road. A little old man came out. 'Do you want to come into my half-finished shelter?' It seemed heaven-sent. We climbed down and settled ourselves on planks left by the workmen. There was a Canadian soldier there who thought that I was a bit crazy when I opened my case and began curling up my hair. I had started while still a child singing at troop shows for Southern Command, and all I could think of was that if I did not curl my hair which was very long, it would be straight the next day for the Sunday show.

After many hours the bombardment stopped and the all clear sounded. Up we came. The devastation was terrible. Shop fronts had been blown out, contents of the shops were strewn all over the pavements and most of the fires were still raging — anyone could have stolen anything that night.

Mrs K.D. Allhusen, a nurse, was on her way to the hospital at 5.30 on the morning following a raid when a policeman stopped her and asked where she was going.

I said 'To the hospital.' He said 'It isn't there.' It had had a direct hit but luckily they got the patients out safely. Apparently a baby had been born during the raid — they had saved it by putting it in a drawer.

Our final Southampton story is from Eva Asplin, a Salvation Army ambulance driver who had moved into her parents' cottage deep in the New Forest after her own flat had been land-mined.

Making my way there one night, I went through one of the most beautiful avenues in Southampton — the whole avenue in flames — firemen with fire-escapes, water pipes filled the road; my pass and SA bonnet hastened me on. Policemen and firemen challenged me, accompanied by a new language I had never heard before! They thought me quite mad! I picked my way ahead — well aware of a full petrol tank aboard; suddenly I saw a staggering man in my path — his gait made me guess 'He's drunk'. Then I saw that he was a soldier with full kit. I jumped out, shoved him in and his kit, helped by a fireman. He had arrived home on embarkation leave, but found no house, no wife, no home. I explained that all the folk in that locality would have left home early evening and gone to the hills. I took him home to my parents. Gradually he calmed down. We led our guest to a made-up bed in the sitting-room. Next morning I came down to take him to the military depot, then to the Civic Centre so that he could find out where those of that avenue were ... but the bed was empty, bedclothes neatly folded and piled up in perfect order. That was the last we ever knew of 'Tommy', all enquiries made everywhere ended in a blank.

Plymouth

Plymouth suffered a concentrated series of raids greater than that of any southern port. The worst period started with the nights of 20 and 21 March, followed by an almost non-stop series of raids on 21, 22, 23, 27, 28 and 29 April. Mass Observation reported that

the civil and domestic devastation in Plymouth exceeds

Plymouth's cathedral, St Andrew's, is blitzed.

anything we have seen elsewhere, both as regards concentration throughout the heart of the town, and as regards the shattering of homes all over the town.

Writes Councillor Jack Wigmore:

These blitzes were pretty horrendous. Many people were killed, particularly in a large air-raid shelter in Portland Square. Fire engines came from far and wide to tackle the fires, including many from Bristol. During this period the Germans had a field day as most of our ack-ack batteries ran out of ammunition; the only opposition to them was from a naval vessel anchored in Plymouth Sound.

Pat Konig, a Wren, worked shifts during this period

which meant little or no sleep, as the nights I wasn't on duty I slept lying on the ground floor of our quarters — we were not allowed in our rooms. I think it was only the foresight of our Wren officer that we are alive today; our quarters were in Devonport near the docks, and as Plymouth had been flattened, she felt sure the Germans would be back to finish off the job. She organised for all of us to be accommodated in private houses in nearby villages ... our quarters were bombed the night after we left.

Once when I went with two naval friends to a theatre in the centre, there was a raid during which the theatre bravely continued ... however, the bombs became increasingly loud and we looked at each other and said 'That was close', and then it happened. The stage had a direct hit and the roof and walls all about us collapsed like a pack of cards. At the time I'm afraid it was each man for himself to get out, and then, I remember, stumbling along over all the stones, bricks and debris, diving into the shelter of an already-blitzed doorway as yet another bomb came crashing down. Many were incendiaries causing terrible fires. It didn't seem possible that we would get out of this alive. One pair of us wanted to stay and see if we could help, but our escorts insisted they got us out. Only after we had got back, did they return to help people out of the rubble.

One day when I was walking to the Dockyard where my small boat was moored, a sneak raider let loose with machine gun fire, and I really thought my last moment had come. I covered my face with my hands and pressed my body against the nearest wall and all the time heard bullets splattering all around me, sure that they were going to pepper my back. That was the moment when I really knew the meaning of fear, followed by shock, real shock, because as I walked back to the town, people had died just where they were sitting or standing. I had never realised this could happen, and it was a few minutes before I realised these people were in fact dead. I remember a young baker's boy standing in a doorway with his large bread basket still over his arm. I remember a family sitting at their dining room table with all the walls around them gone. They looked exactly as if they were on a stage, or made of wax.

Charlotte Marsh remembers the strafing too.

It was a daylight raid in Keyham, Plymouth. Children were going into school, 1.45 pm, when suddenly, without any warning, a black object came from out of the clouds and machine-gunned the children. Luckily the teachers quickly grabbed them into the shelters. After that the headmaster said that no child under seven years of age would attend school to be a responsibility for the teachers. Dockyard workers, too, were machine-gunned at 7 am in the mornings going to work.

Olive McMahon lost her husband when HMS *Glorious* was dive-bombed. When he joined the ship, Olive was in the Alexandra Nursing Home, where their daughter had just been born.

I will never forget the day he came in to see me before going away. He went into the nursery and his first words to me were 'She gripped one of my fingers.' On returning home with her I got those dreaded telegrams, then the final one and his medals. Some say it was warfare and that time heals. How can one forget? During the big blitz, while my three little ones were sleeping in the shelter on a makeshift bed — a door taken from a house that had been bombed — I crept out of the shelter after the all-clear and went on to Friary Bridge and watched our city centre burn ... How I dreaded those terrible drones of the approaching bombers every night. My nightly thoughts were always of what my husband said — 'God will keep you safe for me.'

Doreen Jessop (then Herd) was, at 17, one of the youngest ambulance drivers in the area.

My shift was called the mug shift, as we were always on duty when the heaviest raids were on. When a road would be blocked off because of an unexploded bomb, we would have been driving past it all night! A lot of people and children used to go out in the country at night to safety and then come back in the morning. It was like a dead city at times ...

We had a seaplane base, and sometimes the German planes would come in behind ours and drop their bombs before the alert was sounded. They set fire to the oil containers and gas works which were burning for days so was a good target for them to drop their bombs. We were without gas, water and electricity and had to rely on water lorries. My mother cooked meals on an open fire and baked in a biscuit tin. On Sundays we would put the meat and potatoes in a roasting tin and take it to the bakery up the road and he would charge sixpence to cook it.

One night a land mine dropped on a park where there was a maze of underground shelters, full of people, and I had to take the ambulance with a squad car of men to take the injured to hospital. When I arrived the scene looked just like a deep glen with lanterns at the side, like hills. It turned out to be soldiers with lights digging people out at the sides of the crater. Some were just parts of bodies and, where it was possible, we had to attach a label to the body or parts, with my name, and the name of the first aid post and whether it was male or female. We then went into the shelter, and there were all the people just sitting, some with children still on their laps, people with glasses on, and the glass still intact, and they were all dead, killed by the blast. The thing I saw, which was different, their hair, looked like wigs, sort of lifeless, and dusty.

There were phosphorus bombs, and they caused terrible burns and injuries and splashed all over the people's bodies, which was difficult to treat before getting them to hospital.

My feelings during the blitz was, we had a job to do and got on with it, and if it had my name on it, well, that's it. But in between raids, we would get a bit depressed, at the people who had been injured and made homeless, and some of the sorry sights, but then we would think of a funny instance and have a laugh.

Mrs J. Taskis (née Summers) remembers a very cool father.

Once after the five houses behind us had been hit and we returned to find windows out, doors and walls down, soot everywhere, etc., we were clearing up the kitchen and found an unexploded incendiary bomb which had crashed through the window and rolled under the gas stove. When my father arrived home (a trained fire-watcher), he calmly took this bomb out to the back yard, unscrewed the fuse and shook out the powder very carefully, then screwed it up again and put it in a galvanised bucket. He gave it to me to take up to the air-raid warden who was on duty at the top of the road ... I remember now, carrying this up to him, whereupon he went white, until I proudly told him about my dad!

Michael Anderson, then a gunner stationed at Deal, still has a letter his mother sent him during the big series of raids.

Dear Son,
It's 3.30 and I'm rushing to catch the post. So very sorry not to have sent before. I fetched your photos dear and silly like should have asked Shepherd to forward some, but have had a very busy time: three nights blitz and the second was terrific. It took the stuffing out of our sails I can tell you, as Devonport has now gone and Plymouth. I had to climb over the

debris to get to the meat market on Saturday — the Soper is still there, several are gone. There's no Bank Street at all! Saturday afternoon Scott took Greta and me to the College to see Noel Coward's play 'Hay Fever'. It was excellent, but very poorly attended, Shakespeare (Society) did it for the League of Pity, they had to pay £9.9.0 royalties, so only made a couple of pounds, I think. We did enjoy it so. Scott [on leave from the RASC] hasn't laughed so much for a long time. It was very subtle. Scott has to go again tomorrow so we shall miss him. Aunt Meg is here staying again and Auntie Alice is sleeping here so the house is very full at present. They're talking of evacuating children from Plymouth. We were very lucky, only one pane gone from the breakfast room, but others cracked. Thick earth, etc., on back and front steps as well as the scullery roof. I had a heavy time brushing and clearing up, although Daddy is back now and again now and we are beginning to get more normal. The road is very busy and Mutley Plain like the City of London with everyone shopping there. Dingles and others opened there yesterday for foodstuffs. We're all safe and well and look forward to seeing you again soon. Glad you enjoyed the parcel — am afraid food will be tightened up again soon but will send you while I can. Glad you had no ill effects from the inoculation tho sorry to hear about David — poor dear! We picture you being an NCO, tho try and catch your thief as food is very precious. Can't you set a trap for him and mark your stuff? Had four of the cast (Shakespeare) to tea. They went all over Mutley Plain and couldn't get a cup. I bumped into them and brought them over here and they were so grateful as they did an evening show too. This morning Paddy brought an armful of flowers from the 'Four Invaders'. It was a kindly thought. Must fly dear. Fond Love. God guard you through this cursed war and bring you safely back to your job.
Your loving Mother.

To this he adds a sad footnote: 'It was her last letter to me. Before the following morning the house received a direct hit and the whole family was wiped out. My mother, father, brother and two aunts, one of many families killed in those dark days.'

Our final Plymouth story is from one of the survivors —
Betty Wilson, then 15-year-old Betty Brown.

My friend Iris and I left the cinema when the air-raid warning
came onto the screen, and found the nearest public shelter —
in a park. After about half an hour the shelter shook like an
earthquake. We were terrified as dust and stones came down
the entrance, making us all cough. When the noise abated, we
decided to try to get home so that our parents wouldn't
worry. We made our way to the park exit and a bus stop. We
were really scared of the dark — and all the planes could still
be heard and searchlights sweeping the sky. Suddenly we
heard a whistling bomb and dived into a deep shop doorway,
a man was there also, he said nothing. We were both hugging
and crying and wishing we were home, still the man said
nothing. I said to him, 'I hope we shall be fairly safe here, we
are going home on the bus as soon as we can.' He didn't
answer. We shone our torches on him, his eyes were open
and staring blankly, he didn't blink or shade his eyes, we
knew he was dead. So we went into a pub on the corner and
told some men about it, and they went back with us. The
man's jacket had caught on a hook, and that was keeping him
up.

Mum and I were in one bed at home when 'Whoosh, bang'.
A smell of burning came from the landing, we put the light on
and saw smoke seeping through the roof. We put on our
trousers, dressing gowns, coats and shoes, got our gas masks
and cases, threw out the pillows, bedding and rugs through
the open window onto our small lawn below, my mum got
me onto the window sill, and told me to jump. I couldn't
move, I was terrified, the bedroom door was blistering. Mum
said 'Betty, jump or fry alive' and she pushed me out. I
screamed all I could. I landed on all the bedding OK, and
watched Mum jump. Voices and water were heard, but I just
wanted to sit there, huddled up to Mum in a blanket. Then
there were some neighbours around us with tea, but I
couldn't hold the cup. I was shaking badly. Mum and I cried,
we had been so close to being burnt in bed. We relived that
jump many times. The house was patched up and livable, but

the fear was always there as I tried to sleep, 'Will I have to jump again?'

The raids eased off, but dear old Plymouth had taken a battering, it was so sad to see the devastation, it was hard to imagine that Plymouth would ever arise again. The teenage years I had went by, running from raids, terror, sadness and memories. I don't really remember being a teenager. I had to grow up quickly, and take my chances ... I was one of the many lucky ones to live on.

Merseyside

'Liverpool was the terminus for our Life-line with the USA and so the most important port in the country.' These are the words of Norman Ellison, from Wallasey, a fiercely patriotic Merseysider who kept a detailed diary throughout the war. His first entries show how relatively minor incursions became such a part of everyday life that people were unprepared for the first big blitz when it finally came on 28 November 1940.

9 August — On Aug 9 Merseyside experienced its first night raid with a few bombs and one casualty on Birkenhead.

10 August — Just after midnight, Wallasey had its first air raid with six killed and 80 wounded by the 15 bombs dropped.

13 September — Ferries stopped running as the Mersey had been mined from the air.

17 September — A sneak raider came up the Mersey in daylight, bombed Speke and made off. The action of a brave pilot and crew.

27 September — After a recent raid on Wallasey, a woman, whose house had been bombed to the ground, came to my friend Ben Kelly, sergeant in the special constables, and borrowed 2 pence to ring up her husband working a night-shift. He overheard this laconic conversation — 'Is that you, Fred? ... Well, don't come home to the house — it isn't there. Go to mother's for breakfast. Goodbye.'

An injured woman being helped to a reception centre from a First Aid Post after her home was bombed in the May blitz on Merseyside, 1941.

28 September — Argyle Theatre, Birkenhead, completely destroyed. A landmark with many happy memories.

10 November — On every night for the last three months, with very few exceptions, Merseyside has been visited by German planes. Many visits in daylight. At first the warning sirens were taken seriously during the daytime and all haste was made to the nearest shelter. Buses, trams and ferryboats stopped; offices and shops were locked up and their staff retired to basements and cellars. The streets became deserted and the whole life of the community was paralysed. Sometimes there would be five such stoppages during the working day, yet no bombs were dropped and nothing happened. So now we carry on — sirens or no sirens — and do not seek shelter until the guns open fire or bombs are dropped. At night it is mines — so the sirens are heeded and cover taken quickly.

29 November — 524 enemy raiders dropped 356 tons of HEs and 860 canisters of incendiaries each containing 36 bombs. It was the first time we suffered from the devastating effect of land mines, each about the size of a pillar-box, slowly descending by parachute. Some became hung up in trees or from the roofs of houses, suspended by the parachute cords and swinging in the wind. It is not possible to praise too highly the bravery of the bomb disposal squads who rendered them harmless by removing the live fuses. Indeed, many lost their lives in this extremely dangerous duty.

Doris Wallington lived in Liverpool before joining the ATS, and remembers

travelling each morning across the River Mersey by ferry boat, appalled by the sight of another wreck ... the sailors had risked their lives to save us. They'd run the gauntlet of German submarines and stormy seas only to be sunk at anchor in the 'home' river.

We had barrage balloons floating from barges along the river and batteries of guns on each shore, but still enemy planes found their targets. Towards Xmas the blitz became worse, the park shelters were full. Anderson shelters were being issued slowly, but as the raids became heavier, neighbours clubbed together to buy their own concrete shelters ... We were always glad to see the dog leave the shelter ... the all-clear would go seconds later ... Once my uncle had to spend the night and every time a bomb or gun-fire sounded, he would hold his flat cap inches above his head. He was frightened, we were all frightened, not knowing if our home had survived the night.

Lots of children, evacuated to Wales, had come home for Xmas, but there were very bad air raids. The sirens wailed again so the children were hastily evacuated again.

Bad indeed. Over the course of three successive nights, from 20-22 December, a total of 500 bombers hit Merseyside. The first night was a Friday, and Ellison noted that

The raid started 6.30 pm and continued without cessation until 3.30 am. Very heavy. In and out of the shelter for protection against the constant shower of shell fragments. At 4 pm ALL Liverpool appeared to be on fire. The whole eastern sky was ablaze — a terrifying sight. A thick pall of smoke over everything.

Nancy Nossiter, a Wren petty officer, was in charge of a watch in the teleprinter office on the first floor of the Liver Building.

Two watches were caught on duty — we came off watch at 1800 and another watch arrived just before to relieve us, when it started, and the Liver Building was quickly ringed by fire, an ammunition ship in one of the docks alongside was on fire and exploding. The city was soon alight, and the German planes were strafing people on the streets — we went up on the roof of Liver (STRICTLY forbidden!) to watch, and the planes were actually below us, machine-gun firing, in the light from the huge fires everywhere — the sky was bright red, we saw people shot down about us in the streets below. The noise was terrific. All the telephone lines were out of action, but for some unexplainable reason, one of our tele-printers, a direct line to the Admiralty, worked, and as you may know, teleprinters automatically turn themselves off after 30 seconds if not used — ours never got a chance! As fast as one signal was sent, another came in , and anyway, we took it in turns to stay by it, like some precious article — which it was — to see it didn't go off! Otherwise, all other signals were sent by despatch riders — VERY dangerous — or radio, or direct signals (semaphore/morse flash) to the ships.

We had Perspex eye-shields in our gas-mask cases, and these we took out to give to the firemen, who had no protection for their eyes, and they were badly affected by the smoke, of course.

There were two Wrens on watch at a time, so four of us took it in turns to mind the machine and send messages, and the others tried to get a bit of sleep — and a bit of food ! We were trapped there for 48 hours, before our reinforcements arrived, by which time most of the fires were under control, and four very tired Wrens arrived back at the Wrennery — Ackerley House — on the outskirts of Liverpool. There we were immediately sent to sick bay, and sister bathed our eyes, which were as bad as the firemen's pretty well — the smoke was everywhere, as all the windows had been blown out of the building, and even though they were boarded up, a lot of smoke was around! Then we were given 48 hours off ... I slept for 24 hours straight when I got to Gran's.

Joy Alfree was nine years old, and living at Bebington, just across the river from the city.

During this week of attacks my mother took me over to Liverpool to buy a siren suit à la Churchill. All the centre of the shopping area was a terrible mess, but some of the big stores were managing to carry on amongst all the damage. I got my siren suit and with the innocence of a nine-year-old proclaimed in a loud voice 'I hope we have a raid tonight, then I can wear my suit!' What a frightful child. We had a raid, I wore my suit and the only time in my life I wet myself and the navy blue dye came out over everything.

Norman Ellison again:

Saturday 21 December — St Nicholas church still smouldering when I passed on my way to the office this morning. Great devastation everywhere. Another raid started 6.45 and continued until 4.30 am. Much heavier than last night and more local. Many bombs all around us — more than 40 houses demolished within a good stone's throw. We stayed in the shelter and seemed to have bombs whistling down on us all night through. Many incendiaries too. We had three opposite the front gate and got them out — very lucky. Never so glad to see the dawn before. What a mess we are in! Not a window or windowframe in the house. Doors blown in, slates mostly gone, walls cracked. Water, gas and electricity all cut off and a bitterly cold east wind blowing through everything. Molly Peterson came round and offered to cook some grub for us at her home. Flak-driven glass had ripped the curtains to ribbons; it was embedded in the walls, pictures and furniture — but the weekend joint was under cover. We collected other homeless people and later that afternoon dozens of us sat down, some on the floor to a most welcome meal.

He and his wife were forced to leave their home shortly after this and got to stay in a friend's attic. While they were away their old home was looted. There was a period of comparative peace, but the massed bombers returned in March 1941, on the 13th and 21st. He noted down, following one of these raids, that

bombs destroyed the main water supply to Wallasey and for nearly a week there was nothing. The corporation erected canvas-screened army-type latrines in public parks and on waste ground ... troops had been drafted in to clear the roads. Convoys of heavy lorries brought in water. People lined up with jugs for drinking water. All who could leave Wallasey were going.

Stephen Woodcock, the warden down in Kensington, heard about the same raid in a letter from his friend Lena Roberts, written on her return to Birkenhead from London.

We got the 5.30 all night from Stafford and travelled in complete darkness. Crewe informed us that many planes were about and would everybody please hurry in getting out and into the train, keeping close to the walls of the station for safety. The train simply raced to Lime Street, searchlights and AA following us all the time. Liverpool seemed fairly quiet except for some fires, so we got to the underground and came to Birkenhead Park. We were welcomed by the most awful explosion a few yards away, and such fires! Birkenhead was well alight. I wanted to shelter in the station as the guns were going terrifically, but Maud insisted on going and luckily we did so. We'd gone just five minutes walk to the entrance of the underground shelter in the park when Maud told me to look — there were two parachutists coming down ... I didn't have time to see the invaders — with a terrible bang and then another, we were blown into the shelter — and then further in by another blast. The place rocked and Park Station was no more. After that until 3.30 Birkenhead knew the worst.

There were quite a lot in the trench shelters and others kept coming in who had been in houses destroyed over their heads. People were amazingly calm. A few women wept, thinking of the comfortable houses they had so carefully tended and which were no more, and husbands petted and comforted, saying 'Don't worry, after all we're alive!' I shall never forget that night. These trenches rocked with explosions and blasts swept them away again and again. It is these hideous land mines — they scatter such awful destruction. There are miles of streets with hardly any habitable houses and pathetic treks of carts, vans and even by bicycle with precious salvage. We are having a husband and wife here until they can find another home.

Flo Rigden, from Birkenhead, recalls one night when the incendiaries were dropping all round.

My mum said they looked like they were dancing on our road. Then we got a lot of heavy stuff coming down. It was really bad. Mum and Dad made a bed under a heavy table under the window in our basement kitchen for myself and my younger sister and two younger brothers. A high explosive bomb came down across the road and our whole house shook. We had a heap of soot and smoke down the chimney, my sister, brothers and I were thrown from one side of the kitchen to the other, and an old man, a friend of my grandfather's who lived in the house, was terrified, and all we kept getting from him was 'It's an insanitary bum down the chimley', he kept saying this for about ten minutes. My father calmed him down. But I bet we were the only house in the UK hit by an insanitary bum!

Flo has another story about her mother during the war. It seems that her elder sister, Lily, was attached to a mixed AA battery near Woolton, Liverpool.

She came home one day during the blitz and told Mum she had seen a terrible sight at Liverpool Pier Head. A naked man who had had his penis blown off. Poor mum was very shocked her daughter had seen this terrible thing, a naked man. Then Lily laughed and said the man was only a stone statue that stood at the Pier Head.

A bit of Scouse humour and courage came in handy at this time. On Friday 25 April, his 48th birthday, Norman Ellison wrote in his diary:

I have no home, my furniture is stored in no less than five places, my wife has been away for four months nursing Uncle George and goodness knows when she will rejoin me — yet I am as cheerful as possible, for I am fully determined not to allow this insane war to get me down.

Six days later he needed all the determination he could muster, for the following Thursday, 1 May, saw the start of seven straight nights of bombing, with over 800 bombers taking part. When the shock was over he sat down and wrote the following account.

At 10.50 the first bomb fell on Wallasey, the prelude to a full week of night raids with the object of destroying the Port of Liverpool. In a supreme and concentrated effort, the enemy aimed at total destruction of the great dock system itself and to break the morale of its inhabitants. Official reports say — 'It was an attack more severe in its weight, its concentration, and its continuity than had been experienced by any other area except London, and more severe perhaps in its concentration than even London had experienced. In Liverpool, for instance, the killed numbered more than 1,400 and there were more than 1,000 seriously injured. In Liverpool, Bootle and the adjoining fringe of Litherland and Crosby, nearly 90,000 houses were destroyed or damaged. This total represented about 40 per cent of all the houses in the area concerned. In Bootle, which had the greatest weight of attack, about 80 per cent of the houses were affected in some degree by bombs, or blast or fire. In Birkenhead, out of a total of about 34,000, over 25,000 were damaged. Over 1,600 were hit as many as three times. In Liverpool, no fewer than 7,500 persons had to be evacuated owing to damage to their houses.'

An aged Liverpool couple gaze at the ruins of another bombed house and shattered car, 4 May 1941.

Doris Wallington remembers that on the Monday morning they went to work

past smouldering ruins, stepping over fire-hoses, looking with disbelief at the rubble of once fine buildings stretching from Paradise Street to the waterfront. Even in daylight the pall of smoke darkened the sky and the smell of burning spread for miles around. Miraculously, Queen Victoria's statue was standing in its cupola, imperiously surveying the devastation. The three-storey building I had left on Saturday lunchtime was just a smoking hole in the ground; however within a few weeks we were back in business in borrowed premises. The safe had been salvaged and the ledgers, which had been packed very tightly together were still legible, although charred round the edges. The reinforced cellars and basements weren't so lucky. The gas pipes had melted with the intense heat above and anyone sheltering there would have burnt to death, as had the rats which had caused such a problem in these old buildings.

And Norman Ellison ended his account by saying that

for seven consecutive nights Merseyside was bombed with a concentrated intensity which showed how important the enemy regarded the closing of the Port. At 4.30 on the morning of May the 8th the all clear sounded and the wonderful Civil Defence services, weary beyond belief, prepared to snatch a little rest before the next raid came. It never came. The enemy had exhausted itself. He had thrown all resources into a supreme effort and failed. The morale of Merseyside was severely strained, but never broken. That week, the all-pervading smell of burning and the halo of smoke above the city, soldiers clearing the streets of debris . . . tottering walls and the skeletons of fine buildings against the sky; a ferryboat bombed and sunk at her moorings — great tangles of firehose blocking the streets, and everywhere, tired, unshaven faces. Liverpool was groggy but very far from being down and out.

Clydeside

The people of Clydeside just didn't believe it would happen to them. The war was more of a nuisance than anything else, and Mass Observation reported in March 1941 that only one Glasgow resident in eight thought that there was any chance of heavy bombing in their area.

This sense of complacency was dispelled on the 13th and 14th of that month by what Angus Calder describes as 'a two-night blitz of classic ferocity'. And it was the small town of Clydebank, just north-west of Glasgow, which suffered the most, with only eight of its 12,000 houses remaining untouched.

Ritchie Calder, it will be recalled, had singled out Clydebank for the inadequacies of its shelters in the course of his tour of Britain the previous autumn. Things had scarcely improved. The people had the choice of cowering in their flimsily built tenements or taking to the brick surface shelters which offered not much more than token protection. And once the incendiaries had started to do their work it was the same sad story as in so many other places; vital water mains bursting; fire equipment brought in from outside with couplings that didn't fit. Most soul-destroying of all, according to Mr A. Campbell,

was to see the waterfront shipyards nearly all missed and the brunt taken by the local people — especially the housing estate on the hill behind the main target.

Betty Anderson says that it all happened so fast that many of them stayed in their homes.

We could have got killed going up the street to the shelter. My friend next door said goodnight to her boyfriend and never saw him again. The spiral staircase was the only thing left in Morrison Street Co-op, I believe the fire-watchers there were all drowned. There was a tramcar split in two; a girl conductress who was only identified by the badge on her lapel.

The 'Holy City' from Singer's Clydebank factory, 13–14 March blitz 1941.

Rosetta Racionzer, then nine years old, remembers

the large fire ball in the sky made by the Singer Company wood pile, and Radnor Park School ablaze just across from where I lived on Kilbowie Hill. We lived on the ground floor and neighbours came down to our little corner of hall. There was at least 16 of us and Mrs Morgan had a bottle of holy water which she sprinkled every time a bomb fell near. As the night went on she had to sprinkle more sparingly and by the all clear only a drop was left.

Mrs W. Devlin was sheltering with her family in a neighbour's house

when a bomb dropped not far from us, blew in the windows, glass cut my son's face, it went right through a factory roof. The fire-watcher on duty on the roof was blown into the graveyard opposite with his head already off.

Mr M. Wilson was on night shift in the Royal Ordnance factory when the office stores caught light.

While the bombs were raining down, the Laird of Haldane and myself volunteered to go up 60 feet on a straight ladder with a stirrup pump to put the incendiaries out. When we came down a landmine blew up down at the quayside and blew us against a baffle-wall cutting me badly on my hands and knees. I went into a shelter and then out again to help three security police who were all badly injured when the Gatehouse was bombed. I got them into a motor-waggon and drove along Dumbarton Road through all the rubble and broken glass when first the tyres burst, then the rim broke and was running on three wheels till I got to Yoker where the Whisky Bond was on fire, where the police stopped me. They said they would take the wounded to hospital and they stopped another car to take me home — but I landed back down at the factory again where one of the tenement houses was bombed, collapsing on the people who were sheltering in the Close. It was a mess. Nothing but blood running out of the Close. The Laird said 'Get some whisky' as a lot of the helpers were in shock and the Maggie Scots pub's doors were blown open anyway. Whisky steadied the nerves. I decided to get my brother down at the factory to help. As I got to the Bridge I heard an old couple screaming as their house was blown down on top of their shelter. I took some of the stones and rubble off and told them to stop in it as the bombs were still raining down. The fire brigade were still trying to put out the Ordnance offices, which had nobody in them. I kicked up hell at them as the whole city was in flames and women and kids in trouble . . . but I got the same answer as I got up at the Whisky Bond . . . they would run me into the police-jail . . . But by now my leg was in a mess and it was four in the morning, so I carried on home and got my mother and father to pack some clothing and go down to Balloch to relatives, as I knew the bombers would be back.

About 40,000 people were hurriedly evacuated, though most returned before long to find Clydebank looking like a vast demolition site. Rosetta Racionzer says that they managed to get a lift in a car out of Clydebank to Balloch but had to be helped by men with helmets and navy uniform over a handmade bridge as there was an unexploded bomb at my aunt's house and she was going too with her two-week-old baby. The gentleman who gave us a lift put a sum of money in my mother's and aunt's hand.

We spent the second night listening to the planes go over bombing Clydebank where father and grandmother were left behind. Grandma's sons saved her house. It was the only one left standing in the row. They took a hatchet to a window frame and put out an incendiary bomb lodged in a chair. Later, they made soup in the garden on a bunker of coal that had caught fire.

Mr Thomas Walker reports that

some miners from the Gilnhochill coalmine came and dug out all the dead and injured. Dead were loaded on to vehicles and taken to 'Crossmyloof' ice-rink which was used as a mortuary and for the preserving of the dead.

Clydebank, during those two nights, suffered the greatest proportion of damage of any British town during the war. But Glasgow did not escape lightly either, with some 790 dead, nearly double the number in Clydebank. Mary Corke (then Marner) was at the pictures with her friend when it started.

During the film the lights went on and two ARP wardens stepped onto the stage and cried out that there was an air raid and everyone was to leave the pictures to go home or stay in the building if they wanted to. The Salvation Army workers came around with tea and biscuits and a man played the organ as we all sang 'Pack up your troubles' and other war songs, to keep us from being afraid. After staying for this, my friend and I made our way home. We were so afraid because we did not know what was happening. There were policemen, ARP wardens, Civil Defence men all running around, and whistles blowing and they were calling to us to make our way home as soon as possible or we would be killed. It was a very bright moonlit night and we could see the German sign on the plane above, as there were four big searchlights shining straight on it. There was also pom-pom guns going up Ruglean Road, firing at the plane and trying to shoot it down. We could hear the shells from the gun hit the ground, so we dived into a doorway, where we hid and cried, too afraid to move. It was called Two Maxes factory. Just then two ARP wardens went by and once again told us to get off the road and to the nearest shelter. My friend ran home her way, and I ran as fast as I could down Florence Street to where I stayed. When I came to my door my father came running over shouting at me. He was ARP warden on duty and he also told me to go to the shelter at once.

After he had left I just went into my own house. I was fed up running back and forward to shelters every time there was an air raid. I went in, changed into my pyjamas and sat in the big chair near the window and read a book. I knew I'd be all right there as my father had put a bed-tick under the bed with blankets and pillows. The bed was propped up with wooden blocks to hold it. I just thought to myself, if anything happened I could just dive under the bed. The reason my father had done this to the bed was because my mother was crippled and in a wheelchair. It was a good job the hospital had taken her in the day before, as we would never have managed to and from the shelter. Florence Street and the chapel were straight across from me.

As I sat in the chair, there was an unearthly flash of light and a bang then everything went black. I never knew what hit me, I was just screaming, the chair was blown away, with me in it and I landed right under the bed. The blocks flew out from beneath the bed and everything landed on top of me. I just screamed and screamed until I heard voices shouting through the broken glass in the windows. It was the ARP wardens who were pulling and lifting everything from me and carrying me out on a stretcher. I looked up and one of the wardens was my father, as they were lifting me out the ceiling caved in on top of him and I never seen him for two days.

I was taken to hospital for stitches and there were quite a lot of casualties there. One lady came in and said she was just looking out the window at the plane, had glass sticking out of her head. Another woman came in with three kids, whom we all thought were black. She had been sitting with her three children around the coal fire telling stories and singing to keep the children's spirits up and waiting for the all clear, when the chimney blew out and they were covered from head to foot, so they were not coloured children after all. We all had a good laugh. I knew it was not funny, but she took it all in good fun. All the casualties were taken to Battlefield School, where Civil Defence, ARP, nurses and all the people who lived there came with clothes, blankets — everyone was stripped, washed and cleaned in school basins, although people were afraid and crying. Then everyone had new clothes right down to their shoes. The Salvation Army, auxiliary workers, ARP wardens and Civil Defence workers came in with soup and food and put tags round our necks with our names and addresses on them, then gave us gas masks to carry, then put us all into different classrooms, with an army blanket around our shoulders. We all lay down on top of the kiddies desks to sleep, we were all crying and calling for our families, some by this time didn't have any. I was crying for my mum in hospital.

Next morning everyone was lined up and put into buses. I kept asking them about my father. They said they would find him for me, not to worry, just to go with them. They took us to Adelphi Street School, took us into classrooms, put down army camp beds and the Civil Defence came in and gave us our dinner and told us just to stay there until we were sorted out. I was there for about an hour then two ARP wardens came in. I was so happy I started to cry because one of them was my father, he had his arm in a sling as he had a broken shoulder and he was so moved as he could not find me, it was just luck that he had spoken to the lady with the 'S' Block children who told him where I was. He then took me to the office where we were issued passes so we could be let in and out for our bed and food. Then he took me to hospital to see my mum, she was in the best place. He said I was lucky when I told him I was standing in the factory doorway; they said it had been flattened to the ground and also our house and the

Collecting water from one of the water carts which were brought in from Glasgow — the March blitz on Clydebank, 1941.

school and the chapel in Florence Street. He said that they had shot the plane down over the Clyde. They had tried to bomb the gasworks in Florence Street, but instead they dropped it on the Gorbals. We stayed at the Adelphi School which was our home for four weeks. Later I worked in Baron Strouds ammo factory; at least I thought I was doing something for the war.

Mr J. Spence was 12 years old at the time, four years younger than Mary.

When we returned to the house after the raid, we found it covered in a pile of soot brought down by the vibration. We all stood in the stair entrance, or close, which had been reinforced with pit props. There were baffle walls at the edge of the pavements opposite every close mouth, to lessen the effects of the blasts. I looked out and saw shrapnel falling in the street. I also saw tracer bullets over the full moon. We only had two fighters to defend us. A landmine landed on Kelvin Bridge and there was a brick and concrete air-raid shelter in the street opposite, and the blast blew in the sides and the people were killed by the concrete roof falling on them. A high explosive landed on Dr Kennedy's house in Peel Street. It was full of policemen who may have gathered to help the injured. It took 12 days to dig them out, and the last one out said he had heard a girl moaning near him, but by the time they reached her she was dead. I knew that girl.

The best account we have of the March raids comes from a letter written to a young evacuee, now Mrs Anne Sandys, and her brother by their father who had stayed behind in the city.

Dear Anne and Neil,
Today I went with an officer who had to visit that part of Glasgow which took most of the blitz. Some of it was pretty ghastly. Poor families who had lost everything they possess ... they just have nothing left which has any connection with their previous existence. Quite dazed by it all they are taken away in lorries and so on to places in the country; some come back in the daytime to try to collect something out of the rubbish. There was one little crescent of neat small houses in neat small gardens; they had all been very friendly and good neighbours. They had Anderson shelters in every second garden; during the blitz they went to their shelters, most of them; a bomb landed plumb in the middle of the crescent and one house simply disappeared. The other houses were no longer habitable; all the people in the shelters were safe; it was amazing. A little old lady all by herself was sorting out some odds and ends in the little garden in which stood the roofless skeleton of her house. She said it had been noisy and terrible and she had lost some good friends who had not gone to their shelters; then she clenched her hands and exclaimed 'I don't care if he comes 50 times again, I have lost my fear of him,' and yet she does not know where she is going to live now. I don't think I shall ever forget that scene; a frail little old lady with the heart of a lion; 'I have lost my fear of him'; him, Hitler. It made one feel so ashamed of one's own fears.
We talked to lots of people; men going back to work in

shipyards; women who had been bombed out of their homes. I never heard a word of fear. Sorrow for those who had suffered, yes. One party who had had a miraculous escape but lost their home, thinking of those who had been killed in their houses, said 'We've got much to be thankful for; we've been spared.' I don't think I've ever been so proud of being British. And today the children are playing in the streets in the less damaged areas; the shops still trade with boarded up windows.

Perhaps that is enough for one letter.

Best love to you all

Daddy.

The bombers returned to Glasgow *en masse* on the nights of 5 and 6 May. Clydebank was spared that time; it was the turn of the little town of Greenock. According to William Sutherland, then serving in the Royal Artillery,

The Greenock blitz was far worse than anything else in Scotland apart from Clydebank, and was the result of a real mix-up between the army and RAF chiefs which left Greenock at the mercy of the *Luftwaffe*. My anti-aircraft battery was stationed at the top of the 'Whins' on the fateful night in May 1941. We saw it happen. The *Luftwaffe* came over in their hundreds about midnight. Our battery fired about 13 shells at them, and then got the orders from the command post to cease firing, as the RAF were on their way to engage the *Luftwaffe*. The RAF failed to appear. The accuracy of the German airman's bombing was truly uncanny. The first bomb hit a brewery, the second hit a sugar refinery and the third hit the centre of town. I'm sure the accuracy of the bombing was due, in no small measure, to lack of opposition.

Mary Kirk was a child living in Greenock at that time.

For most of the war I lived in a tenement block of 12 families. The entrance-close to the building was our only shelter in times of air attacks. It had been reinforced with metal beams which we all called 'trusses' and the doorway was protected

Undefeated — a Clydebank girl keeps smiling.

by sandbags. I often wonder whether the close afforded any protection at all. People said that we were told to go there so that our bodies would be easy to find if our building was hit. During the day the children all played around them and swung from the girders. We were told to go into the close when an alert was sounded, usually at night — I remember how cold it could be. I often slept through the nights, although we always missed school the day following a raid. My granny never left her bed in the top floor of the building, preferring, she used to say, to die in comfort rather than go down to the close during the air-raid alerts.

One night I was carried out by my cousin, a Royal Marine on leave at the time, to see the fires at Clydebank. It must have been many miles away, but the whole of the sky had turned a deep, bloody scarlet.

Around the time of my seventh birthday, for some continuous nights Greenock itself was the target. I will never forget the throbbing drone of the German aeroplanes above. They seemed very close. We could feel a tremendous jar as the entire building was shaken by the blast. Some seemed closer than others, but the building shaking terrified me far more than any of the noise. Some adults tried to entertain the children, but most people huddled silently; except one woman would sometimes yell out 'Oh God help us! Oh praise God, save us' when a bomb sounded particularly near by. She made everyone more anxious.

One night a voice yelled in 'Walkers has been hit!' That was the sugar refinery where my father worked. My mother left the building to walk a mile or so through the raid to find out how he was. My father survived, but a lot of men were killed in the refinery.

The mornings after a raid the streets were littered with rubble and debris. It was alarming to see how near some of the bombs had fallen. Some buildings had been completely smashed and resembled missing teeth in a row.

South Wales

The noise wailed inhumanly over Cardiff. First one siren, then another sounded in the distance like an echo. Sombre, admonitory, the noise fell away into the wind, was carried away with the smoke blown from thousands of chimney-pots, carried forward and away with the paper blown through the night streets. The trees stood at attention on the pavements, waiting, under a moon threading bare the soap-sud clouds. In expectancy, the City stopped for a moment, listening to itself, to its own footsteps. The mood of landscapes abruptly became sinister, the church on the hill, the secretive street leading to the municipal baths, the deserted garage at the crossroads. In the cinemas a notice fell across the screen distracting the audience of flickering, uplifted, tired faces from Bette Davis or Gary Cooper. It read: 'An Air-Raid Warning has sounded. Stay in your seats. Don't panic. Be British.' Soon the film ended in a close-up of a kiss and, as if by magic, out of the dark pit the juke-box organ ascended, gaudy, elephantine, changing colours as it wheezed out the popular tunes:

I'll be seeing you
In all the old familiar places

Outside, the trams, long blue-tit phantoms, jerked to a halt, and motor cars, wearing slotted masks over their headlights, speeded swiftly down the dark avenues of absence. Somebody was knocking at a door.

'Mr Morris, your curtains aren't properly pulled.' And the chink of electric light leaking from the third-floor window was promptly stopped up. Others hurried through the black-out with their hand-torches extinguished. Hurried home in the dark, anonymous, nameless.

'Excuse me, I'm sorry. Is that you, Dora? I'm lost. The moon's gone behind the clouds.'

Be British. Don't panic. The organ rode down into the pit again and the audience clapped perfunctorily. A horizontal beam of light splashed onto the screen and the Metro-Goldwyn-Mayer lion roared. Outside searchlights floundered in the sky, spooky and curious. Spiritual cold devices poking the clouds that sailed high over the balloons, high over the patched roof-tops. In the distance, like a throb of a dying pulse, the malignant sound of aeroplanes. In the distance, the white fur of fire of the ack-ack guns touching and fumbling briefly the hillsides all along the coast.

'Swansea's 'aving it tonight.'

'Barry's 'aving it tonight.'

'Newport's 'aving it tonight.'

from *Ash on a Young Man's Sleeve* by Dannie Abse

Cardiff itself was attacked several times, with a 125-bomber raid on 2 January 1941, when Llandaff Cathedral received a direct hit. But it was Swansea that suffered most, especially during three successive nights of the following month. It started, in a minor way, on Friday 17 February, as Laurie Latchford noted in his diary.

Sirens started at 7.30 pm. Within 10 minutes the air was full of the throb of enemy planes flying very high ... 'Volunteers wanted for Swansea' said Greaves, a warden, running up from the post. 'Everybody ready?' said somebody with a tin helmet on her head and a man's civilian mackintosh over her dance frock! She was the young driver, and without a tremor, she turned the car towards the red glow. We were now out of the area of fields and scattered houses, and were approaching the outskirts of Swansea. A battery of guns near the road was firing as we passed, giving the car a hard slap every time the gun fired. Army lorries were posted at intervals all along the road ... At the hospital we could hardly see for smoke. Casualties were being taken from ambulances. Ghostly figures were moving in the strange smoke-shrouded light. A chapel was burning red, topped by volumes of slowly twisting smoke. Guns were firing continuously. A huge bomb exploded towards the docks. Areas of leaping fire were in all directions ... we drove over fire-hoses thrown all over the road in great curves. Debris showed dark on the wet, fire-reflecting roads ... We helped put out fires and checked shelters. It was snowing quite heavily. One thing was very marked among the men of the ARP and regular services. Whether tackling fires or fire-bombs or dealing with HEs, damage or with injured people, not one of the experienced men rushed about, or talked more than was necessary.

It was two days later, on the 19th, that the big raid started.

About 7.30 a plane went over as I was on the Mumbles train leaving the office. Then the alert sounded. There was a greenish flash and a sharp report (amidst real thunder and lightning). A short pause, then the hill to the north of the town was patterned with intense white points of light from many incendiary bombs — the green flash from a 'Molotov breadbasket' ... There was a curtain of white above a stone wall seawards. More incendiaries. Another, then another 'bread basket' falling in sweeps. To the north, at the back of the town, the white glare was giving way to sullen red glows as fires started. The docks were flooded with the intense light. In the gloom of doorways and walls were occasional figures with sandbags, members of the newly-formed householder fire-fighters. The train cleared the immediate town and was on the curve of the bay. The docks were in clear view. So many incendiaries had fallen that from the distance they seemed to be almost touching. Where they struck a hard surface they jumped high, showed a reddish flash or glow, then flared up. Some, after a short time, exploding, scattering white burning metal high ... in the docks higher than the dock sheds. As we watched, the white glare over the town and docks began to fade away. Only one red glow marked where a house had caught fire on May Hill.

But again 'breadbaskets' threw down their loads of incendiaries, and again the town and the docks were swept with a deep wave of white light. Overhead the sky was yellow with flares. 'Volunteers wanted for Swansea', Greaves said. I had answered the call for last volunteers. Now I felt tired, and had had no food since midday.

During my meal I was preoccupied. I wasn't too pleased with myself. Incendiaries were still falling on Swansea town and the docks. I counted as many as 10 parachute flares in the sky at one time. Searchlight beams crossed and gathered in the sky, red tracer bullets streamed upwards trying to shoot out the flares, and occasionally breaking pieces away. The guns fired with heavy ground flashes and orange sky bursts, and as a background was the white glare of incendiaries and the sudden red up-burst of HEs behind the outline of trees and scattered buildings. All the time the planes throbbed overhead.

By then the glow of the burning town could be seen from miles away, as we were told by Siân Phillips, the actress.

I was a little girl living in a village in the hills above Pontardawe. My mother woke me up in the middle of the night, wrapped me in a shawl and carried me out into the garden which was very big and very high above the valley. And she said, 'I want you to remember that I'm reading the newspaper by the light of Swansea burning', and Swansea was nine miles away, and I think it burned for three days and three nights, and night didn't really fall for about three or four days because the flames were so intense. And that is my only recollection of the war.

One person who has more vivid memories of that first night is Laura Vaughan-Rees, who remembers that Lord Haw-Haw (William Joyce), broadcasting from Germany, had already announced to the people of Swansea, 'the Gower Peninsula will be your graveyard'.

I hadn't been out for weeks, what with a young child, and fancied an evening at the pictures. I left my son at home with a cousin of his, a nurse, who'd come over to spend the night, and went to the early show, intending to be back by about seven. While we were in there the sirens started; nobody took much notice, but we went out eventually only to find that bombs were dropping all over the place. I went across to a hotel opposite the cinema and managed to phone home to say I'd be taking shelter in town, because it was out of the question to walk home; it wasn't just the bombs, it was a nasty rainy winter night.

After a couple of hours the hotel itself was bombed, so we managed to get round the corner to Marks and Spencer's, where they had a shelter in the basement. It was absolutely packed out, and the manager was walking up and down and he came up to me and said 'You look very cool and calm and collected, would you like to help me?' I said I would because I was feeling bored just sitting there. So he wanted me to go round the shelter and take the names and addresses of everybody, then go upstairs, stand at the door of the store, do the same for anybody who came in, and cross off the ones who went out, so we'd know who was here in case the shelter was hit. So I said to him 'We'd better have a duplicate list, in case one of us gets killed' and he thought that was a good idea.

Several people did come in, and the most frightened of all were some officers off a Norwegian ship, they were absolutely terrified. (In fact my husband was scared stiff when he was home on leave and there was an air-raid. And he'd lost two ships by then!)

A lull came eventually and by that time I was so bored that I grabbed a pile of rugs, put them on the floor and fell asleep.

The all-clear went and I walked home. Going up the hill to Gwydr Crescent there were bits of legs and things all over the place. So I got home, and two or three doors away from us was living a young man who was the driver for the Swansea chief of police and he came in and said, 'For God's sake don't go out!' — we couldn't telephone, the lines were all down — and his uniform was all pitted with holes from the shrapnel.

Eventually my in-laws got through and said that Michael was to go to his uncle and aunt's in Tumble.

That evening Laurie Latchford, tired out, still found time for his diary.

Thursday 20 Feb — In the clear sunlight, the snow-covered roads, beaten hard and shiny, were closely scattered with little heaps of sand, or earth, or charred sandbags where the incendiaries had been 'doused'. There was practically no traffic moving or very few pedestrians. Most home windows were broken. Practically every roof showed broken tiles. Over all Swansea were houses and shops broken open and torn by HEs or burnt to rubble-filled cellars. Some from previous raids, some from last night's. The fresh wounds showed stark without the thin covering of snow.

That night the alert sounded before the sun had set. Fire brigades from Camarthen, and Gloucester and police from the country, and from neighbouring forces were already in town.

South Wales families emerge from their Anderson shelter after the blitz.

Jerry came in then from the west. The night was made as hideous as the night before. At midnight the all-clear sounded.

Friday 21 Feb — The noise of gunfire, bursting bombs and aeroplanes was worse than I had experienced before. There were leaping flames over the whole stretch of Swansea. The fires seemed to run to the sea-edge and beyond. The gently-moving sea was aflame with reflected light. At the distance there seemed no division between fires. The windows of the houses on the hills overlooking the town mirrored the flames so that it seemed that the houses themselves were alight. All clear at midnight.

Nancy Bosanquet had by now finished her training in London, and was working as an ambulance driver in Cardiff. As she told her mother in a letter, she too was in Swansea on that Friday.

My dear Mummie,

I have been having a pretty busy time lately so I will tell you all about it while I have the time to write. . . .

The third night [of Swansea's first blitz] was my turn on one of the cars. At 9.15 the message came through to stand by at the transfusion centre. I went there and then on to pick up the doctor — a pathologist who is his deputy — a sister and two nurses. They had a message that SWANSEA was having a bad time, so they decided not to wait till a message came through for them and at 10.30 we set off. By the time we got to Neath we could see the light of a terrific fire in the sky and the road was a stream of fire engines coming from as far as Reading and Swindon — and guns and cars, all going in the same direction. It was fun driving my party as the police were looking out for me and I had orders to ignore red lights so I willed them all to turn red as I approached so that I could importantly shoot over.

We got to Swansea eventually about an hour before the all clear, with searchlights waving about the sky and everyone much harassed. Driving was not easy as we only had side-lights, the night was dark and the fire ahead blinded one. It was also very difficult to find our way about because of constant detours round unexploded bombs. We went to Cefu-Coed Hospital about 2 miles outside Swansea — it is really a mental hospital with one wing turned into an emergency hospital and quite full of casualties — a depressing place with long dark stone passages along one side and endless large and small wards, each block exactly alike so that I continually lose my way. I pottered about for about an hour till the doctor, sister and one nurse were to be taken to the other two Swansea hospitals. And then I drove them —first to Towy Lodge past blazing buildings and bomb craters, using only my sidelights, as the whole place was lit up by the fires. We waited a short time there while homeless people filed into the hospital as being the only place they could go — and then on to Swansea General Hospital — the way there was down a fairly narrow street flanked on each side by the technical college which was all on fire, with shooting flames and glowing pieces flying about the air — I rather expected to detour this but I was told to drive straight on, so I wound up my window, and drove past — between the firemen and the fire — but we didn't get soaked with water as the water had given out — in streets on fire I only saw one small hose being used, and the firemen were just standing about their yards of hoses. They had some nasty rescue jobs — I heard of one husband and wife who were pinned onto their beds by debris. Firemen worked for hours and in another ten minutes might have released them — when the gas caught fire — and the man begged them not to leave them as the firemen all fled for their lives. That fireman was still having nightmares I think.

After the Swansea General, we went back to Cefu-Coed where they had the worst casualties, and for the rest of the night I tramped round the wards giving a hand here and there, getting water and tea for patients and nurses ... At four some of the nurses went off duty as they were coming on again at 7.30 and the other driver (who had brought a surgical team from Cardiff), a red-headed young soldier actually also a patient, and myself found ourselves in charge of a large ward and some small ones, with most of the patients in the large ward needing attention and none of us at all sure of ourselves. I found myself not so much affected by the sights as the sounds. There was one child who was delirious and called out to his brother, another who screamed for his mother in her sleep, one woman who mooed like a cow the entire night, and a lad with a broken shoulder-blade who groaned all the time in great pain, etc. Numbers of them had had hardly any treatment at all. The screaming child's face was black and bloody on one side, and her pillow soaked in blood, and the man next door to her had a bloody lint across his eyes. The latest patients seemed to have oddly black faces, etc., etc., but the sounds I heard haunted me for days, and the stench of unwashed patients — some because they were that type and some because they were sweating with pain. One old man had several blood transfusions but when I last saw him I could hear the rattle of his breathing in his throat and he died before morning. There were a number of amputations and for that sort of operation I believed blood transfusions are

Nurses survey the damage from their bombing near miss at Swansea General Hospital.

most useful — they restore a very shocked patient to a state in which it is safe to operate on him.

We finally drove back about ten — most of my cargo asleep, and then I got back to headquarters again after a sleepy lunch with the two doctors. That day I spent recovering while the rest evacuated the General Hospital which was surrounded by unexploded bombs ...
Love
Nancy.

And the wardens, too, were eventually able to rest, as we learn from Laurie Latchford.

Saturday 22 Feb — Near the town centre, fire and bomb damage was almost continuous. Firemen were still playing jets on burning material. The market in Swansea, that had been a glass-covered area with high brick walls, was now a mass of twisted girders — but the market wasn't dead. It was Saturday morning and the Saturday morning market was functioning from the back of several lorries which had found their way into town along the major road from the west. Apparently, people had come out of their front doors, slightly above street level, like terriers, doused the incendiaries with sand, and then disappeared.

I relieved a warden in the S. West. The three wardens on duty hadn't been relieved for three days. There were many UXBs in this section. Waited for another raid, but it didn't come. The many small dwellings of Town Hill and May Hill were sad, desolate places; bomb-holes in the roads, houses with fronts blown out, and carpets, chairs, toys and rubble all intermixed. Terraces with houses blasted out showed rough gaps. Over all was sunlight and a Sunday quiet. All the wardens were very tired out but prepared to continue. The post was without doors and windows, and the ceilings were down. The internal partition walls leaned at strange angles ... against one wall was a large sack of dud incendiary bombs piled one above the other like wine bottles; there must have been several hundred. They had been brought in by wardens during the three nights of bombing.

Belfast

Belfast didn't receive a single bomb until 7 April 1941, when six Heinkels — possibly detached from the major raid on Clydeside — caused relatively minor damage.

It was the most unprotected city in the United Kingdom, with only a handful of ack-ack guns and not a single searchlight, and so could offer little resistance when the first big raid came eight days later. Among the almost 900 killed and 1,500 injured in this Easter Tuesday raid were some of the 1,000 people evacuated from England to 'safety' there earlier in the month.

As with Clydeside, the *Luftwaffe* failed to cripple the dockyards and other industrial targets; it was the people who suffered. However during the next major raids, on 4 and 5 May, this was reversed, with fewer than 200 killed and massive damage to industry. But the workers of Belfast did their best and, to their credit, production at the shipyards was back to 40 per cent within three weeks.

Both water and fire-fighting equipment were in short supply during each of the three raids. James Gunn, of Newry, explains how some appliances arrived from a perhaps unexpected source.

On the night of the April blitz I was on duty in the local telephone exchange. About 1.30 am I heard the drone of aircraft overhead. An hour later I felt vibrations. The work drill was to follow instructions from Telephone House, Belfast, which I expected from there. After approx. one hour a most urgent call came from the Provost Marshall to say Belfast was burning and they could not make contact with Dublin. I contacted my Dundalk counterpart and a contact was established with Prime Minister de Valera. All help was ordered North, and the RUC opened border roads to permit free passage of Dundalk, Drogheda and Dublin fire brigades to do their neighbourly duty.

Newry fire brigade with its voluntary crew, although a Nationalist town, went to Belfast that morning and worked tirelessly to extinguish the fires.

Aftermath of the blitz on Belfast, 15 April 1941.

Madeline Corken was nine at the time, third in a family of five.

Our family and neighbours spent hours in a dog-kennel-shaped air-raid shelter trembling and praying for the Germans to stop their rain of bombs. The constant bombardment of the anti-aircraft guns was terrifying. I was mystified why my mother constantly nursed her tummy amidst stifled groans and we all made a hasty exit from the shelter to our own house across the street. My father rushed out into the night amidst falling bombs and flying shrapnel to return later with the midwife. Not long after we heard the cry of a baby. I couldn't believe it! You can imagine our joy and relief (not to mention my mother's), and I think the sound of the all-clear was the most beautiful thing I ever heard.

Sammy McBride was just four years older than Madeline.

It was holiday week and I was allowed to go to the Alhambra

Theatre where I sat roaring at the antics of Stan and Ollie in *Saps at Sea*. This laughter was soon to turn to fear in the following hours, which turned out to be a nightmare when the *Luftwaffe* turned the city into a blazing ruin ... and later, the endless processions of coffins ... a macabre reversal of roles which meant that the loved ones passing had to be reported to the boys and girls serving overseas.

In York Street, the world's largest spinning mill was badly damaged, it had collapsed on top of nearby Sussex Street and Vere Street, causing a lot of casualties. A large number of soldiers were killed when their barracks in Eglinton Street was demolished; also, W. Wilton's funeral furnishers was burnt down and many Belgian horses perished.

The anti-aircraft gunners of the carrier, HMS *Furious*, in dry dock near the city, were real heroes and fired at the invaders all night.

Scarred Shandarragh Park, Cavehill Road, Belfast after Easter Tuesday raid, 1941.

Herbert Woolsey was on the police special constabulary stationed at the harbour on Belfast Docks.

On the night of the big air-raid, I saw a large parachute coming down and what appeared to be a man holding on to it. Two men ran past me shouting they were going to get him, but the man turned out to be a mine attached to the parachute and the men were blown to bits. The Germans had previously dropped bombs on the shipyard but they had not had the desired effect as the ground was too soft. The next day when on duty at the shipyard, the sirens went off and I observed a German twin-engine plane coming between two rows of ships with a man leaning out of the cockpit pointing what I took to be a gun. He was dressed in goggles and a leather cap. I simply froze. It was next day I learned it was a plane taking photographs after the raid.

On one occasion when on duty with an RUC constable, the sirens went and we both tried to seek shelter in an iron shelter suitable for one, only about 15 feet from the water. He got in and I squeezed in also by holding the door after me. Then a bomb fell in the edge of the jetty, throwing mud and water all over the jetty. It did not explode. We had difficulty getting the shelter door opened as it was plastered with mud. When we did get it opened and looked at where the bomb fell we could see nothing but bubbles and steam coming up from where it fell.

Once I heard a plane which seemed a long way up, a bullet struck the ground in front of me. I picked it up. It was about 3 inches long. Unfortunately I gave it to an American who wanted it for a souvenir.

Sammy McBride's most vivid memory is of the day following the worst raid when,

in the midst of all the grim sights we saw Union Jacks fluttering on heaps of rubble which had been homes just a few short hours before, and the defiance which showed in tired, dust-covered faces of people who were still digging for the missing.

Hull

Hull suffered 49 raids between the Battle of Britain and its own big raid on 18 March. Major attacks followed on 7 and 8 May, leaving only 6,000 out of 93,000 homes undamaged, while warehouses, food stores and the tall flour mills were smouldering remains. And 24 of the city's rest centres were hit, creating additional misery for the 40,000 people who lost their homes. For Hull, the raids continued for some time after they had stopped elsewhere; 17 July was a heavy one, but there were tip and runs from May to September and again in May, June, July 1942 and March 1944. The citizens of most blitz towns thought that nobody elsewhere gave them credit for what they were going through. In the case of Hull they were certainly justified; Herbert Morrison believed that 'the town that suffered most was Kingston-Upon-Hull ... Night after night Hull had no peace and was an easy target.'

Our three witnesses coped cheerfully enough; Gladys Lamb, a young woman staying with her mother, said:

Cascades of smouldering grain from Rank's Clarence mill slide into the River Hull during the second big attack on 7–9 May 1941.

We used to lay on this mattress in the gas cupboard. And one night there was a really heavy raid on and Mother said 'Oh Glad, isn't it awful', opened the door and pulled the blackout back and all the city centre was afire. It was tremendous. You know, they'd bombed Hammonds and some insurance buildings, there was a lot of people killed under that building ... My mother was bombed out of Havelock Street ... we could hear the screech as the bomb came down. Of course, for all you were in the shelter you automatically ducked, it was the natural thing to do ... it was a land mine, there was no crater no nothing. It hit the top of Scarborough Street and knocked half of it down and half of Havelock Street down. My mother was stood on the doorstep, there was no windows, no doors, nothing. I mean half of the house had gone and she was stood on the doorstep. And this bloke called Tarran, he was the councillor, he came to my mother and he said 'Have you got everything you need?' and she said 'You silly bugger, I've got more than I need.' It was terrific, night after night after night, you know, the bombings.

Digging for survivors off Prince's Avenue in West Hull during the May blitz.

Joan Geraghty, then a schoolgirl, remembers that

After the three very bad night raids in May ... the bus could only get so far down Anlaby Road and then we walked to the centre of town and all the sets of the road had been lifted up and buckled with the heat ... and everybody was walking to and fro looking for friends and relatives, I suppose, and getting to work. It never occurred to people not to go to work even after the bombing, even the shop assistants all turned out and cleaned up and did whatever they could, and when we got to school eventually, we found it was a sort of centre because there had been some bad bombing down Buckingham Street and the people who had been bombed came and sat in the school looking very grey and drawn and dirty, everything was so dirty, and eventually the WVS brought tea and cakes, you know, bread and butter round. These mobile kitchens were really marvellous, the work they did, and eventually they set up our school as a feeding centre and they brought soup and people came and either ate in the school or took food home with them.

Winifred Hipwell was one of the many who carried on going into the city to do her shopping every week, ignoring the frequent alerts.

After one severe raid we went in as usual to find the city centre a mass of rubble where the main shopping centre had been. One department store had taken up residence in the municipal museum, from which most of the valuable exhibits had been removed before the war. There was one exhibit left — the skeleton of a dinosaur hanging from the ceiling, its huge skull looking down on displays of lingerie and perfumes and watching the parade of the women shoppers. Shortly afterwards the museum itself was burnt to the ground but the department store had returned to temporary buildings on its old site and, along with other stores, was carrying on business as usual.

We always took our dry-cleaning to one particular firm and that, too, was bombed and we found only a heap of burning rubble under which, we assumed, was our cleaning, lost for ever. A short while afterwards we received a card saying some garments had been found and would we please call at their new address. We could claim only a waistcoat but it proved there was business as usual. After another interval we received a card stating simply 'Your cleaning is now ready, please collect.' I found my suit that was thought lost, cleaned and pressed, with only a water-mark on the lining to show the ordeal it had been through. It had been found in the firm's Liverpool headquarters which had also been bombed but had carried on business as usual.

It was not all gloom and despondency. There were dances and entertainments and at Christmas time we went carol singing, trudging from farm to farm, falling into ditches and stumbling over ruts, then to emerge on a hilltop and look out over the black expanse of the vale of York. Not a glimmer of light pierced the darkness, the shape of the range of hills was just visible on the horizon, the stars were brilliant and low in the sky, hanging close enough to touch.

THE COUNTRY

The war was taken seriously, even in small village communities, as Pat Briggs tells us in her recollection of life in rural Yorkshire.

We never had a blitz, we had a war in Bishopthorpe. What I distinctly recall is the social ramifications like an invisible ether which surrounded everyone because they had some particular 'wartime work', quite independent of their normal lives. My dad, head warden for an extensive area of surrounding villages, had a MAD order to pay every warden 2/6 a month which meant cycling about 30 miles. On top of this there was an 'early warning' to the head warden which woke Dad and Mum by phone every time planes flew up the Humber and turned off. They were woken night after night for no reason at all; there was only one raid on York in the whole war. Mum was particularly fed up with all this but

DUTY was a real force during the war and my parents simply wouldn't see sense and resign the position. I can remember telling Dad to find some easier way to pay the 2/6 and his rock-like nobility in refusing to do anything so underhand as to defy ARP regulations. Even as a teenager I had more sense!

Well, we had a whistle and a handbell if one of these warnings came when Dad was at work. Mum was supposed to ride round the village blowing long toots on the whistle for the warning and ringing the bell for all clear. We didn't get anything except the first warnings except for one notable occasion — the planes must have flown past York for some reason. Mum, in a PANIC because it was a REAL warning, set off on her bike blowing long blasts of the whistle and did a round tour of the streets blowing all the way. She returned along Long Road and was only capable of 'phew, phew — pherphew' gasping blasts of the alarm. As she passed the house of Mr Stewart the fire warden, his wife came darting out of the front gate. 'Oh! Mrs Briggs,' she cried, 'is it a FIRE WARNING?' Mum stopped for breath, got off the bike and said irritably, 'No, it's an air raid warning.' Mrs Stewart, carried along by her own fears, continued her interrogation. 'Well, you WERE blowing a "short, sharp blast" and THAT is a fire warning.'

It was the last straw and Mum spluttered. 'I know it was a "short, sharp blast". If you'd blown this bloody whistle all round the bloody village YOU'D blow short, sharp bloody blasts!' This was incredibly rude language at the time and Mrs Stewart was so offended she turned on her heel and strode back inside and it took a grovelling apology from Mum and about three weeks before normal social relationships were resumed with our family.

THE BAEDEKER RAIDS

The attack on York just referred to was one of the so-called Baedeker raids in which historic, ill-defended towns were targeted. Named after the well-known guide books, these were ordered by Hitler as reprisals for an attack on Lubeck on 14 April 1942 in which part of the beautiful, old centre was destroyed.

Moonlit nights were chosen to enable the bombers to come in at between 5,000 and 10,000 feet. They started with Exeter on 23 and 24 April. Bath followed on three nights in a row, then Norwich on the 27th, and York on the 28th. On 3 May there was another attack on Exeter, the worst in the series, with Norwich hit again on the 8th and Canterbury on 31 May, then twice in early June. Following this series, the Baedeker towns were left alone, except for 31 October when the Germans mustered some 30 FW 190 fighter-bombers (with fighter escort) for a surprise low-level attack on Canterbury.

Bomb damage to the High Street, Canterbury after the raid on 1 June 1942.

Margaret Tansey remembers the night York was blitzed.

That same evening, April 28th, the editorial in the local *Evening Press* had been on the subject of the so-called Baedeker raids on other cathedral cities and warned the citizens of York that they should be prepared as York might be next. It was indeed — that selfsame night!

There was just myself — a young teenager — and my widowed mother in the terraced house, and we used to go upstairs to bed in the dark as we had not blacked out the bedroom windows.

We were awakened by the frightening noise of bombs dropping and leapt out of bed and realised that the bedrooms were as light as day or even brighter. There had been no warning for some reason. Although we had an air raid shelter outside, we dared not chance going with bombs exploding all the time so we dived into an alcove-cum-cupboard under the stairs and sat there in a very apprehensive state as there seemed no end to the bombs. At one stage we heard machine gunning and I said 'Hurray — Spitfires!' but we heard afterwards that it was low-flying planes gunning the streets.

The bombs nearer to us made an ominous whistling noise as they came down and eventually we heard an extremely loud whistle. We both put our heads down and my mother took hold of my hand saying 'God help us!' With that the bomb dropped with a tremendous explosion. Our chairs were

Bomb damaged houses after the second Canterbury blitz, October 1942. Canterbury was another cathedral city that became a victim of the Baedeker raids.

literally lifted from the floor, the windows shattered, soot and debris shot down the chimney and everything in the house rattled ... we sat there for a long time, shaken and nervous ...

They seemed to have gone, we ventured to the front door. What a sight met our eyes — all across the horizon was a continuous red glow of fires burning over York. Our neighbours were all looking out by now and checking on each other. Two of the men who had been out in the street all the time on fire watch duty would never forget the experience. Many bombs had been dropped in the centre of York, burning out an ancient church and the historic Guildhall.

I walked down the street to check on my aunt and uncle. The road and path were thick with soil and there were rockery stones, rose bushes and debris to fall over. A bomb had fallen in the garden of houses opposite my aunt's — a direct hit on the shelter, fortunately unoccupied — they had dived under the table ... their house looked like a crazy house and two blocks of semis had to be demolished as they were so unsafe.

There was no sleep for anyone after that of course and everyone was filthy after clearing glass, soot debris. I set off to work and found the road I usually took closed due to an unexploded bomb. So I cut through Rowntree's Park and walked along by the river. I was anxious to know whether York Minster was still standing and when I couldn't see it at first I was nearly in tears. However, a little round the bend it came into sight and I was so relieved that I nearly wept again!

Then I wondered whether the Castle Museum where I worked would still be there. To my relief it was all right, however the curator and lecturer's flats were in ruins ... I spent hours helping to clean the lecturer's books which to her were the most important things. The covers were damaged and there was dust and rubble between every page! The contents of a tin of treacle from the flat above had not helped.

A friend of my mother's had a narrow escape. They were sitting under the staircase and heard such a loud whistling that they thought they were 'goners' but before their eyes a huge bomb came through the ceiling in the opposite corner and went through into the ground without exploding! 'It took the wireless set with it' she kept saying . . .

There were a lot of unexploded bombs to be defused and piles of rubbish to be cleared, but everyone worked heroically, especially where people were trapped of course . . .

When I next rode through the city centre on my bicycle I found the road in Coney Street all jewelled with pieces of glass which had melted into it in the intense heat. This was where the shopping arcade and church had burned down. There was a lovely old clock on this church — it had the figure of an admiral looking through his telescope on top and of course it had stopped during the fire. Next day people listening to Lord Haw-Haw broadcasting from Germany heard him speak to the 'citizens of York', saying 'You haven't had much sleep have you? And we'll be back again tonight!' Then he mentioned what time the clock had stopped at, although the little admiral was still looking out, and it was very sinister to hear this. Of course everybody was still very shocked anyway and some fires were still burning. The goods warehouses at York station took three days to be extinguished.

That evening, people brought blankets, etc. and walked up to the Knavesmire (a large open area with the racecourse on it) and they slept in the woods there. This went on for a few nights and then, as there was no further attack, it died out. An anti-aircraft gun was brought in and I saw it in the middle of the road in Bootham the day after the blitz. I think it was to boost morale as we had no defence whatever during the blitz.

TIP-AND-RUN ATTACKS

By this time the *Luftwaffe* had been mainly withdrawn to fight in the East. But for propaganda purposes the Germans continued to carry out occasional small-scale night raids and frequent daylight tip-and-run attacks, mainly on coastal towns.

These could be carried out in comparative safety. Reconnaissance or mine-laying planes carried a bomb or two;

planes seeking out shipping treated small seaside towns as alternative targets. Between July 1940 and November 1941, for example, raids on Tyneside killed nearly 400 people. Great Yarmouth had 72 raids with 110 killed and Lowestoft, 54 raids with 94 dead. S.J. Davies remembers

the River Orwell was like cat's eyes to enemy aircraft. They'd follow it up to bomb the docks at Ipswich and on the way back machine-gun the river (Harwich and Felixstowe also had sea plane stores and fuel depots). The Stour got the same treatment.

Even Cornish fishing resorts were not exempt — Falmouth alone received 33 raids with 31 dead.

Mrs Glad Hammond worked for a NAAFI in Eastbourne, Sussex.

We used to get German bombers coming off the sea with their engines off and swoop over, hit the town and bomb and machine-gun the streets, then back out to sea again. If there was time we would get an air raid warning, which would be followed by the 'cuckoo warning', which meant enemy aircraft overhead.

We had a terrible raid when a Marks and Spencer's copped a direct hit, which killed and injured a good many as it was one week before Christmas, when the store was crowded.

There was so much looting done as well. Many a time after a raid, we would get some of the soldiers bringing different articles in that had been looted and tried to sell them to our NAAFI.

John B. Collins was a schoolboy in Hastings, Kent.

In August and September 1940, the population of the town fell dramatically, mainly because of the threat of invasion. During the winter 1940/41, bombers were very frequently heard at night as they passed overhead on their way to London, but some of the worst raids on the town were by daylight tip-and-run fighter-bombers in 1942 and 1943, when the *Luftwaffe* did not venture further inland during daylight. Heavy raids were made on the town in 1942, in March, and May 1943.

In the March 1943 raid, for example, the German planes crossed the coast to the east of Hastings at 3.30 pm, and flew round the back of the town before dropping their bombs as they headed towards the sea. A number of bombs were dropped at a very low level, bounced on hitting roadways and flew considerable distances before coming down again and exploding. One passed through a local police station where a policeman, who had been on night duty, was sleeping; it took some of the furniture with it as it went on to bounce in Battle Road before finally exploding in Adelaide Road where it killed a retired headmistress who was ill in bed.

During these raids there was considerable pressure for better fighter protection from the RAF and anti-aircraft guns, and a local air-raid warning of imminent danger called the 'cuckoo' warning was introduced. At times even this was sounded after the raid had started! A standing patrol of two RAF fighters locally known as Gert and Daisy, which came from Biggin Hill, was sometimes at the wrong place when raids on coast towns took place as the patrol had to cover the coastline from Eastbourne to Folkestone it seems.

Joan Bowman was in the Land Army just outside Hastings.

Early one morning there was a series of explosions. I came to the door with my landlady and saw a German bomber heading for the coast, his four bombs dropped all round a house. When neighbours ran to see if the occupant, an old lady, was all right, she was standing at the top of the stairs in her nightie and when asked if she was all right calmly remarked 'He never touched me.'

But it was Dover that was really in the front line, subject not only to continuous raiding but also to shellfire from the guns of Cap Gris Nez — only 22 miles away. Helen Anne Sandys (then Ramsay), a Wren of 18½, worked in the Signals Distribution Office at HQ Dover Command, where all the

offices, plotting room, etc. were deep inside the cliff, underneath Dover Castle. Here are some extracts from letters to her parents.

September 1943 — The people of Dover are magnificent, some parts of the town are terribly battered, and resemble some of the newsreels of Russia. Some of the houses are just shells, most of the shops are boarded up, and at first sight it is difficult to make out whether a shop is open, or not, until one sees a notice 'Business as Usual'. The Boy's County School, where I am billeted, is high above the town, and overlooks it. Early in the morning it is rather lovely with mist hanging over the town, the castle silhouetted against the sky, and the sea beyond.

24 October 1943 — Recently we have had some quite noisy nights with the barrage. We have an AA gun about 100 yards from our room, so you can imagine when the planes are crossing the coast what the noise is like — all the coastal artillery really gets going. I expect in due time I shall learn to live through the gunfire. I love the guns. For the last ten days we have always had them once during the night. They are very comforting, as they drown the sound of the planes. One of the guns is only 100 yards away and it is quite uncanny to hear the man shout as they fire.

21 January 1944 — Just now we were told there was a German plane down. We went out and saw it from the cliffs. We could hear the ammunition popping as it burnt. It made a great ugly red flare, and the plane was burning from end to end. I believe there was a terrific show with hundreds of searchlights, and flak bursting. Three planes were brought down. We couldn't get anything to eat as the canteen had closed, and also all the lighting in Dover went out, but we were soon on emergency circuit ... all the nurses, NCOs orderlies and drivers were called out. The ones that remained danced, and talked with cigarette lighters. The band drowning the ack-ack ... This morning I saw a young German being led away blindfolded by three soldiers. One of the survivors. He looked very young, and this time yesterday,

he must have been in the *Vaterland*. I wonder what was going on inside his mind. It is no good being sorry for them, especially as he dropped some bombs, and hurt people.

10 May 1944 — I came off watch tonight at 8 pm and on again having come on at 2 am. I tried to sleep, but suddenly woke up by the bombing of France. I cannot begin to describe one's feelings, lying in bed with the din in the distance, so persistent, that one has to open the door to prevent it rattling. The whole ground shakes, and I stood on the cliffs tonight, and they were shaking again then. June came in late from a dance, and we smoked in the dark, and she turned to me, and said 'This must never, never happen again.' Daddy, I can't describe how one feels, so young at times, and others so awfully old and wise. There are things too big, and strange to grasp, and it is hard to explain how one feels standing on the cliff, listening to the sea lapping in the harbour, with the moon shining on the sea, and then those ghastly rumbles going on incessantly in the distance. It brings home to one, that we must see all this destruction, and futility do never, never happen again. Two days ago we went into a gun site, and looked across to France. As you saw in the papers, it was very clear, and the gun crew pointed out Calais clock tower, and the Cathedral spire. We could see Cap Gris Nez, and the phare at Bologne — but the best of all was seeing their guns. We could see them, through the rangefinder and glasses. Funny to think we have seen theirs, and not our own. (I also remember seeing a German troop train, moving up the coast, with reinforcements for the German army. You could see the sunlight flashing off the windscreens of moving army vehicles. The Channel looked no wider than Morecambe Bay, and I felt great thankfulness, that that narrow strip of water was between us and the Germans.

29 September 1944 — Quite a lot has happened. We have had several unpleasant shellings, five in 36 hours, and another one that lasted most of the day. The press had lulled people into a false sense of security, and one day at lunchtime, they sent over salvo after salvo, killing a lot of people. That more or less unnerved Dover, and since then the town has been

more or less in a state of siege. Only one shop is open. When we go on duty we remain there the whole of 24 hours, messing with the men. The town is one mass of street diversions, and we have no gas or water. The press said all the shelling was over for Dover, and then they got one of their worst, with people buried for 48 hours. Still there is only one gun left, and for the present it is leaving us alone. Yesterday for 2½ hours the sky was black with Halifaxes and Lancasters . . . I have never seen so many planes in all my life.

Undated letter — Thank heavens the shelling is all over. Dover is an awful mess, and the demolition squads are working, I believe many of them from London.

May 1945 — Peace at last! Our routine has not changed so it is hard to believe. We heard the P.M.'s speech at 1500, and at the same moment all the ships in the harbour hoisted their colours and did the V signal on their sirens. . . . The following day we celebrated by having a good dinner in the town, and dancing in the streets with bonfires, squibs, singing and generally being rather rowdy. All we think and talk about is demobilization now. But I'm afraid we will all have to be patient.

6.
CIVIL DEFENCE

They hadn't heard the plane this time; destruction had come drifting down quietly on green silk cords: the walls suddenly caved in. They were not even aware of noise.

Blast is an odd thing; it is just as likely to have the effect of an embarrassing dream as of man's serious vengeance on man, landing you naked in the street or exposing you in your bed or on your lavatory seat to the neighbour's gaze. Rowe's head was singing; he felt as though he had been walking in his sleep; he was lying in a strange position, in a strange place. He got up and saw an enormous quantity of saucepans all over the floor: something like the twisted engine of an old car turned out to be a refrigerator. He looked up and saw Charles's Wain heeling over an armchair which was poised 30 feet above his head: he looked down and saw the Bay of Naples intact at his feet. He felt as though he were in a strange country without any maps to help him, trying to get his position by the stars.

Three flares came sailing slowly, beautifully, down, clusters of spangles off a Christmas tree: his shadow shot out in front of him and he felt exposed, like a gaolbreaker caught in a searchlight beam. The awful thing about a raid is that it goes on: your own private disaster may happen early, but the raid doesn't stop. They were machine-gunning the flares: two broke with a sound like cracking plates and the third came to earth in Russell Square; the darkness returned coldly and comfortingly.

But in the light of the flares Rowe had seen several things; he had discovered where he was — in the basement kitchen: the chair above his head was in his own room on the first floor, the front room had gone and all the roof, and the cripple lay beside the chair, one arm swinging loosely down at him. He had dropped neatly and precisely at Rowe's feet a piece of uncrumbled cake. A warden called from the street, 'Is anyone hurt in there?' and Rowe called aloud in a sudden return of his rage. 'It's beyond a joke: it's beyond a joke.'

'You're telling me,' the warden called down to him from the shattered street as yet another raider came up from the south-east muttering to them both like a witch in a child's dream, 'Where are you? Where are you? Where are you?'

Graham Greene, *The Ministry of Fear*

To the warden this would have been an 'incident', and not a very serious one at that. He or she would have had a quick look around, then returned to the wardens' post to report 'parachute bomb at such and such address, one dead, one survivor just needs cup of tea and a clean-up, no fire, no UXB'. Not much of an incident; all in the night's work.

An account of a rather more serious incident was written on 26 January 1943 by Noel Streatfield for the records of the WVS (Women's Voluntary Service).

A public house in the docklands had a direct hit ... soon there is a clanging of ambulance bells, the shouts for stretchers, the hurried throwing of blankets or sacks over

Rescuers digging for bodies at an incident, 1944.

ghastly remains before the relations have a chance to see them. Digging operations start at once. Teams of men whom we call 'Heavy Rescue' and 'Light Rescue' are rushed to each site where there is a possibility of anybody being buried. Cranes with attachments for removing debris are set working, and all dockside rings with the sound of picks and shovels ... Against this antheap of rubble the district warden takes up his position as Incident Officer. This means he is in charge of all work caused by that particular bomb. All bombs have such an officer, he can be picked out by the blue cover over his tin hat and where he is, a blue flag flies by day and two blue lights mark him by night. On the pile itself scooping the debris up in spades and putting it into the crane buckets are about 80 men. The road is roped off by the police and round the incident ambulances, police cars and lorries are parked. Outside the ropes stands a tragic group. Men, women and some children. A few know for certain who is under that mass of rubble, some are pretty sure they know, and the rest fear they know. Whispered snippets of conversation go round. 'My man usually goes up there about that time, but maybe he was off on a job somewhere else.' 'My mother went to the Jug and Bottle for Dad's pint — she isn't come back ...'

In the rest of this chapter we will look at the different roles of people involved in such an incident, from the warden who set things in motion to those concerned in the aftermath, including the volunteers who handed out tea and comforting words to victims and rescuers alike.

THE WARDENS

The prime role of the wardens was, as we have seen, to get to know their area intimately so as to be able to direct the various emergency services to those places where people would have been gathered when a bomb fell. And as the war went on they had, for the sake of their own survival if that of no one else, to become familiar with the swift changes in the ghastly technology of destruction. Some entries from

Stephen Woodcock's diary show just how quickly these could occur.

Tuesday 4 Feb 1941 — Mr Keogh, Home Guard Section Leader, questioned the instructions I had put up in the hall telling Fire Parties that they must not approach an incendiary bomb for about two or three mins after it ignites, owing to the danger of explosion. After some arguments he agreed that I was right and thanked me for my explanation.

Thursday 20 Feb — Notice to wardens of a new type of explosive incendiary bomb — a wooden circular board showing a light beneath, which may explode any time after 30 mins after the light has gone out. Persons are to keep at least 50 feet away.

June 1941 — To date there have been 1,052 incidents, 244 killed, 1,234 seriously injured, 702 houses demolished, 7,900 houses damaged, 582 HE bombs (50–1,800 kg), 69 unexploded, 39 oil bombs, 4,000 incendiary bombs. The type of bomb now used is a general purpose bomb with a thin casing. It causes more blast and has a sensitive fuse. There are six sizes, from 50 kilos to 1,800 kilos.

Bert Snow describes a further modification to existing bombs, and the discovery of an entirely new type.

All incendiaries made whistling sounds as they rushed to earth, and very soon an evil genius worked on a scheme for fitting some with a device which greatly magnified the sound, so that it became a piercing howl. Another surprise was bombs by parachute. By arriving at a more leisurely rate, they were able to achieve more widespread surface damage. I was one of the surprised CD workers who arrived at an incident where a huge crater now occupied an area enclosed by four narrow streets, in which hundreds of small brick homes had stood a short time before. A warden said to the new arrivals 'an aeroplane came down here', and we thought he must have been right because of the extensive damage, although we were puzzled that there was no sign of aircraft wreckage. It was later that we were told of the new bombs.

A fire alarm still working amidst desolation. Poplar High Street,
11 November 1944.

The development of unexpected types of bomb continued
throughout the war, so those involved in civil defence had
to keep permanently alert. They were caught off-guard in
Grimsby, on one sad night in June 1943, however, when
containers of the new Butterfly bombs were dropped, some
set to explode on impact, others after a predetermined time

or when disturbed. Most of the 163 casualties occurred after the all clear, when people emerged from the shelters and started picking through the rubble of their own homes.

Whatever the type of bomb involved, the warden had to assess the damage and report back to the post as soon as possible, then see what measures could be taken on the spot while waiting for the emergency services to arrive.

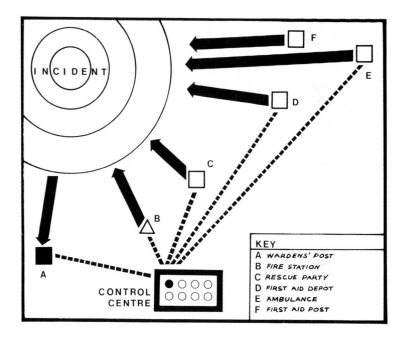

THE CONTROLLERS

Someone at the post, usually the chief warden, would then phone the details through to the control centre for the district. Patricia Cockburn, the wife of writer Claude Cockburn, worked in one such centre, deep under Praed Street in the Paddington area of West London.

Sixty of us sat in the large underground room, each at a narrow desk on which were four telephones, coloured white, red, green and black. There was also a flat, lidless box with three divisions in it. In one division were a number of rings attached to white discs; these represented ambulances, the exact number you had at your disposal. In the next division, rings with red discs which were fire engines; and in the third rings with green discs which were representing heavy rescue machine — a kind of bulldozer with a claw. On the wall in front of the desk was a board with nails sticking out of it in rows, numbered vertically from 1 to 20 and horizontally marked, 'On the way to the occurrence', 'At the occurrence' and 'Out of service'. Above the nail-board was a very large-scale map of the area one was responsible for.

The black telephone was for communicating with the chief warden of one's district, who 'phoned you when a bomb fell, saying 'HE at the corner of Acacia Street and Watt Crescent. Casualties and fire. Request four ambulances and two fire engines.' You then picked up your white telephone and ordered two ambulances to go to Acacia Street, and your red telephone and told one fire engine to go there too, at the same time taking out two white discs and one red one and hanging them on the nail under No. 1, if it was your first bomb of the evening, and on a level with 'On the way to the occurrence'. When you were notified that they had arrived you moved the discs down to 'At the occurrence', and so on. You never gave the warden all the machines he asked for. If you did you would run out of ambulances and fire engines long before the raid was over. If any of them were blown up or broke down when they were out on the streets you moved their discs to 'Out of service'. When you were informed on your white or red telephones that the ambulance or fire engines were safely back in their garages, you took the disc off its nail and put it back in your box ready for the next errand of mercy.

It was exactly like a child's game — and required about the same skill in playing it. Success was largely a question of temperament. At one time I had sitting at the next desk on my right a spendthrift whose district adjoined mine. In an emergency you were allowed to lend equipment across boundaries, and she was always asking me to lend her ambulances or fire engines, having been too prodigal with her own early in the night. To my left was a miser. Anyone unlucky enough to be fire-bombed in his district was likely to be burned to a crisp. I used to overhear him say to his chief warden, 'I haven't got any fire engines available at the moment. Try putting it out with stirrup pumps', and I could see out of the corner of my eye that his tray was full of red discs.

THE FIRE FIGHTERS

At the outbreak of war the 2,300 regular members of the London Fire Brigade were joined by about 23,000 members of the Auxiliary Fire Service, some full-time, some unpaid part-timers. (Similar arrangements, on a smaller scale, were made in the provinces.) By the end of the war 793 firemen and 25 firewomen had lost their lives, with 7,000 seriously injured.

The new auxiliaries had to learn fast. Before the war there were fewer than 2,000 pumps in the whole of Britain; on the night of 29 December 1940 about that number were at work in the London area alone, with 300 more sent in from outside.

The task of the fire fighters was made more difficult at first by occasional friction between auxiliaries and regulars; and that of crews who went outside their area to give assistance was often rendered impossible by the discovery that their equipment was incompatible with that of the host area. This state of affairs was remedied in May 1941 when the creation of a National Fire Service was announced in the Commons. The vast number of different brigades (over 1,500 in pre-war days) were then re-organised into 40-odd 'fire forces' under central control.

Here are some stories from men and women who remember what it was like.

We used to have mobile units in London which would go out to towns to support the local fire brigades. When they got there, of course, things didn't fit, so all that we could supply was the manpower and not the pumping units. Eventually, they installed a national fitting which was called an instantaneous coupling. All fire brigades now are provided with them.

Dick Helyer

At Dagenham there was a lot of division between the regulars and the auxiliaries. The regulars treated us like we were second class. We got lumbered with all the second rate equipment — old taxis for fire engines, old crowbars, they wouldn't let us near the new turntable ladders. They had all the modern stuff for themselves, but because they were controlled by the borough they weren't allowed outside the borough, so most of the time they just sat around with all the best equipment, doing nothing. We were the ones that were called out all the time, all over London to help put out fires, but we didn't have the best equipment to do the job.

Charlie Chambers, AFS

The AFS came in on a watch system and we regulars had to train and take orders from them, because at one time, at the beginning of the war, there was a Home Office order which said that AFS officers carried precedence over ordinary firemen. The first time we went out, our officer was the manager of the Ford works at Dagenham, and he had a rank in the AFS and he told us what to do. And we completely ignored him because if we had done what he wanted us to do — it was only a house fire — there would have been two girls dead up in their bedroom. What he was doing was completely haywire. Obviously the first thing to do with a fire is to see whether there was anybody in it!

Walter Amos, LFB

A control unit is a travelling watchroom and is sent to the larger fires. You plot the fire and firemen come to you for anything they need, such as lifting gear, salvage vans, escape ladders, extra pumps, etc. I liked the excitement of being on it. We were a three-girl team. We had to be quite close to the fire, where we could be seen easily. Sometimes we were there most of the night, and if we managed to get a sandwich it was usually covered in black smuts and tasted of smoke. Still, anything was better than nothing and it didn't seem to do us any harm. It was amazing how many good people turned up with jugs of tea for us too. Little old ladies used to brave the shrapnel, they were marvellous. One lady turned up with a saucepan on her head. Of course she was under the impression that shrapnel wouldn't go through it (what a hope!).

Kathy Clayden, stationed at Wandsworth Fire Station

I was on the Bull Ring job during one of the heaviest raids on our city, even the wooden blocks in the road caught fire as they were covered with tar to preserve them.

Quite often we had to search for water, as most of the mains supplies had been fractured by HE bombs. That would mean a long relay of booster pumps from a canal, river or a 100,000-gallon tank often half a mile away. It gave one a weird feeling seeing shops and offices one knew so well going up in flames, and there was nothing one could do about it until the water supply had been restored.

Most fire stations had a billiards table, and it was most annoying when one was leading by 20 or more points and the 'bells went down' and we had to leave the game and 'go down the pole' to the engine house and away to a fire. I kept hens at the station, which was all right while I was on duty, but every time I came back off leave I was greeted by 'They ain't laid at all while you've been away', but I'll bet some firemen had eggs for their tea!

Arthur Roberts, Birmingham Fireman

The Fire station at Southwark was my life and home when I joined in 1938, being as I was brought up in an orphanage home. I was at Southwark after being bombed out. We were taught first aid, abbreviations of fire appliances like TTL (turntable ladder), BA required (breathing apparatus), etc., with squad drills in the yard of Southwark Fire Station.

At first we were posted to sub-stations with three watches — red, white and blue. The LFB treated us as part-timers, but when in action, they loved us. Remember we wasn't prepared for war really, and we didn't have the fire appliances, we had taxis pulling fire pumps. I was a watchroom-attendant at first, taking fire calls, and we had pegs on map boards in our watchroom marking where our pumps were. We called for help from different stations to move them up (standby duties), even from Kent; when Kent was having flying bombs we were moved where needed, even some of us going to Portsmouth, Coventry, Bristol. I learnt to swear like the men, F... B...s. But the firemen, firewomen were a grand bunch, regarding friendship and comradeship. They were the best years in a way, when you were on watchroom duties; we used to pray for all of them to return, which many, many never did, sad to say.

I decided to become a Despatch Rider. Two weeks training on the cinder track, passed out flying colours. I was then on the road, riding my 350-cc motor bike over water hoses, and reporting to the divisional officer in charge, sometimes having to lift the bike over the fire hoses. I used to see red shrapnel fall, riding on the motor bike, thank God it missed me, and I often helped out folding the fire hoses along with some firemen ,,, we came back to our station, dirty faces, either wet, or dusty tunics and uniforms. We never spoke, our eyes and faces told it all, of the terrible sights we saw, bodies lying around, and parts of bodies. While the firemen fought fires, the Germans would drop HE bombs in the fires; many firemen got killed or thrown to the ground. They were a lovely lot of guys ... We never knew if we would ever get back to our stations, once the air raid warning went. We were fully dressed and out as soon as the bombs fell. I still hear the stations bells ringing and still can't forget the smell of burning flesh, it's a smell you can never forget, ever.

Hilda Carter, London AFS

THE WATERMEN

Dick Helyer worked on the Thames, supplying water to those fighting fires close to the river, a vital job when mains could easily be pierced by high explosive bombs. (See photograph on page 17.)

I joined the London Fire Brigade in 1938 from the Royal Navy.

(On the river they was all ex-matelots, bar one I think.) I was stationed on the 75-foot-long river fire-boat at Blackfriars, the *Massey Shaw*, which had already made many crossings to rescue the troops from Dunkirk. This had two four-stage centrifugal pumps which could pump out 3,000 gallons per minute. It formed a jet capable of reaching the top of a six-storey building, her main job being to relay water to fire-fighting appliances ashore. We also had about 20 emergency fire-boats, and barges with four pumps put in them for water relaying. We had boats from Teddington lock right down to Southend, and some nights they were all out water relaying.

There was a control boat which you would report to if there was a big riverside fire. That would go out to the fire and detail you where to go. We were the first, I think, to have wireless communication installed.

I remember seeing one night the turntable ladders putting a jet into a building at Southwark Bridge Road and the jet just faded out because they dropped bombs on the water mains. We used to put fire boats to supply people on the land in those circumstances. We just dropped anchor and took the hose ashore on a skiff, which was a very difficult job I might say. With the tide flow you got, a certain amount of skill is required to take a length of hose ashore. We had to pull straight ahead of the fire boat, then at the word GO put the arm over and pull hard for the shore and hope that you were carried ashore by the tide. If you weren't, you went downstream and had to start all over again because the tides were so strong.

It was worse when the tide was low. I remember one time when I was laying off of Queen Victoria Street, anchored out ... there were some parts of the river, which needed a bit of holding to your anchor ... when you got your hose ashore you would start drifting down the river because of the tide. He was crafty enough to have his very heavy raids at very low water so that what you had to do was get your hose to the water's edge, try to get it over the mud and have a line to give to the chaps on the shore to pull it ashore, but the mud used to come up to your knees and you had a hell of a job.

You've got to realise that directly you had a big dock fire

you knew that you were in the target area and it wasn't a very pleasant feeling. On one occasion when the Thames was really well alight on each side of the river just below Tower Bridge, the water looked as though it was boiling. You see the fires were consuming so much of the oxygen in the atmosphere that you got a down-draught which went along the top of the water into the base of the fire. That'll give you some idea of the intense heat that was generated by these fires.

THE RESCUERS

In this organised chaos, in its stage setting, there were moments that leave themselves in the memory — those moments when silence is called suddenly and everyone stands immobile listening, trying to make contact with the people beneath. To be buried alive — the most pagan of all deaths. Unforgettable that silence, with no sound but perhaps one bit of plaster falling from the roof.

Those words are from the diary of Moyra Macleod (then Wren Charlton) describing something that took place, not in the East End of London, nor on Merseyside, Clydeside or any of the places one associates with the blitz, but in Dartmouth, on a sunny February day in 1943.

It was the rescue squads, usually men experienced in the building industry, who were mainly responsible for such work. But, as Walter Amos explains, it was not always possible to wait until they arrived.

We [firemen] were always called out first with the police. Then we got heavy rescue in if they were needed. We often had to shore up buildings. Once we got the message that there were some people trapped in the basement. When we got into the basement, there were two lady ARP wardens bent double taking the weight of all the debris on top of their backs, supporting it with their backs so it shouldn't fall on the young children beneath them. And the biggest job we had then, once we had shored up, was to get these girls straightened up. We laid them on the ground and got them warmed up and we fetched buckets of warm water from a hotel and we bathed them.

Sometimes it took time to reach those trapped and, as the Reverend Markham recalls,

these tunnelling jobs were strange affairs, so chancy in their outcome. One night I was summoned to a small house, which had been demolished by a bomb. We managed to crawl under the collapsed bedroom floor, held up precariously on one side by a tottering wall. There, by the light of our torches, we found a man still sitting in a kitchen chair at a table, his head and body bowed down to the table top by the weight of the flooring which had trapped him, injuring his head. He was greasy with mortar dust but conscious. We got the rescue party, who sawed off the legs of the chair, and so released him to be whisked off to hospital. We found his daughter, lying dead in the debris a few feet away.

The deaths of children are recalled with particular clarity. As Walter Amos told us,

One of the things that really sticks in my mind was when, at the beginning of the blitz, the fire service was still running ambulances, and I went to pick up a child injured by an air raid. When we got there, there was a beautiful little girl, she was eight years old, she was the sort of girl that you see in the old Pears soap adverts. When we looked at her, we could find no injury except that a piece of shrapnel had taken off the back of her skull and she was lying on the ground. She had a beautiful smile on her face. We took her to Hendon Cottage Hospital, and I told the doctor that I thought she was dead. (She was, but we weren't qualified to say.) A young doctor came out to certify; he took one look at her, took off his white coat and went off to join the Air Force, because he wanted to drop bombs on people who were dropping those on us.

Tragic discoveries, sometimes at the end of hours of patient labour, were so common that many involved in rescue work prefer to recall incidents where something odd or humorous happened to soften the pain. Mr J.B. Stephens, a Waterloo fireman, tells us of the day that an HE dropped on Waterloo rail station during the morning rush hour.

We were the first on the spot. A double-decker bus had the whole top deck sliced off, killing nearly all the passengers except one City gent who was trapped under the seat. When rescued, he was found to be only slightly hurt, but refused to enter the ambulance until his bowler hat and brolly were found. He could not arrive at his office 'not fully dressed'. We found both on the bus, both battered, returned same to him. He smiled his thanks, put the hat on his head, gripped his brolly, then blacked out. We put him in the ambulance, hat and brolly still in place.

And on another occasion they were called to the back of Tennyson House, facing the Oval.

We placed our ladders against the open gaps in the brick-work, proceeded to clear the rubble, etc., covering a trapped woman, chatting all the time to keep morale up. Suddenly her face and feet were visible. 'It won't be long, dearie,' I said, 'before we have you out', and continued to remove more debris. Suddenly she cried 'No more. Please don't. I ain't got nothing on! I'm naked!' Off came my uniform jacket to cover her blushes as we removed the last of the rubble to expose a plump middle-aged female ... Meanwhile in the next flat one of my crew was trying without success to get a female, dressed in a nightie, to step on the ladder. She was afraid of heights and ladders. He decided to carry her down using the fireman's lift, and was on the top rung when she tried to pull her nightie over her exposed thighs, thus blinding the rescuer as it fell over his head. Result! A very shaky down-the-ladder operation ... and the lady had lost control of her bowels, so the poor fireman had to clean his head and face from the first

Helping walking casualties to the First Aid Post.

aid hose. Red faces all round, but a good laugh by all when we reported back to base.

A good laugh was needed; humour, especially what the Germans call *Galgenhumor*, gallows humour, was often a safety valve to enable all civil defence workers to cope with reality.

As early as September 1940, according to Margaret Kennedy, her husband David, a warden in London, was noticing

the deliberate callousness and brutality which the younger wardens, of both sexes, assume when talking of casualties. 'We got five bods out of the pub at the corner. Or five and a half bods, to be exact.'

He commented on this to another middle-aged warden, who is rather a pal of his. [He] said they are just like young medical students in their first year, who always make a point of being tough and saying raw things about operations and post mortems. He says it is a sort of self-defence against shock when you get your first encounter with the physical horrors of life.

Four more years of war gave people a chance to build an even thicker carapace around them, if we can count as typical a conversation that S.N. Behrman reported in the *New Yorker* on 27 January 1945. In the course of a train journey to Cardiff he spent some time with a young warden who, having regaled him with a variety of horror stories, added

'It isn't all unrelieved gloom, though. Sometimes funny things happen.' I encouraged him to tell me a funny thing. 'Well,' he said, 'one day we were clearing out a badly blitzed house. We found a decapitated man. We looked and looked for his head but couldn't find it. Finally we gave up. As we were carrying the torso through what used to be the garden into the van, we heard a chicken clucking. Hello, I thought, what's that chicken clucking about? There's certainly nothing left for him in the garden. We went back and followed the clucking till we found the chicken. It wasn't in the garden at all but in part of the rubble and it was clucking at the missing head.' I was happy to find that there was a lighter side to the man's work.

But the laughter couldn't always be sustained. Margie Bruce, an ambulance driver in Finsbury, has a story about a group of heavy rescue workers who

had been working away for 10 days, and the archway that went down into this bomb-site was made up of the bodies of six children. They were all dead and the men were saying, 'I don't think we'll be able to get nothing more up out of that now ... I think we'll 'ave to close it in and it's dangerous.' And then one of them suddenly said 'Listen, I can hear somebody. I can hear somebody talking.' And we all listened, and you could hear a voice somewhere or other ... and those men turned, and they worked ... and they had been working there the whole time, they must have been exhausted; they had odd times off, of course, but they all went back down there like fresh things to get the person out. And then one of the big chaps who was down inside came up, and in his hand he had a birdcage, and inside the birdcage, rocking on its perch was a parrot who had had all but his tail feathers and a few on his head blown off and he was rocking backwards and forwards doing what was known to us as the three Bs ... 'Blast! Bloody! Bugger! ... Blast! Bloody! Bugger!' And at the sight of this, those men sat down and started roaring with laughter ... and then it all turned into tears and they were sobbing. And you realised then just exactly what a strain it had been to them not showing emotion all those 10 days and doing that ghastly work.

For Walter Amos it was the discovery of some unexpected victims of the blitz which moved him to tears. It was one morning in the City and they were allowing streams of water to pour out over the remains of the previous night's fire to prevent it re-igniting.

The lower half of Golden Lane had been devastated by fire. Across the road from where I stood was a badly fire-damaged building, so imagine my surprise when a man came out of it leading a horse. The animal looked terrified and the man was having trouble controlling it. As he passed me I asked him 'Where did you get that horse?' and he said 'Over there', pointing to this particular building. This aroused my curiosity, and off I went to have a look inside. To reach the upper floor I had to walk up a cobblestone ramp; the heat was so bad I could feel it through the soles of my top boots. I was not prepared for the sight that greeted me on reaching the first floor; it looked like a huge room and down either side was a range of stalls and at the far end was what I think was called a loose box, so obviously the building was used as a stables for a local carrier. Lying on the floor down the centre of the room was what looked like huge joints of roast meat. It took a little while for me to realise I was looking at a row of dead horses that had had no chance of escape and had been burned alive. I am not ashamed to admit it was the only time during the war years that I just stood and cried.

But for some rescue workers the strain became unbearable. From Birmingham a confidential report was sent to London saying that

some of the rescue personnel ... are said to be suffering from strain caused by having continuously to handle so many mutilated bodies. To use a colloquialism, the men are said to be 'going crackers'.

Firemen, too, were under similar strain, as a story from Fred Gibney, a Smethwick warden, illustrates.

We had had a rough night, but no incidents on our patch. The ack-ack guns had been busy blasting away all night; these acted more as a deterrent to keep the bombers away from sensitive targets, but on this night they had hit one of the bombers.

He came down on houses just off our patch with all his

load on board and the resultant fire had incinerated all the poor folk who had had no time to take shelter. When I went around to see if I could be of any help, the fire brigade and the rescue squad had arrived.

At the foot of one of the fire tenders lay the remains of one of the German crew, only the torso remaining. Suddenly one of the fire crew took a running kick at the remains of this poor soul lying by his tender. No doubt he was frustrated at the futility of their impossible task of dealing with the holocaust caused by the plane's landing on the houses, and, looking back I can understand his reaction, but may he be forgiven on the day of judgment.

But, as Walter Amos explains, it was not just the horrific sights that caused firemen to crack up; many faced a moral dilemma which was literally irresolvable, that between duty and the simple demands of human compassion.

We had several weeks of continuous night bombing, which is why so many firemen finished up in the mental hospitals. I mean you were going out there every night, you were just standing on the box ... One of the worst features of this was when you were sent to a fire and our orders on leaving the station were 'on no account were we to stop for houses on fire, we were to go to the factories, the factories were essential to the war effort, and they must be saved'. On the way, people would stand in the road and try to stop us. Their houses were alight, the families were trapped, and our orders were to go on. What do we do? I know the answer. Several people got rescued that shouldn't have got rescued, several factories got burnt that shouldn't have got burnt ... if you had a crowd of women standing in the middle of the road and if you went on you were going to run them over, or kids were in the road ... you had to stop.

THE AMBULANCE TEAMS

Those responsible for rushing the injured away also had to

learn to steel themselves. Brenda Rhodes, shut away in a convent boarding-school until she was 17½, then pitch-forked into the war, could not have coped without what she calls

the camaraderie of 'mates' — people from every walk of life, a ballet dancer, an orchestra musician, ex-school teachers, shopkeepers, a boxer with true cauliflower ears, an ex-nanny, a chorus girl, a cook and parlour maid (they came together as they were sisters and had left 'service' to do their bit). They were wonderful people and to them I owe my education, my growing up and knowledge of 'the facts of life'.

Brenda worked first as an attendant then as a driver.

If you could just imagine the vehicles we used you'd find it scarcely believable. We had large, commandeered cars — Humbers, Austins, etc. These were to be used for walking casualties. Light vans or lorries that had had the rear adapted to hold either two or four stretchers. Very rough and ready they were too — leaving a wooden shell like a three-sided box, the back open, with curtains to draw across the first aid kit, it was quite rudimentary. And imagine trying to find roads in the blackout with only a 1½-inch slit of light in your headlights, and, having found the road, finding the building!

A vivid memory is of being high up on a hill and looking down at the Thames with docks and riverside on fire as far as I could see. Then I did cry — there was I, starting my adult life with what at that moment seemed the end of everything. Could we win? Could we POSSIBLY overcome all this?

We could only help and comfort and move to the hospitals the many, many casualties, to those dedicated medics in the hospitals — bombed and damaged themselves.

Seeing all this death and destruction around you each working day seemed to numb you; you tried not to let it get to you, otherwise you would not be able to continue.

Brenda carried on with her job, despite being bombed out three times at home. On 18 September 1940 her colleague Bert Purdy had to face something even worse.

We received a call to Saundersness Road School, Millwall, situated well in the Dock area. I knew that it was being used by all different sections of the civil defence — hundreds of people, including my own young brother, Ernie. The school had received a direct hit.

We assisted in removing the casualties to Poplar Hospital. On returning to the school, I was informed that my brother was still trapped with his team mates. I was allowed to remain at the school for two days, identifying the bodies, but they still hadn't found Ernie yet. Several days later I was told that Ernie had been found and my other older brother Will had identified the body. It was a tragic experience. Ambulance personnel engaged on emergency accident work get hardened to dealing with all types of incidents, but where children and your own family are involved, it is a different matter. We also suffer.

Most of the injured were looked after at hospital. But in many cases, as Bert Snow told us, the hospital had to come to them.

The mobile medical teams were called in special circumstances such as when trapped victims were suffering pain and some other serious conditions. I saw one of these teams in action when a little boy of about five or six was trapped in a damaged shelter with his mother and sister dead alongside him. He was not responsive to anything that was said to him and would occasionally whimper with fear and confusion, then lapse into unconsciousness for a short time. Efforts were made to release him from an opening just above his head, while a man climbed through another opening in the side of the heaped-up earth, but was unable to reach him because his dead mother and sister blocked the way. A medical team, consisting of a doctor and two nursing sisters, in a specially-equipped van, responded to the call for help, and by the light of torches the doctor gave the little air raid victim an injection, which allowed him to sleep peacefully, while his rescuers worked to release him. Some CD workers reached a state of nervous exhaustion under the strain and tension cause by fear, anxiety and inadequate rest. I marvelled that there were not more afflicted in this way.

But there were moments of peace, too, even of beauty. Bert remembers nights

when flares were extensively used and, as they slowly floated down at various heights, they presented a beautiful sight, in spite of their fighting purpose. Those of the chandelier type were especially attractive.

And David Kennedy (Margaret Kennedy's warden husband) could write to her at the height of the September 1940

Searchlights during a raid on London, September 1940.

bombing to marvel at the 'real beauty of London in the blitz'.

He says it thrills him when he goes out on patrol; the blackout makes the houses look much grander, like precipices standing up in the moonlight, and the geometry of search-lights across the sky.

Such moments were rare, perhaps; but they helped many of those working in civil defence to get through the long, deadly nights.

THE AFTERMATH

But even when the fires were out and the last injured removed to hospital, the work was not over. The rescue squads might have to stay on to shore up the building, or demolish it, if it was too dangerous to be left. At times, as Bert Snow reminds us, 'there was the more grim task of digging out a decomposing body that had been previously overlooked'.

The Reverend Markham also had work to do.

Once we had dealt with the safe delivery of casualties to hospital, nothing helped their recovery more than the know-ledge that their personal treasures were safe. The usual prac-tice of those who took shelter was to put all their cash, savings certificates, items of personal jewellery, and personal papers such as birth and marriage certificates, in their hand-bags, which they left under the chair on which they were sitting, or by their side if they were in bed. As soon as it was daylight, I used to take two of my wardens, and tunnel through mountains of rubble to find these handbags. We dared not leave them, even for a few hours, or they would be gone.

As soon as we recovered dead bodies, I had to put them in an empty room, under the guard of two wardens, until a stretcher party could remove them to a mortuary. Otherwise their clothing would be rifled, there in the midst of the darkness and dust, and falling bombs. I often said in those days that it was a good thing that I was not armed with a pistol or a gun: I would probably have shot those whom I suspected of this kind of activity. It used to make me very angry.

There were the survivors to think of, too. And by 1944, when George Beardmore was active as a warden, the procedure was more caring, and considerably better organised than in the early days of the war.

The Home Office had learned that nothing reassures the bombed more than the simple word 'Information' printed on a card and stuck as near as possible to the site of the disaster. What had been a private catastrophe was turned by this word into a matter of public concern. In an office thus requisitioned, lists were compiled, principally gathered by the WVS, of the people who had been in each of the affected houses before the bombs fell, and of those who could be traced afterwards. Some inevitably were never traced or identified. It was then my job ... to acquaint the nearest blood relations of the deceased or seriously injured and in hospital, or to see that this was done. First and foremost I had the job of helping the injured or homeless to begin life again by directing them to the nearest rest centre, handing out certificates which could be used as evidence to railway booking clerks that the holder had been made homeless by enemy action and should be given a free ticket, and in some cases obtaining money for them from the Public Assistance Department. Also present was a WVS lady in charge of their store of second-hand clothes. Apart from the loss of life in his family, a man might present himself in his pyjamas, having lost all he possessed; in wartime, when papers such as identity-cards and ration-cards were necessary for existence, a good deal of grief might follow, and replacements for these, too, might be found.

THE BOMB DISPOSAL SQUADS

Finally, the most dangerous work of all might have to begin. Our first description comes in a letter already quoted from — that written to the young evacuees Anne and Neil by their father back in Glasgow.

An enormous bomb of a new type — or it may have been a land-mine, but anyhow something new and of enormous size was found unexploded. The area round it was cleared of people. A naval officer — expert on explosives — and one rating moved cautiously towards it. At a certain distance the NO told the rating to lie down and not come any nearer. He walked on alone, reached the enormous bomb, put his ear to it and shouted to the rating 'She's still ticking; get right away back; have the cordon moved hundreds of yards back.' Alone he started his task. According to the account given me by a senior officer, it took him 45 minutes to remove the enormous nose cap. She was still ticking. He got quite a lot of his body inside the enormous thing and then slowly and deliberately he set about disconnecting the clockwork from the explosive. Remember that this was something new, not something that he had been able to practise on before. It sounds incredible but I was told that he remained half immersed in the infernal machine for another 45 minutes and then wriggled backwards with the clockwork in his hands. When later he handed the clock to someone else he remarked 'Well I got the teeth out.'

Our second account comes from just such an officer, Major (then Lieutenant) G.R. Ovens of the 25th Bomb Disposal Section, Royal Engineers.

In 1940 the drill for dealing with a UXB was roughly as follows. After a raid the local police and ARP warden's post would do a reconnaissance of their area and report any suspicious holes in the ground. Sometimes the very concussion of a bomb hitting the ground and not exploding would be sufficient alert to suspect an UXB until proper inspection could be carried out. The BD Officer would confirm or otherwise.

223

Pioneer Corps with a UXB in Brockley, 1941.

When action was called for the immediate area to the UXB to be evacuated, a squad from the BD section would start digging down the hole to expose the bomb. Once the bomb was exposed, the squad would retire to a safe distance until the officer was able to get to the bomb to defuse it. Once, when the squad had retired and I had climbed down to examine the bomb type and position of fuse(s), I came back to the surface to get something and to my surprise saw a fellow staring at me over a nearby garden fence. When I enquired what he was doing there he replied 'I saw you was an officer so I thought there can't be no danger if 'e's there.'

But danger there was. One morning in October 1940 Lt Ovens ('in circumstances of great gallantry and at imminent risk to his life', as the letter of commendation reads) managed to remove the charge from a 250-kg delay-action bomb by suction, a hitherto untried procedure. Not everyone was lucky enough to escape with their life, though, as Bert Woodhouse can bear witness.

When we went on a job, we would draw lots to decide who

had the first go at defusing or moving the bomb — we'd each take a turn down the hole with the bomb, 20 minutes each, one at a time. When we got it out often we'd drive it out at full speed to Hackney Marshes or Barking Marshes and explode it. Anyway, this particular day a 1,000-lb bomb fell at Cummings Road, Dagenham, and as a matter of course all the streets around were evacuated. Nobody knew very much about bomb disposal in those days, including us — we were just squaddies. We were terrified but we tried not to show it. Anyway, we were winching the bomb out of the hole when it exploded. There was a terrific blast and I was thrown onto the floor, covered in rubble. A chimney-pot landed on my head, I was bleeding from both ears and I was crying. My three mates were right next to the bomb and they were literally blown to pieces. There was nothing left of them apart from a bit of leg in a wellington boot, which was all they discovered of my mate Jackie Lewis.

THE QUIET CARERS

In stories of the Home Front the names of two voluntary organisations keep cropping up: the Women's Voluntary Service and the Salvation Army. They stepped in right at the start of the blitz when official bodies were found wanting; their distinctive uniforms were to be seen at every moment of crisis, helping and consoling. Here is a brief account of the two organisations, using the voices both of those who served and of those who benefited from the services.

The WVS

The WVS was founded in 1938, and by early 1940 had half a million members. 'Only capability counts,' said their formidable founder, Lady Reading. 'A titled woman is subordinate to a typist if the typist is the better worker.'

An unnamed WVS worker describes how they helped in the early days.

Inside the trench shelter, the older occupants gratefully thank WVS canteen girls who have defied the blitz to bring them their early morning cup of tea.

On Sunday morning, Sept 8th, we congregated at headquarters and telephoned to the centre organisations to stand by. Communications were bad but, as we anticipated, our warning was superfluous, for many of these faithful women had been up all night assisting the LCC in their gigantic task of accommodating the homeless ... Gradually news trickled through from the centres that extra mobile canteens, clothing and volunteers were urgently needed. Squads of women collected at HQ and were sent to answer the calls, accompanied by quantities of clothing. In most places [during the next weeks] our centres were working for 12 hours a day ...

By October Whitehall and the LCC had now to face reality; the blitz had come to stay and the emergency services for the homeless had to be overhauled and increased to compete with far larger numbers than hitherto expected ... Through the foresight of WVS headquarters, some boroughs had been provided with fully staffed mobile canteens which were never off the road, and as they had been able to prove their value, so the cry went up for more and more ...

The Reverend Markham confirms how their help was appreciated.

Among the many different services, I think that the Women's Voluntary Service deserves a special mention. Every night during the raids, they drove down to my post area, for instance, as they did for all others, carrying urns of tea or soup, to be distributed in the public shelters. My messenger, Jenner, used to tell me how he met girls in their vans at the edge of our area, to guide them round the various shelters. This often had to be done, while the bombs were falling around them. He remembered many times seeing incendiary bombs bounce off the bonnet of the van. They also provided much appreciated mobile canteens for the personnel working on a big incident. I do not know if any of those young women received medals, but I certainly think they deserved them.

And this passage, from *The Story of WVS Clothing* by Barbara Banks (1941).

The messenger boy gives a helping hand; Winchester Street, Pimlico, 6 June 1944.

Black with soot, or grey with dust from the rubble of fallen masonry, what little clothing they had dirty and torn, the people crowded the Rest Centres. The value of clothes in helping to restore morale was immeasurable. Within a few hours, the scenes of distress and confusion would be changed. Tidied up, dressed in warm clothing, the men would be ready to face the new day. Girls in neat frocks would have combed out their curls and powdered their noses. There was Mrs Ainger who, minus all her clothing had to be popped into bed in the sick bay at the Rest Centre ... Some clothes were found that pleased her very much; while one worker went away to change the dress that was too large, another helper produced a hat that really did take her fancy. All her resilience came to the surface. Dressed only in hat, vest, knickers and woolly bedroom slippers, she pirouetted gaily, singing snatches of cheerful songs. Outside in the dark street, her little home was wrecked; Rescue Squads were still trying to find bits of her friends, but for the moment she was released from her horror.

The Salvation Army

Helen Brett was a member of the Balham Corps in London.

I was one of a small team which went out every night of the blitz to the many shelters with pies and tea, and although none of us had a tin-hat not one of us was hurt, although shrapnel and bombs fell constantly near to us. At first, under the direction of a very caring Officer, Major Matthew White (who was often seen trundling along the road with replacement furniture for unfortunate bombed-out people), we had little equipment, but used what we had! Part of our 'effects' consisted of an old pram. On this we had to balance the urn — borrowed from the Home League (the Sisterhood) — it just, and only just, stretched across the top of the pram frame. Underneath it we had also borrowed cups and a large box of pies which we got each day from Walls. One night, going very gingerly along the pitch-dark blacked-out streets, we ran the pram into the kerb and there was an almighty

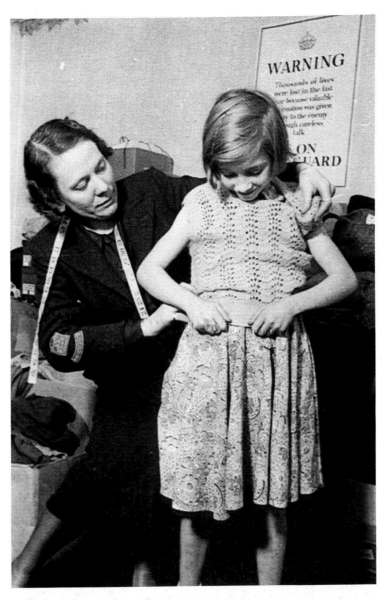

A WVS worker helps choose a jumper for a little girl whose home was destroyed the night before, and she lost all of her clothes. The British War Relief in the USA sends clothing to Britain.

crash as it overturned. On the instant whistles blew and from all directions tin-hatted wardens came rushing along calling out 'An incident . . . there's been an incident!'

The Salvation Army Hall in the High Road was open for people to take refuge and one night, when an unexploded bomb meant evacuation, we had many people sheltering in there. It was especially poignant to see a young mother on a stretcher, with her new-born baby, lying on the Mercy Seat which was reserved normally for people seeking special prayer, and which bore the words 'Room at the Cross'.

One night which was particularly heavy with anti-aircraft and the resounding thud of bombs, I had been giving tea and pies at the shelter on Tooting Common, having been dropped there earlier by van. I had to get back to Balham and a warden said he would take me. I therefore sat on his cross-bar as he cycled through the terrible noise, and he said placidly as I cringed in front of him 'This is nice, isn't it, we must do it again!'

The Salvation Army catering for children in London's underground.

George Woodhouse, the fireman, remembers them out in the middle of the great blitz of 10 May 1941.

When no. 23, Victoria Street came crashing down, I was one of a crew from 76x sub-station (Holloway) working in one of the adjoining streets. In the early morning hours we were wet, cold, tired, when we were approached by a fire service officer who told us there was a canteen van parked in Queen Victoria Street and if we went two at a time we could get a hot cup of tea. Imagine our surprise to find the van manned by two Salvation Army lasses who were handing out cups of tea and a biscuit as if it was a Sunday school picnic. They appeared to be completely unaware of the bombs falling around them. I have often wondered what the word courage meant, but on that night those two lasses had it in abundance.

Brigadier Winifred Hughes was based at the Greenwich Salvation Hall, which had an underground shelter.

The façade of the Salvation Army Headquarters at 23 Queen Victoria Street, Blackfriars, collapses in the aftermath of the heaviest attack of the entire blitz on 10 May 1941.

We had facilities for tea-making, so charged a penny for tea and biscuit each evening. And we took tea to the six cellars beneath the shops in the main street which had been turned into shelters. One night the warden came to ask me to break the news to a young woman that her husband had been killed. They had been married 18 months, so I went at about 2 am and stayed till about 4 until the all clear went. Before going home I offered a prayer for the now widowed young woman and felt God drew very near and blessed us all at such a sad time.

Another night a couple were bombed out and the warden brought them along to me. They had taken shelter in a brick shelter with others, which you had to knock so many bricks out of the side to get out – the door part was covered in debris from the houses. In less than two hours after, they were laughing about the woman, who was plump, getting stuck in the hole in the side and those outside trying to pull her through and those inside trying to push her out! The spirit and courage was remarkable in those days, of all the people in the blitz.

7.
LIVING WITH THE BLITZ

One seems to spend half one's time trying to buy a sack of coal because electricity has failed, or trying to put through telephone calls on a wire that has gone dead, or wandering about looking for a bus — and this is a miserably cold, slushy winter. The night life of London has almost ceased, not because of the bombs but because of the shrapnel, which is often plentiful enough to make it dangerous to go out after dusk. The movies close early and theatres have stopped altogether, except for a few matinees. Only the pubs are much as usual, in spite of the now enormous price of beer. On nights when the raids are bad the deafening racket of the guns makes it difficult to work. It is a time in which it is hard to settle down to anything and even the writing of a silly newspaper article takes twice as long as usual.

George Orwell, January 1941

If there was ever a time when one should wear life like a loose garment, this is it. I particularly admire the little tarts who wander about the streets of Mayfair every afternoon and evening in their finery. When everyone else is hurrying for the air-raid shelters, they are quite indifferent and continue to stroll undisturbed.

General Lee, 15 September 1940

Living with the blitz was never easy; though, as the two extracts above show, some coped better than others. Working, sleeping, travelling, shopping — all were rendered at best difficult, at worst impossible. Even the simplest habitual tasks of everyday life were affected. By mid-October

Housewives delivering their linen to a mobile laundry in the London area, April 1944.

1940, with sirens wailing all day and the nightly raid starting earlier each evening, Vera Brittain wrote that

when the all-clear sounds an hour before twilight, London's hot-water loving citizens make a swift and universal calculation: 'Can I get through my bath before the all-night siren goes?' Usually, in my own experience, one doesn't quite manage it; one is half dry when the familiar shriek echoes across the city, and lucky if one has reached the basement with one's cumbersome equipment before the bombs begin to fall.

Mrs Clara Milburn, a Midlands housewife whose published diaries are a delight, reveals another worry shared by many women of the time. On 3 October 1940 she wrote

On this day did hie me to the barber's and there did get my poll neatly trimmed. In other words, I have been bobbed! [We] set off about 10 am for Coventry, where, to the hairdresser's surprise, I said I would have my hair cut and permanently waved. Months ago I thought I should not like to be having a permanent wave if the sirens sounded in the middle of it — and that is exactly what happened!

This fear was played on by the manufacturers of Jamal, the 'Superlative Machineless Permanent' which promised 'perfect results in salon or shelter' without the risks associated with the traditional salon machine. But men had an even greater fear, that of sitting at the barber's, an open cut-throat razor inches from their throat, when the bombs began to fall. Two days after the start of the London blitz Orwell asked his barber if he carried on during raids. 'Oh yes, he carried on just the same. And one day a bomb will drop near enough to make him jump, and he will slice half somebody's face off', he thought.

The next month, on a sunny September morning, General Lee was being shaved in the barber's shop at Claridge's when the sirens started wailing.

Almost at once I heard a bomber overhead and had just started to remark that it had arrived undetected when the whistling scream of the descending bomb was evident. The barber fell flat on the floor and then as the first bomb went off and we heard another coming down, scrambled to his feet and shouted for me to come with him. With my face covered in lather I followed him into a strong niche or passageway at the end of the barber's shop, where we waited while a third bomb came down and went off. Then all was quiet, we emerged and he resumed shaving me. He had seemed so distraught at first that I wondered whether it was safe for him to wield the razor, and after he had finished I congratulated him on having such a steady hand. He held it out for a moment and contemplated it with satisfaction, for it did not waver in the least.

Such matters were of little concern to those who were children at the time, many of whom looked on the war as a great game. S.J. Davies, then a schoolboy in Felixstowe, writes that

With our parents at work all day and into the night, very little control was exercised over us kids.

Recreation for us during air raids was to get up the heath with the soldiers. My brother and I used to be engaged passing the clips of Bofors ammo to the gunners whilst firing at the aircraft, or getting it from the dumps to the guns; this activity was self-imposed, no one told us to, if it was our misfortune to be killed it would have been worth it, better to do something in retaliation than nothing at all.

The war could even reach the smallest of villages, including Great Wakening, near Southend, where Mr M. Smith lived as a youth.

We had a mine dropped just below the house. The pilot must have thought he was over the shipping lanes of the Thames. It was rather a misty morning. The plane went around two or three times then suddenly we heard the engines rev up and the swish of the mine descending and one almighty blast, dirt and rubbish flying everywhere. Stones whining their way overhead just like bullets out of a gun. My friend and I dived behind a hedge. It damaged a roof or two, but luckily it landed in a field.

Just below this field, a Heinkel 111 crashed with the occupants running hell for leather down the hill towards a farm. They sought refuge in a chicken shed, but were flushed out by the army. The airmen were put into an army truck. Disgusted at being caught, they tried to take it out on us who had gathered there to watch. They spat on us and shouted abuse, although they didn't expect stones, clumps of earth and grass to be thrown at them whilst in the back of the lorry. Anyway, while everybody was still busy with the intruders, I had a good look all over the Heinkel. What struck me first was the distinct smell of the interior. I sat in the pilot's seat, pressing these rather large fat pedals. I did take something from the plane; what it was I've no idea, but I hid it by the pond, and never did retrieve it.

All around our seawalls we had a 15-yard minefield, about 10 miles of it. To get across one had to follow the tapes, but my grandfather got blown up by them. A young lad a few doors away threw a big wooden stake onto a mine, but alas it came back faster than he imagined, and entered his stomach — fatal of course. When they were laying the mines we used to unscrew the detonators, take out the explosives, put it in a hole in one of the trees and put a match to it. We must have been mad.

It was not only boys who were fascinated by the war. Beryl Bainbridge, the novelist (then a little girl of seven), used to spend long solitary hours in the pine woods of Formby, up the coast from Liverpool, playing war games.

You couldn't just go to Woolworth's and get toys in those days so I made my own gun. My father was quite proud of it. It was like a wooden rifle, with another bit of wood at the front for the barrel and a piece of knicker elastic at the top on a nail with a cork on the end, cos my father was a traveller in corks. So that when you pulled the trigger you let go of the cork and it snapped out on the elastic and went off like a bullet.

I also had another huge piece of driftwood. I tied a piece of string round it and that was my dog, 'Blaze'.

There was so much time to play after school, with it being double summer time. I'd go out barefoot, then cross the road to where I kept my brother's old cast-off trousers hidden in some bushes, take my gymslip off and change into the trousers. Then I'd be away, dragging the dog in one hand, with my rifle in the other, and I'd hide behind little hillocks and just go 'Bang! Bang!' at anything in sight; hour after hour, it was lovely. I used to go all through the pine woods, which were pitted with bomb craters, past great notices saying 'Keep out' because of the unexploded bombs, then down to the shore, which was covered with rolls of barbed wire. And it was littered with exciting objects washed up from all the ships which had been sunk. I didn't worry about the signs, I'd just wriggle under the wire or walk round the end of it and see what I could find. I'll always remember the log books, great saturated ships' log books, I'd pick up. And I once found half a horse, all bloated; I don't know which end it was, it can't have been the top end, I'd remember that. Then a big green ammunition tin I still have.

Squadron Leader R.F. Bullers, whose house in Blackheath was damaged when a bomb hit next door, explains that for someone of his age

there was a tremendous interest to investigate, to find out what had happened. It was all new experience for me and perhaps in my youth I was unable to concede 'that it would never happen to me'. Perhaps it was a feeling of fatalism. For many years in the war I believed there could never be a future, another way of life from the one we were leading — that we should always be at war and that there was no point in planning for tomorrow.

It may have been this feeling of fatalism that led some children deliberately to court danger. Many of them certainly were, in the words of Helen Sandys, 'completely war-minded'. Helen, a Wren stationed at Dover in 1943, noted in her diary on 27 November that

The main entertainment is playing 'soldiers' in the street. Very realistic actions round a telephone box — armed with toy machine guns — accompanied by the appropriate noises, these youngsters, sometimes three year olds, tear up and down 'shooting' each other — the victim, with much groanings and clutchings, then falls to the ground ... one couldn't help but wonder what sort of a future these little kids have got. It is bound to have a great effect on their later life.

Beryl Bainbridge, looking back, is not surprised that she and the other children of her generation were war-minded.

If you're very small and all you hear is people talking about bombs and who's dead, you do become morbid about most things. That's all we ever really talked about. It's nonsense to say that children hardly knew the war was on. I think that

239

boys and girls were totally immersed in the war; and enjoyed it.

Children were often just left to their own devices. Most fathers were away and the women too tired after an exhausting day to pay much attention.

Mrs Keene remembers the long journeys into central London.

The District Line became at times a nightmare, we would be on the train for a long while due to disruptions. If we got a seat we were lucky and then out came the knitting and needlework. In fact, it became competitive, because the same people seemed to occupy the same carriage, and we would watch each other and try to get ahead of each other or buy a more complicated pattern. Eventually some of us took up smoking (Wills Weights), which were awful, but it was understandable as the journey to and fro got worse ... The man in charge of our office, Mr Thornton, was so thoughtful to us, always in the winter evenings he insisted we left together, sometimes there were as many as six; he would accompany us down to Blackfriars station with the aid of a hand torch, just a small hole in the centre showing. We were glad of this, because walking through some of the alleys from Ludgate Hill to Blackfriars station was an experience we could well do without.

On occasions we would learn that Covent Garden or another market near Holborn, or Leadenhall Street Market, would have fruit for sale, so two of us at a time would be allowed to go and queue. This was disastrous as on one occasion a land mine was dropped and the two girls were killed along with a large number of people, so from then on we were forbidden to go out during office hours. We had our own shelter below the building ... so that W.R. Royle could keep their business open ... in the basement were emergency beds and emergency food supplies (also rats), very little in the way of toilet facilities and often there was no plumbing at all. I know we kept using the toilet basins and the smell was awful, but somehow and at some time they got emptied. We never had any heating in the winter and office duties were done wearing all our outdoor clothes and mittens used for typing ... the telephone switchboard was a 10-line one with cords that you plugged in, and you wore headphones. It was often out of use because of the bombing.

We continued going up and down to the city for the first 18 months and just accepted treading over the hose pipes and rubble, seeing bodies covered over and buildings demolished. The continual drone of aircraft and guns just seemed to go on and on.

Another Londoner who often had trouble getting home was Mrs Crook.

One night, as usual, the searchlights were moving around the sky, an air raid was in progress. I had fled into the tube at St Paul's, stepping over the bodies asleep on the various platforms. Having made my way to Holborn I managed to get the last train to Manor House. Now it meant waiting to get a bus, if a bus could get there — or a nice long walk. It was a very dark night, no vehicle was even lit except for a tiny slit of light at the front and rear. All windows were boarded up. There were about 20 people waiting around, all hoping for some transport or other. Suddenly in the darkness, the outline of a taxi. The driver, who of course I could not see, shouted 'anyone going towards Edmonton?' I thought it was a move in the right direction, I would have to walk the rest, so I hopped in. The cab was empty I thought, the darkness impenetrable. There were no more takers and the cab moved off. Suddenly a man's voice said 'Good evening, where have you been?' I froze. Peering in the far corner, I could see a military uniform. 'Have you enjoyed your evening out?' he enquired. I was tired and hot and a little fed up with having to struggle home on my late duties; my husband of a few months in France or somewhere; our armies taking a terrific bashing; nothing but darkness, rationing, air raids, running from shelter to shelter; and he was asking me if I had enjoyed my night out! After going through the whole saga of misery in my brain I managed to tell him I had just left work in telecommunications and was fed up to the teeth with this war. He assured me that it would not last much longer as long as we kept our chins up and kept going. When we reached Tottenham, he got out of the cab. The driver said he would go another mile or two but the big guns started firing again and the searchlights crossing the sky, and a little further down the road at the Angel Edmonton the cab driver stopped and said that now it was getting too bad, he wanted to go home to his wife and family, and did I mind walking the rest? On offering to pay him I was told the serviceman had paid my fare and had asked the cabby to take me as far as he could. I always wished I could thank that soldier.

Norah Turner didn't have so far to travel, but her hours were even longer.

I worked a 52-hour week, plus overtime when we were extra busy, at a local factory in the East End for such a meagre wage that we had little energy or resources to 'live it up' in our spare time, and a Saturday night in the cheapest seats at the cinema was the highlight of our social calendar.

At the beginning the war held the promise of the unknown, change, excitement and adventure. The gas mask fittings were a giggle, and many jokes went the rounds when men began digging deep pits in our back-yards for the Anderson shelters. Seeing little kids being sent away from their parents into the safety of the country, and brothers, sisters and friends called up for the forces, age group by age group, took much of the frivolity out of the 'adventure', and the blitz washed away the last vestiges of our romanticising. Life became a dreary round of going to work, more or less straight from the shelter, spending a large part of the day in transit between the work-bench and the shelters (four storeys down), then home, before the sirens went if we were lucky, to a hasty meal before de-camping to the Anderson for the nightly incarceration. Hearing bombs whistling down, the rumble of buildings collapsing, the shattering of blasted windows, while the skies were lit with a red glow of fires, was a terror to be disguised, and endured, night after night, as we tried to sleep on the mattress-covered floor of the corrugated iron shelter in the yard, which felt just about as secure as a tent in a field full of rampant bulls!

Beryl Mullins worked at Coutts and Co. in 440 The Strand, travelling up from Eltham Park to Charing Cross station every day.

Whenever there was a raid, after the all clear, my mum would phone the bank — fortunately there was always a reply — she'd put the receiver down without speaking. I wonder how many other mothers did that? We lost all, no most, of our windows at home, and once when our front door was only just holding on to its hinges, the lock had blown off, Mum came back into the cellar where we slept saying 'We'll be OK, I've stood a chair by the door. Nobody will get in.' I didn't remind her they could just step in the window. Not that there were anyone else around to come in! We seemed to be the only house that was occupied for streets around. One particularly horrid night when stuff seemed to be dropping all over the place, Mum disappeared up the cellar steps — I thought she'd gone to the loo. She came back a few minutes later. 'Everything will be all right now,' she said, 'I've got my corsets on!'

Life was no easier in the provinces. Edna Smith (who later became a gunner in a mixed AA regiment) worked as a clippie in Birmingham.

I loved it and thought I was great, my hat on the side of my head, with curls pinned all down the side with hair-grips. I learnt to stand without holding while the bus went along and could run upstairs and not feel out of breath. Then the bombing started and B'ham was being bombed mostly every night. We were told we had to run the bus all the time if people were on it, even during an air raid. When it got really bad we would pull up at the nearest air-raid shelter and go down ... what a sight, people everywhere, some sleeping on the floor, men playing cards, people singing, everyone didn't seem to care. There we would be, me and the driver sitting there, me with my money-bag round my neck. We always managed to get a cup of tea, then the warden would come down and say 'all clear', off we would go. I would call out, 'Anyone for the Bull Ring' (the market place) — on they would get, happy, singing, grateful I think that the all clear had gone . . .

When the bombing was very bad you could leave your bus near the depot and go home with your money, and pay it in the next day — also you couldn't take the trolley buses into the depot because of the head arms flashing while going in . . . some days you would go out and couldn't get past all the water-hoses blocking the road.

After that we spent lots of time down air-raid shelters and it was a relief to get a day shift; at least I could spend the evening and night in our own shelter with Mum, who was very worried.

Another Birmingham resident, Michael Longmore, was able to spend all his nights in the family shelter; but then he was only six at the beginning of the war. At first they used their cellar as a shelter, but then were issued with an Anderson. He describes it as

a standard corrugated steel shelter which was half buried by the family in the garden such that the bottom of the entrance hole was just level with the surface of the ground. Then earth was piled on top to afford extra protection. Following that, an earth wall was added to the entrance to act as a bomb blast deflector. Sacking or old pieces of rug (not carpeting, that was definitely middle class) were then hung over the entrance hole. The earth base of the shelter would then be about 3 feet below the natural level of the garden. There always seemed to be the obligatory 2 inches of water to avoid.

Every night, it seemed, following the rising and falling wail of the alert sirens, my family, consisting of mother, father, grandmother and uncle (mother's brother) would get out of their beds, throw on top coats and stagger and stumble out to the bottom of the back garden where the air-raid shelter was.

The whole of the sky would be illuminated by the criss-cross beams of searchlights and I could never understand where these came from. We would clamber down into the shelter by means of a sawn-down piece of old ladder provided by a local window cleaner. Once inside the shelter we would sit on old stools and wooden crates or boxes around the sides of the shelter. We would pass our time playing cards by candlelight, and because of my uncle's thick spectacles I could read his cards reflected in the lenses. The game was 'knockout' and I became quite good at it.

It was very cramped and the heat of our bodies would soon condense on the curved arch of the galvanised corrugated roof and run down the corrugated steel walls. The structure was held together by red-oxide-painted angle irons running round the middle and bottom of the shelter and fastened with large nuts and bolts and square washers. This part particularly sticks in my mind because of the light provided by candles. All of the time there was an immense amount of noise from a mixture of exploding bombs and various anti-aircraft guns pounding away. In the brief pauses between explosions we could hear the noise of aeroplanes. It was a common belief that the enemy planes could be distinguished by the alternating droning of their engines whereas our planes had a steady hum to them. It all seemed very normal.

The Latchfords in Swansea had already worked out a sheltering routine, almost military in its precision, by June 1940.

Before going to bed, the fireplace in the kitchen is closed and covered with newspapers. The kitchen table is pushed into the corner and overlaps the fireplace a little. A groundsheet is then spread underneath the table and a blanket and some cushions follow. A mattress is then pushed out on to the table top. Games, sweets, paper and pencil and first aid box are collected in an old shoe box. The shelter is completed by pushing the heavy gas-washer on one open side, and an old-fashioned pedestal folding card table on the other. A pail of water is to one side. On going to bed, unless a raid is in progress, a torch, a candle, a box of matches and my false teeth are placed under the bed, and a small case which holds the insurance papers, and another shoe box containing valuables, Essie's asthma powder, matches, and all our cash are put on the small table at Essie's side. All clothes are folded neatly on a chair near the owner's bed in the order of putting on, including shoes and stockings.

While another family, the Barratts in London, seem to have made their shelter even cosier than the house.

We made [it] from very strong timber and of course got no condensation, which was one of the problems of the Andersons. We had Li-Lo beds for our two-tier system of bunks capable of taking my mother and father, my sister when she was at home on leave, and myself — and a little bit of space in the middle for our Alsatian dog, who always succeeded in beating us down to the shelter. There was a supply of water and a few tins just in case the house did go up. We had electric light and a point for a Pifco toasting machine for either a bit of toast and dripping at night or boiling a kettle, and also it kept the shelter nice and warm. We had a radio and books and generally we had a comfortable time ... It was warmer often than in the house because in those days the houses weren't centrally heated ... but we found that once you got into the shelter, shut the door, a nice cosy atmosphere existed and we were all very happy.

Beryl Bainbridge's mother would have loved a shelter like that. Their Anderson just filled up with water and the local communal shelter in the back field was only tried out once or twice by the family, rather to young Beryl's regret.

We had that very yellow sandy soil; there were boards laid against it, but there were little gaps, you could pick away at it and the sand would trickle down, it was rather nice. And there was a lovely smell about the shelter in a way; later it was cat pee and stuff, but at one time it was just that nice soily smell, mixed up with ciggy smoke and candles. But my mother stopped us going into the shelters; 'They weren't nice people, a bit common.' In fact my mother didn't like the ordinary brown paper that people stuck over their windows, that was common, too. She painted ours black so that it looked like leaded patterns across the brown bits.

When sheltering with neighbours some people felt they had to make a special effort. Marion Talbot tells us of a Miss Harding, an elderly lady who used to share the family shelter in Forest Gate.

My father used to fetch her from home and help her down the rather steep steps. She was a lady of some substance and great dignity. Each time she came she was dressed immaculately, as if for making a social call or taking afternoon tea, and once established she would sit upright and seemingly unflustered throughout the raid. Most people let their hair down on these occasions but she always maintained her dignity.

So too did the people in the store where Mary Palmer (later a firewoman) was working at the start of the Bristol blitz.

It was a large, long-established ladies' outfitters and draper's with exclusive customers. When the siren went, we all filed down into the cellar, but the customer/assistant relationship had to be preserved so all the staff sat on one side of the cellar and the customers on the opposite! We usually took our knitting with us and made quite a few comforts — gloves, balaclavas, helmets, etc.

Few public shelters would have been so cosy. Many of them, as the Reverend Markham explains, were erected in great haste during the phoney war period.

They were mainly meant to be used by flat-dwellers, who had no Anderson shelters. They were originally built very rapidly out of brick and lime mortar, their walls sitting unkeyed on to the concrete of the railways or pavements, and topped by a slab of reinforced concrete about 9 inches thick, which was

A street in Islington showing a row of houses demolished by a flying bomb. The street shelters stand intact.

also unkeyed by any reinforcing to the walls. Later on, these were known to us as 'the Morrison sandwiches' shelters, because in the actual blitz, too often the blast of a bomb would suck the walls outwards and the concrete top would sandwich the occupants to the ground. Eventually they had to be strengthened with reinforcing in the walls and down into the concrete base.

In addition to these street shelters, two more public shelters in our area were provided. One was a smallish underground shelter near the Walworth Road shops, the other was constructed out of the basements of unfinished flats which had only reached ground level. They were cellar-like rooms, down rather steep stairs, with little ventilation and very thin concrete roofs, intended as floors for the ground-floor flats. There was no form of heating and they were damp; but they did eventually house some 5,000 shelterers, and were a constant problem.

As well as my crypt there was the recreation ground shelter, where there was no water except for one standpipe in the open playground above, necessitating endless journeys up the steep stairs from below to get cans of water for the thirsty children and their parents. Likewise there were a few

Elsan closets behind sacking curtains in cubby holes off the narrow trench-like passages, where the 9-inch-deep wooden benches were so close to the opposite ones that the knees of the shelterers almost touched. During the raids, the parents of small babies had to bed them down on the concrete floor under their benches. Mrs Jackson often tore up sheeting to make nappies for the babies, when supplies ran out during the 12 hours that some spent down here in the height of the bombing.

I hardly ever went down into the crypt shelter during raids, unless I was needed for some problems. When I did so, I had to tread delicately between the bodies of the shelterers, lying like sardines on a variety of beds, mattresses, blankets or old carpets which they brought down with them. Some sat in deck-chairs, some lay on the narrow wooden benches provided by the borough. The stench from overflowing Elsan closets and unwashed humanity was so great that we had to buy gallons of Pine Fluid, the odour of which I cannot abide to this day. The shelter wardens had a whip round among their flock to buy electric fans, which did stir the foetid air a trifle, giving an illusion of freshness. I suppose you can get used to those sorts of conditions if you stay in them for 12 hours, night after night. At least one family of parents and young children stayed down there almost 24 hours, rather than go home and risk losing their place. Places were as precious to the regulars as seats in some theatres, so that queues formed outside hours before the siren wailed, and I had to provide wardens to regulate the flow of would-be shelterers, some of whom came from some distance, even by taxi

When one of the shelters developed scarlet fever, the borough health officer promptly forbade us to allow more than the official number of 230 in the crypt the following night. I refused to put the burden of dealing with the 400 or so who would have to be excluded on the shoulders of my wardens, and told the authorities that the police would have to be responsible. That evening, two burly sergeants and six constables were sent to regulate the intake. By physical force during two hours, they were able to keep about 100 shelterers outside the churchyard gates, which they chained. Naturally, this crowd did not take this treatment lightly. The warning went; the police returned at once to the Carter Street Police Station; the crowd broke open the gates, and piled pell-mell into the already crowded shelter, causing much more confusion than would have been present if we had been allowed to fill the shelter methodically with the regular shelterers.

That the 'Morrison sandwich' shelters were far from safe is confirmed by John Freestone, who lived not far from the Reverend Markham's parish.

One evening when I was 15 and my friend, Dickie Faulkner, 14, and Bert Mail nearly 16, there was a heavy raid on and we were nearing Vauxhall Street when there was an explosion. A man came along with two children, one on each arm, he was very distressed. 'Go and help please, boys, they have just hit the shelter in Orsett House.'

We came upon a scene of destruction, a large part of the concrete roof had fallen in on the people. We started to get the women and children out first, but the task was too much, we couldn't shift some of the concrete laying on people. There was no other rescue team there at that time, there was pandemonium everywhere, when it occurred to one of us that there was a heavy rescue unit in Vauxhall Street school opposite my home in Malmsey House. Bert stayed behind to help the dazed and bewildered people while we rushed to the school where the duty men were playing darts and drinking, etc. We told them what had happened, they said 'Sorry son, we have to get it official.' One man did come with us and he rushed back and soon everybody was there helping, and ambulances arrived, and we gave a sigh of relief. Bert Mail had come across his aunt and young cousin, both dead, but his eldest cousin lived as she had just gone upstairs to the flat to make a drink when the bomb dropped.

We made our separate ways home, dead beat, filthy and needing a clean up and a cup of tea. We were too young to drink. We didn't belong to any rescue unit, we were our own elite force of three young working boys who had to go to work the next day.

With such buildings evidently unsafe, many people looked for alternative places to shelter. Railway arches were a popular choice, the most notorious being the Tilbury Arches in Stepney. Nina Hibbin went there on behalf of Mass Observation and can still remember the shock of her first visit.

It was like the black hole of Calcutta. People should not have had to put up with those conditions in addition to the hell of bombing. When my eyes adjusted to the gloom inside all you could see was thousands upon thousands of motionless people lying on the ground head to toe, knee to buttock, without a pinhead of space between them. Some were even sleeping on boxes of margarine and piles of rubbish ... and the stench was nauseating. Dung left by the horses in the daytime was trodden into a huge layer of litter, discarded food and children's urine. The only lavatory facilities were a row of six buckets for a shelter population of about 12,000.

Considerably more salubrious were the caves at Chislehurst — several miles of passageways with a series of larger spaces up to 20 foot square. The caves were owned by a Mr Gardiner, who used them to grow mushrooms. At first it was just locals who went there, but within a few weeks of the start of the blitz word had spread to the East End and people began pouring in. They were charged a ha'penny a night, later 6d a week, which Mr Gardiner used for improvements. The younger men and women travelled to work daily, getting up around 5 am.

Mr Gardiner organised matters well, appointing 'captains' to be in charge of between 50–200 people each. Ashbins were used as toilets, with donkeys carting them away for dumping. The local district council and central government took joint control from the beginning of November 1940, by which time some 8,000 were using the caves, with hundreds locked outside pleading to be let in. Jill Lewis, a child at the time, remembers it well.

At first it was almost like being back in the caves in the Stone

Age days. The smell down there was really pretty grim you know, you'd got all the people, you couldn't wash. After a while we started to get improvements; we had electric light installed, we had canteens where you could go and get a cup of tea, penny a cup, which was really good tea. We had cinemas, a dance hall, the children's cinema. It was nice, and we had bunks to sleep in. And there was a children's chapel down there that we used to go to every Sunday morning, really used to look forward to that, we used to have a lovely service, sing hymns altogether, and it was quite the event of the week really for all us children. In fact it was like a city under the ground really.

Charlie Draper only knew the caves after they had been transformed.

When I first came down, I was amazed. It was like a city under the ground. I found my Gran, and she's saved me a bunk. They had two tier bunks, and they was sort of a luxury then, and she's saved me one. So I put my blanket and my pillow out, and put me tools under the bed, and I said I'm going to have a roam round, and I went up a few caves and found there was a dance hall, and there was an old piano where people was sitting there having a sing-song, and outside that there was a cinema the other side of the cave. And the tea room was sort of a couple of tables, where the WVS used to work on, they were selling pies and sandwiches and cakes, and you could get a cup of tea for a penny. And then further along was the hospital where the children was learnt to line up to get their cough mixture and that sort of thing, give them a sweet if they would take their cough mixture. And further on there was a little chapel, and on a Sunday I used to go by the chapel and see the kids all singing away, hymns and that sort of thing. And there was a bit of luxury, they even put in wash rooms, and facilities, like men's and women's toilets and that sort of thing. So it was quite nice. I enjoyed it.

Even the mass shelters back in London improved in time,

initially through the efforts of the people who used them rather than from any initiative on the part of the authorities. Nina Hibbin again:

One afternoon the air-raid siren went when a huge crowd was waiting to get into the Tilbury. There was panic as the crowd surged forward to get inside, and a child was trampled to death in the stampede. The Shelter Campaign Committee which had been formed to try to improve the conditions for the shelterers immediately drew up a list of demands, for things like tickets for shelterers, so that this sort of thing wouldn't happen again. I remember there were about 50 of them and they went to the local ARP headquarters to put their case. When they got there they were told to wait outside and the director would come and speak to them. But he never came. Instead the mounted police charged them; they were slashing their batons to the right and left knocking people down, sending the young and the old flying. Anyone who protested was beaten with truncheons. I was so horrified I rang up the *Daily Express* news desk. 'It's news all right', said the night editor, 'but we can't touch it. Morale and all that.' He hung up.

But it was the beginning of a better and more organised Tilbury shelter, which did eventually become a kind of model shelter, but it took that much anger and that much organisation to get things done.

At the other end of London a very active shelterers' committee was set up early in the blitz. Mr D. Silverman, who was involved from the beginning, explained that

conditions in the air-raid shelters deteriorated and became very disorganised. That prompted me to start a newspaper in one air-raid shelter in Swiss Cottage underground station; this I did mostly as campaigning, also as a link between the shelters, and it did produce some results and bunks were installed, tickets were issued and so everything became regularised. It was published in November 1940 and opened with ... 'A battle is being fought in the station, a battle against

Some of the worst conditions for shelterers were in overcrowded tube stations such as Piccadilly Circus.

shameful apathy, indifference amounting almost to callousness, neglect, soulless contempt for elementary human decencies. The *Swiss Cottager* is against red tape, authority, [and] officialdom.'

It was the people who, whether by direct action or lobbying, brought about immediate improvements in shelter conditions. The authorities showed their concern from early on, but often failed to react as quickly as the people would have wanted.

Gradually, tube-sheltering became an accepted way of life, with lines drawn on platforms to separate the shelterers from actual travellers. Charlie Draper, a young teenager in 1940, remembers how things improved.

I don't know about storming the underground, but you had to be there early for your pitch. I would take my pillow and blanket down the Oval and sit and wait till it was quiet, then lay out my blanket on the platform. My dad and grandfather would come down later and I would save them a space. Attempts by the authority was only porters or station masters who would stop you laying out your blanket too early. Later they even put bunks in the passages and you could sleep in them. I used to take a shopping bag with me to the Oval, a pencil and a piece of paper. Once I had my spot laid out about 9 o'clock, I would go round asking the old people if they wanted anything in the pub. They would give me the money for some light ales, brown ales or stout. I would make my way up to the entrance where there was always a warden or a special PC. They would tell me if it was quiet. If so I would nip round and get the drinks. If it was noisy they would send me down again.

The bunks started appearing from mid-December 1940, and by April 1941 some 600,000 had been provided. On 1 March George Orwell noted that

The Tube stations don't now stink to any extent, the new metal bunks are quite good, and the people one sees there are reasonably well found as to bedding and seem contented and normal in all ways — but this is just what disquiets me. What is one to think of people who go on living this subhuman life night after night for months, including periods of a week or more when no aeroplane has come near London?

Not near London, perhaps, but certainly elsewhere in the UK. During the period 19 February to 12 May 1941 there were 61 raids involving 50 or more aircraft, only seven of them on London (though these included The Wednesday and The Saturday, it must not be forgotten — see next chapter). The majority were on the great ports, as well as on Birmingham and Coventry. But smaller towns received their share, too — Gloucester, Yeovil, Hythe, Poole, Folkestone, Shanklin, Ipswich, Norwich, even Fair Isle. These places had no underground railway system, and their surface shelters were certainly no better than those of London (in some cases rather worse). What, then, were they able to do?

Sylvia Cooke, six years old at the time of the main raids on Plymouth, recalls being able to use a tunnel hewn through a quarry on the edge of a nearby village.

The children slept on old settees and camp beds. I have a vivid memory of a candle stuck in a niche and a damp course with water trickling down the rock face beside my bed. Many hours were spent in the tunnel, and after I'd been hauled out of bed, and dressed quickly in a siren suit, my father or mother would carry me across a couple of fields to the tunnel, often to the accompaniment of gunfire and the sound of aircraft overhead. The local vicar would conduct a service there on Sunday evenings. After all, if the village people were afraid to walk up the hill to the church, he thought it better to join them in the tunnel! The hymns were accompanied by the local sub-postmistress on a piano-accordion, and the singing always seemed very loud to me. On May Day, a lady from the village dressed up as the May Queen, and danced through the tunnel and back again.

In Bristol, according to John H. Smith, the old port and pier railway tunnel was used.

It was a sorry sight, men, women and children huddled together sleeping on mattresses, planks or straw. Some had corrugated iron sheets or old pieces of sacking and canvas placed overhead to catch the water that dripped from the rocky roof of the tunnel. The air was thick with the fumes of oil stoves, oil lamps and various odours of cooking food. Some had stopped until closing time at the local public houses before coming to the shelters. When the corporation employees opened the doors in the mornings the stench and fumes came from within like a fog. It was a picture of Dante's Inferno. Many of the people were nervous wrecks. People stayed in the tunnel by day, afraid to lose their places. Many were young people. There was hardly any room between the rough beds. Some performed their natural functions alongside the beds. It was unbelievable that people could be driven by fear to endure such conditions. The authorities had to step in and clear the place out in the end. It nearly required an armed party to persuade some young fellows to leave.

The battered people of Dover, subjected to constant tip-and-run attacks as well as bombardment from the coast of occupied France, were also able to take refuge underground. Helen Sandys paid her first visit to any public shelter when stationed in Dover in November 1943. Next day she wrote in a letter:

I shall never forget it to my dying day — the sight of these old men, and women, and young children sitting there. We were at the end of a tunnel dug into the cliff. On one side of the tunnel there were double-decker bunks, on the other a bench. Some of the people of Dover were already installed in the bunks, rather like those in the underground stations. Small children came in alone, or in the charge of a girl of about 12. The unsavoury atmosphere was dreadful. As there is no current of air, you can imagine what it was like, when slept in, night after night by those with no homes, and little facilities for washing. Rather like a rabbit hutch. We were the only people in uniform. Sitting next to me was an old lady, shrivelled and sunken, very frail, and all alone. She was sitting there just staring ahead of her — waiting. I noticed that her right arm hung rather limp on her lap. She had no hand. It was severed at the wrist! A little later her two grandsons came and joined her, two little Dover toughs. A sight like that one cannot easily forget or forgive.

But few provincial cities or towns offered tunnels or caves for the shelterers. For those unwilling to stay and face the bombers the solution was what came to be known as 'trekking'; just getting as far away from the bombs as possible each night. It affected all the blitzed provincial cities, and here are just a few representative accounts. John H. Smith describes what happened in Bristol.

Often the warning siren sounded at about six in the early evening and lasted right through the night. People began moving out of the town for the night, sleeping in cars, huts, tents in the country. It was a sight to remember; crowds of people in cars leaving by exit roads. In the morning the ARP activities were much hampered as the roads were often jammed with people returning to the town.

Norman Ellison, while home on leave in Liverpool, noted that

Every afternoon thousands of people left the densely-populated areas of Merseyside to spend the night in the surrounding countryside, sleeping under hedges, in barns, etc., returning early next morning to work. An hour before dusk families could be seen trekking with their bedding to shelters in the underground railway stations at James Street and Central. At first they slept on the bare boards of the platform, but later three-tier bunks were erected.

The Waller family had rented a room in an old farmhouse near Plymouth. Barbara Waller recalls that

down in the farm kitchen there was a row of chairs against the wall where exhausted people used to come during the blitz and hire a chair for the night while their poor city was being flattened. The farmer's wife kept a big black cauldron over the fire and once a day we bought a meal from it. I remember pieces of black flesh being doled out — what it was I have no idea, but we were hungry and gobbled it up.

Betty Wilson, then a teenager, was one of those Plymouth trekkers in 1941.

When we were all weary and sad at the loss of our friends and neighbours, my mother and I decided we would take a bus out to Yelverton, a village about 7 miles out of Plymouth. We took blankets and newspaper, intending to do as many others had done, to sleep in the hedge, anything to get out of Plymouth. It was open country, cold, silent, and the Dartmoor ponies roaming about snorting at us all. There was a raid that night, and we could hear the guns pounding out all they had, the planes going over seemed endless. There were search-lights everywhere, and besides picking out the *Luftwaffe*, they were also lighting up the fight tactics between both sides; it was awful, frightening, but very real. We all wondered what devastation we should see when we returned by bus later. The bus was full when it got to us, and no other for 1½ hours, so we all started the long walk at 7.15 am.

Another night six of us went with pillows, blankets, etc., in a borrowed dockyard lorry. It was raining and we huddled under cardboard pieces, umbrellas or sheets until we arrived at a farm in Widecombe-in-the-Moor to a brother-in-law's family, cold, wet and bedraggled. We had soup and then up to the empty barn, shone our torches and some oil lamps and the bats zoomed around us. Terror struck us all, and we got our beds laid out as quick as we could and put the lights out. The bats settled ... gradually we all dozed off ... but a scream woke us all up. It was a friend who felt something scratching on her blanket. It was a rat ... we all shone torches ... which attracted the bats, and there were rats running everywhere. The lorry had to be back in the dockyard by 8 am. We didn't get much sleep and wondered how much more of this could we take.

We stayed home for three nights, a couple of hours' sleep, then it was up again, shove on slacks, jumper, dressing gown, coats, socks and shoes, get gas masks and little case with complete change of clothes in it and run like hell to the shelter. 'Boom, boom, bang bang bang', whistles, whining bombs, voices shouting, the big guns pounding out shells on the waste ground opposite our house, a plane caught in crossed searchlights and all hell had broke loose on the ground — suddenly it was hit and disintegrated, a sickening sight as bits flew everywhere amid the smoke. We all wondered where the bits and pieces would land. Soon it was morning and we all went into our house to breakfast and some to go to school and some to work. I had a job now, but I was so tired the movement of the bus made me nod off. Only because my head went to one side and a person knocked it did I wake up in time for my stop. Others were asleep I noticed.

Mary Joy Miller arrived as a young bride to join her soldier husband in Belfast the morning after the Easter Tuesday blitz.

I was very scared as the ship trailed into the lough between a line of buoys. We seemed to be holding our breaths as we all stood on the decks. Fires were burning round the docks. When we arrived at our digs in Cave Hill we were amazed to find the doors open and no one in the house and the roof was off. We slept the night there and then we went to the police again. We found no one in the streets and written in chalk or white paint was this message in large letters — 'THIS WAY TO THE HILLS' — on the pavements. The police told us everyone had fled and dumped their house keys on them, so we chose to stay at one house near where my husband was on duty.

The family of Mrs G. Smyth, then a little girl of six, were among those who fled Belfast, and her written account makes us understand why they did so.

Every night before we went to sleep I had to take all my books out of my school bag, Mum wanted it for to put the death policies in and a few sandwiches, just in case Jerry paid us a visit and we would have to flee. The air-raid shelters were not built then, and we lived near the large linen mills, so every night Jerry tried for the mills — he missed them, hit bottom of our street, cleared almost 30 houses. When all clear went, we went to see what damage was done, I remember air-raid warden finding some of our neighbours dead. Her son, who was in Navy uniform, had his arms round his mum. They say they had to break his arms to separate the bodies. I think the sister was lying dead beside them. We had what was called the coal hole; it was a place under the stairs. We cleared all the coal out of it and slept in. Dad whitewashed the coal hole — put blankets in, a candle, so during the raids we hid in the coal hole. Then the bombing was coming regular so we took to the fields. This was called bone fields. One night sirens went, so it was Mum, school bag, May and me. Dad did not go, he stayed behind to put the fires out and help. I tried to tell my Mum I only had one shoe on. She kept saying you're OK, not far to go now, hurry in case planes come. When we got to the fields it was everyone huddled together. Mum says where is your shoe? I says 'You never put it on, Mum.' We had an undertaker near us called Wiltons. It got hit with bomb, all the horses broke out, they ran wild in our street, the smoke rising from their bodies and red hot flesh. Mum said she thought she would send us to a friend's in the country, thought we would be safer there. I did not like it. Mum and Dad came by bus every weekend to see us. I used to sit on our friends' step waiting on the bus coming. My Mum would bring me down my favourite pork sausages. I liked the big fat ones. I told Mum after a few weeks I was not happy here, so she brought us back home. That weekend our street again was hit bad. Street was flooded out, all gas pipes were ripped out, we had to put railway sleepers from footpath to our side to get across road. We lived near the picture house. Jerry hit it one night. After all clear we went and saw that the billboard of the picture house was hanging by a thread. It said 'Now showing,

Mother Riley Takes The Air'. Everyone was laughing they said Mother Riley did not half take the air last night.

Some of those who stayed despised the trekkers, and Sammy McBride, then 13, remembers seeing on a Belfast wall the chalked message

> Be a man, not a mouse,
> come from the hills and defend your house!

To which had been added in another hand

> Be a mouse, not a man,
> you can't put explosives out with sand!

It is not our intention to discuss the comparative merits of leaving or staying put. (But it is worth drawing attention to the evidence, carefully set out by Tom Harrisson in *Living Through The Blitz*, that among the trekkers in some places were various local officials who should have felt duty bound to stay.) What must be said, however, is that the vast majority of trekkers made strenuous efforts to get to their places of work the following morning. Of course many would have lost pay had they not done so; nevertheless it is clear that the people of the blitz towns — stayers and trekkers alike — showed great determination, rebuffing the attempts of the *Luftwaffe* to disrupt industrial production and instil a spirit of defeatism into the population of the United Kingdom.

Betty Wilson describes clearly what would have happened to her family had they not left central Plymouth on one occasion.

We got on a bus to the suburbs where a man said he had a spare room for a night. His house was untidy and haywire . . . another restless night, plus quite a bit of itching. The next day we had flea-bite marks all over us and were glad to get the bus home, but when we got home we saw that people were digging at the shelter of our next door neighbours — a bomb had dropped in the garden ... and because we stayed in that shelter sometimes, found out that they were digging to find us too, assuming that we were there. My young friend Eileen was in there with her mum and grandad. Her dad had gone up to the toilet and was killed coming back, Eileen had the back of her head blown off, only her mother survived, poor woman was in a daze and never really recovered. It was the blitz of 13 April 1941, and Eileen's 13th birthday.

But even a flight to the countryside was no guarantee of safety. Some bombs were deliberately aimed at the centres of little communities; others were hastily dropped at random by frightened pilots anxious to gain height; quiet village streets or fields full of harvesters might know the sudden shock of a strafing attack. Indeed we have one sad story of a man who sent his parents out of Coventry to the peace of Kenilworth where they were killed within a week by a stray bomb.

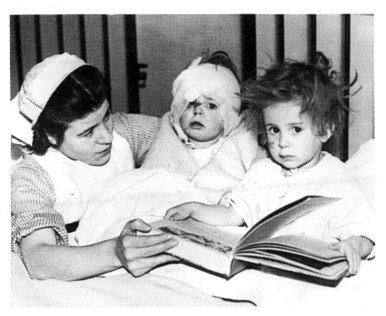

A nurse comforts two babies, Sally Smith aged two and her sister Barbara aged one, the survivors of a family bombed during a raid on London. Their father, mother and brother were killed; 21 March 1941.

263

Neither did the London underground offer a certain haven. Twenty shelterers were killed by tiles blasted off the walls at Marble Arch on 17 September 1940. Even worse was the incident on 11 January 1941 when a bomb exploded in the booking-hall of Bank station, causing the biggest crater in the London blitz. The roof simply caved in and blast killed 38 people sheltering on the platform.

Those involved in dealing with such tragedies have never been able to wipe out their memories of the grisly aftermath, though Walter Amos, the fireman, can no longer recall the name of the station to which he was called one night.

A bomb had gone down the lift shaft, impacted at the bottom, and all that was left, splattered all over the wall, was pieces of human beings, men, women and young children. We didn't have plastic bags in those days, there were ordinary jute sacks. We had to take shovels and put the pieces in the bags. They were taken up, put on lorries, taken to the outskirts of

A large bomb during one of the big raids which made a large crater in a street, breaking mains, twisting tramlines and partly engulfing this bus, 23 January 1942.

London where a big pit had been dug, and there were ministers of every denomination round the pit, reading the burial service, because these sacks contained the remains of human beings, thrown in. I don't think anybody will ever forget that. I never will.

For Mr Woolridge, an ambulanceman, it happened the night a bomb dropped in Balham High Road.

When we got outside Balham tube station we saw that a bomb had made a huge crater in the road outside and a bus had pulled up on the verge of it. Then the bus slid down into the crater which was getting bigger all the time because the burst mains underneath were causing subsidence. Suddenly I heard people shouting, 'Down the tube, down the tube!' and I realised that the crater was above the station platform where people were sheltering.

We made our way down the tube where people were rushing up the staircase which we found later was from one platform, but the other platform we couldn't get to. And all you could hear was the sound of screaming and rushing water. We managed to get to the platform by wading along the flooded track, and then the sight there was terrible. People laying about there and a great pile of sludge all over the platform which had buried all the other people who were sleeping there. People had been killed by the bomb blast or by the fall of sludge and ballast which buried them alive. Lots were curled up in sleeping positions. And the bomb blast had ripped all one porter's clothes off and he lay there naked. We put them on stretchers and carried them away through the water. We carried up about 10 people, then there were others that we couldn't possibly get out because we had no utensils to get them out. They had all to be dug out. We didn't pick up any survivors that night.

Even more people were to die in Bethnal Green tube on the evening of 8 March 1943, but this time only indirectly due to enemy action. Bernard Kops heard about it and rushed to the scene.

When we got to Bethnal Green tube station there were crowds of people near the entrance; police, wardens and rescue workers and ambulances. There was a strange silence. Somebody told us that a couple of hundred people had been crushed to death in the entrance. I was sure my mother and sister were in that crush and we rushed forward, trying to get information. The rumours were flying thick and fast. The only thing we did know was that no bomb had dropped closer than two miles away.

We waited for hours while they brought the bodies out. The longest hours of my life. No one seemed to know what had happened. A policeman was telling another that the bodies were piled on top of each other and that some people on top of the pile had suffocated while others at the bottom were trapped but still alive.

Almost the last person removed was a seven year old. The child stood up and walked to the first-aid post unaided.

When we finally managed to get inside, I could see lumps of hair in the entrance. We passed the bunks of white-faced silent people, and I was afraid to look as we neared our bunks in case my mother and sister were not there. But I heard her crying, and she cuddled us when we arrived. She thought my father and I were in it; told how the police had rushed along the tunnel from Liverpool Street station to tackle the wedge of people from the other side.

In the morning we learned the facts. There had been no panic, but the new type shells bursting in the sky had made people rush in the entrance. A middle-aged woman with a bundle and a baby tripped over at the foot of the stairs. A man fell on her and people just went over like ninepins while masses more crowded in the entrance. It was all over so quickly. One hundred and seventy-three people were crushed to death, the majority being women and children.

By this time many people had taken to spending the night in the comparative safety of specially constructed deep shelters, work on which started in November 1940. Eventually there were eight in all, each holding 8,000 people at depths of between 80 and 105 feet. S.N. Behrman described what these were like in an article for the *New Yorker* in January 1945.

The deep shelters are amazing. They are cities hundreds of feet underground. A companion and I timed the descent to one in the lift; it took several minutes ... The interminable, brightly lit corridors curving beside the endless shelves of bunks have the antiseptic horror of the German film 'Metropolis'. These shelters are really safe. The one we visited has a long bar-canteen which serves cocoa, milk and sandwiches at nominal prices. There is a fully equipped hospital with nurses and doctors in attendance. We walked miles on concrete platforms while the loudspeakers blared 'Dardanella' and 'Tea for Two'.

A good-looking, very neatly dressed man of about 40 was sitting on a bunk beside a boy who must have been his son, about 12 and also very nicely dressed. The boy's hair was brushed smooth and he looked as if he had got himself up to visit a rich aunt. I talked to the man. He said he had lost every possession he had in the world except the clothes he and his son were wearing. They had been living in this shelter for eight months. In the morning he went to his work and the boy went to school. The problem in the shelter was to get up early enough, before six-thirty, because after that hour lift service, except for the aged and crippled, stopped, and there were 700 stairs.

But it would be a mistake to imagine London as a city of people cowering underground, with a few hardy souls patrolling the surface. A shelter census carried out in early November 1940 showed that in central London only 9 per cent slept in public shelters, 4 per cent in the underground (though, as Angus Calder says, 'some accounts of the blitz make it sound as if almost everyone took to the tubes') and 27 per cent in shelters at home. Later in the war many people took to sleeping in the new Morrison shelters, a kind of reinforced cage erected inside the house; but there were still many who simply wouldn't shelter.

Leonard Woolf, in his autobiography, explained that he had only once been in a shelter and that was enough.

I hated the stuffiness and smell of human beings, and, if a bomb was going to get me, I preferred to die a solitary death above ground and in the open air.

Like so many convinced and fervent democrats, in practice I have never found human beings physically in the mass at all attractive — there is a good deal to be said for solitude whether in life or death. When death comes, I shall choose, as some wild animals do, to go off and meet it alone — but not in an air-raid shelter or underground.

Another committed anti-shelterer was Rose Macaulay, who complained in a letter to the *Spectator* printed in November 1940 that

A man sleeps in a stone coffin in the vaults of Christchurch, Spitalfields.

268

There seems to be no doubt that we are settling down ... to be a race of troglodytes ... Is it too late to try to stem it? To start a propaganda campaign for sleeping in bed? One does not want to be a kill-joy, but are all these incitements to the shelter life an intelligent idea? Mr Morrison [the Home Secretary] lately spared a kind word for 'those calm folk who sleep in their beds'; more such words might be timely ... It is a choice of risks; but obviously the chance of one's house stopping a bomb and oneself being killed, badly damaged or buried longer than is healthy ... is a slighter risk than that of discomfort and illness from a shelter.

And when one reads the descriptions of some shelters, even considerably later, it is easy to understand the reluctance of many to use them. In July 1944, when the VIs had started sending people underground again, Orwell wrote about

disgusting scenes in the Tube stations at night, sordid piles of bedding cluttering up the passage-ways and hordes of dirty-faced children playing around the platforms at all hours. Two nights ago, about midnight, I came on a little girl of five 'minding' her younger sister, aged about two. The tiny child had got hold of a scrubbing brush with which she was scrubbing the filthy stones of the platform, and then sucking the bristles. I took it away from her and told the elder girl not to let her have it. But I had to catch my train, and no doubt the poor little brat would again be eating filth in another couple of minutes. This kind of thing is happening every-where.

Small wonder that the Leonard Woolfs and Rose Macaulays preferred to take their chances on the surface. And so did many young people, who were able to use the anonymity of the blacked-out cities for exciting adventures, or at least what they hoped might turn out to be so.

Young John Mortimer spent such a night in the winter of 1940–1 with his friend Oliver Pensotti. While at school they had spent much time wondering if they would be killed before finding out what it was like to go to bed with a woman. They were especially intrigued by what role, if any, the breasts would play. Now, perhaps, they would have the answer.

We went for a drink in the bar of the Normandy Hotel where Oliver got into conversation with an ATS named Jeannie, as the bombs started to fall. The sound of breaking glass, the sweet taste of gin and lime, the peril of arbitrary thuds and the silent presence of the rather chunky Jeannie, who smiled but hardly spoke, added to the excitement of the evening. Months before, a fire-bomb had destroyed the kitchen of my father's flat in the Temple and he now lived all the time in the country, potting up, pricking out, trying to get enough petrol to keep the grass cut and getting up early in the black-out to travel to London to deal with the rising tide of divorce. So we went back to the empty flat and sat among the dust-sheets and the ruins of the kitchen. I found several bottles of port which we drank; descending on a foundation of gin and lime they made the room lurch like a ship at sea. I started to tell Jeannie about Lord Byron and his fatal love for his half-sister, but she was looking at Oliver in a strangely fixed sort of way and whispered words I found extremely enigmatic, 'Have you got a rubber?'

Almost at once they moved into the bedroom. I was left alone with my memories of his fatal Lordship's love life and pulled down, from my father's dusty shelves, a book of his poems:

> So, we'll go no more a roving
> So late into the night,
> Though the heart be still as loving
> And the moon be still as bright.
> For the sword outwears its sheath,
> And the soul wears out the breast,
> And the heart must pause to breathe,
> And love itself have rest.

The crashes were coming nearer. I had a momentary fear of my roving being put a stop to before it had even begun, my sword being laid to rest before it had worn out anything at all.

In due course the happy couple re-emerged and the ATS went off to rejoin her regiment.

'Well,' I said to Oliver. 'How on earth did you manage?'

'Manage?'

'About the breasts, of course.'

'Perfectly all right.' Oliver gave a smile of satisfied achievement. 'You hardly notice them at all.'

8.
LONDON FROM MID-NOVEMBER 1940 TO 1944

As I write, highly civilized human beings are flying overhead, trying to kill me.

George Orwell, 19 February 1941

On 14 November 1940, as we have seen, the Germans switched their attention from London; firstly to Coventry, then on to Birmingham, Bristol, Southampton, Sheffield, Merseyside, Manchester, all of which suffered major raids in the final weeks of the year.

General Lee failed to understand the strategy behind the Germans' apparently random pattern of attacks, noting in his diary of 7 December that

there was not one bomb on London last night. This is the first time that this has happened in my recollection. The whole bombing campaign against England has been so erratic and so varied in its objectives that I cannot believe it is being directed by a trained soldier or airman. It may be the political campaign by Hitler himself, who is a good deal of a mystic, and who is also a man who never has had any contact with the British and has no idea of their dogged endurance.

Whatever the reasons for switching targets so frequently, at least the people of London had some respite for a few weeks in the December of 1940. That was to change on Sunday the 29th, however. Gwladys Cox heard a knock on the door of her new West Hampstead flat and opened it to find her neighbour, Miss Brockmore, whispering urgently to her.

'You really MUST come up and see the fire from our windows — the whole of the City of London seems burning.' So we went upstairs and from their top floor window, facing south east with its wide, uninterrupted view of London away to the East End, we watched almost speechless, a spectacle of the most terrible beauty I have ever witnessed. It was a dark, moonless night, and the whole sky to the East above the City was a vivid sheet of fire and we realised, at once, that the conflagration centred around St Paul's again. Volumes of rose-pink smoke, and many-coloured flashes from explosions pierced again and again the blood-red clouds, which, brooding and angry, hung for miles over the City. We could only guess at the destruction wrought by each explosion.

Cecil Beaton visited the City next morning and found it

still in flames after last night's raid when eight Wren churches and the Guildhall were destroyed. It was an emotionally disturbing experience to clamber among the still smouldering ashes of this frightful wasteland. It was doubly agonising to realise that, had precautions for fire-spotters been taken, much of the damage could have been avoided. But it was too late, and some of the best churches have gone with little to indicate what was there before.

St Bride's in Fleet Street is now just a gutted orangery; St Andrew-by-the-Wardrobe, a hideous black mass with a molten copper roof like a blanket pall over the charred remains. No signs can be found of Gog and Magog at the Guildhall, and only a few baroque memorial tablets with sorrowing cupids and skulls remain at St Vedast's.

In the biting cold with icy winds beating around corners, James P[ope] H[ennessy] and I ran about the glowing smoul-

The night of the Great Fire, 29 December 1940. The City seen from the dome of St Paul's, with Paternoster Row in flames.

dering mounds of rubble where once were the printers' shops and chop houses of Paternoster Row. We have trundled under perilous walls, over uncertain ground which, at any moment, might give way to the red-hot vaults below. We have known Ypres in the heart of London. We could not deny a certain ghoulish excitement stimulated us, and our anger and sorrow were mixed with a strange thrill at seeing such a lively destruction — for this desolation is full of vitality. The heavy walls crumble and fall in the most romantic Piranesi forms. It is only when the rubble is cleared up, and the mess is put in order, that the effect becomes dead.

The Germans had timed their raid well; a low tide, to make the task of the firemen more difficult; a Sunday night, with most of the buildings in the city locked and deserted. As Mollie Panter-Downes commented in her next 'Letter from London' in the *New Yorker* (date 4 January):

Up to that Sunday night, incendiaries were looked upon as tiresome annoyances incidental to a raid. Now that the really serious gap in the air-raid precautions of the big cities has been seen, there is talk of possible hasty legislation providing for the imprisonment of owners of industrial plants that are destroyed by fires that spread because of neglect of proper precautions. Citizens also have been asked, and have shown a willingness, to form communal fire-fighting squads, which are to take turns patrolling the streets, armed with the keys of absent neighbours, so that fires in empty houses can be quickly reached and controlled.

It would not have taken much to reduce the destruction of the night of the Great Fire. Florence Richter, a wartime Waaf, describes how the presence of a couple of people up on the roof saved one historic church from destruction that Sunday.

My mother's cousin, Henry J. Alldis, was verger of St George's, Hanover Square, and became an air raid warden. One night when the bombing was intense, incendiaries were coming down like rain. The wardens were out for a very long time; as a rule they would call back every so often to see if everything was all right in the vault. We waited a long time that night, growing more and more anxious, but eventually the two missing wardens turned up, tired, dirty, but unharmed and safe. They had been on the roof of the church putting out incendiaries — not the most comfortable place to be even in broad daylight; in the dark with the bombs, dangerous to the extreme. We learned later that many churches in the city were destroyed or badly damaged that night. St George's, Hanover Square would have been amongst them, had it not been for two World War I veterans.

The lesson was not learned immediately, though. Two weekends after the Great Fire General Lee noted in his diary that

the blitz last night really wrought quite a lot of havoc, particularly along Piccadilly, where Devonshire House and Rootes's automobile place and Stratton Street are pretty well knocked about. There was also a considerable amount of damage in two buildings where there were no roof watchers. Hitler is a smart fellow and makes these attacks over the weekend, when the British automatically forsake their posts.

But official action was swift. A fire guard scheme was introduced, for men aged 16–60 at first but extended to include women from 20–45 in August 1942. When this was further extended to men up to the age of 63 it meant that the country had, in theory, an army of some six million watchers. Some people managed to wriggle out of their duties, of course, and the prolonged lulls later in the war made people increasingly reluctant to turn out on cold nights after a tough day's work; but the scheme did ensure that many properties which might otherwise have burnt to the ground were saved by the timely intervention of a pair of hands and a bucket of sand or stirrup pump.

By January 1941 Londoners were learning to live with the blitz. The non-stop nights of bombing had given way to what so much of the country was then experiencing — frequent sights of the odd raider, interspersed with occasional blitzes of savage ferocity. To sum up life in London that January, George Orwell included the following extracts from his diary in his 'London Letter' written for the March/April issue of *Partisan Review*.

The aeroplanes come back and back, every few minutes. It is just like in an eastern country, when you keep thinking you have killed the last mosquito inside your net, and every time, as soon as you have turned the light out, another starts droning ... The commotion made by the mere passage of a bomb through the air is astonishing. The whole house shakes, enough to rattle objects on the table. Why it is that the electric light dips when a bomb passes close by, nobody seems to know ... Oxford Street yesterday, from Oxford Circus up to the Marble Arch, completely empty of traffic, and only a few pedestrians, with the late afternoon sun shining straight down the empty roadway and glittering on innumerable fragments of broken glass. Outside John Lewis's, a pile of plaster dress models, very pink and realistic, looking so like a pile of corpses that one could have mistaken them for that at a little distance ... Regular features of the time: neatly swept-up piles of glass, litter of stone and splinters of flint, smell of escaping gas, knots of sightseers waiting at the cordons where there are unexploded bombs ... Nondescript people wandering about, having been evacuated from their houses because of delayed action bombs. Yesterday two girls stopping me in the street, very elegant in appearance except that their faces were filthily dirty: 'Please, sir, can you tell us where we are?' ... Withal, huge areas of London almost normal, and everyone quite happy in the daytime, never seeming to think about the coming night, like animals which are unable to foresee the future as long as they have a bit of food and a place in the sun.

No part of London was now safe from the bombs. Chelsea, in particular, suffered badly at this time, a fact that we are aware of from the number of people then living in the area who wrote about their experiences then or afterwards. One of the latter was Theodora Fitzgibbon who, in her autobiography, describes what happened to their much loved local pub.

The King's Road was full of activity: clanging ambulances, fire-engines and wardens racing up towards the Town Hall. We hurried on to find a cordon round the Six Bells, and massive chunks of heavy masonry on the ground. The front part upstairs had been hit, and toppled into both the road and garden a matter of minutes before closing time. People were trapped in the back. We helped to clear the rubble and brick; it was hard work and made us hot, despite the cold. A small entrance was made and the stretcher bearers, wardens and reserve police went through. The lights still blazed, and someone yelled, 'Turn that bloody light off.'

Several dazed but unhurt people were led out by torch-light; one had a bottle of brandy which was passed around, and we all had a swig. Some were 'regulars' who recognised us. The one with the purloined bottle said jauntily: 'What happened to you tonight that you didn't cop this lot?'

There were more inside, trapped, probably dead, as they had been sitting near the front door. Curly, the Irish barman, had gone down to the cellar and was found, his rimless spectacles still on his snub nose, but he was stone dead, an unbroken bottle in his hand. Almost-full pints of beer were standing unspilt on tables in front of customers who stared at them with unseeing eyes, for they too were dead from the blast.

Christopher Mayhew, then working for SOE and living in Chelsea Cloisters, wrote to his family about a fairly typical raid of this period.

I have just returned rather breathless from putting out some incendiary bombs which fell with a loud metallic 'plop-clatter' in the street outside my window. I careered downstairs and managed to get a bomb to myself, which I put out with much gusto and waste of sand. Some dozens of enthusiastic cloisterers were pouring into Sloane Avenue and the little streets off it, some frightfully efficient, carrying sand-buckets, others just enthusiastic, and all most unsuitably dressed — in pansy suits or smart frocks or bedroom slippers. It was a queer scene — little groups of men and women running about like that with buckets of sand in the erratic orange glow of the incendiaries.

I was in the cinema when the blitz began. Rather a close one came down and the building swayed unpleasantly. The audience let out a momentary, collective, giggled 'phew', then was suddenly quite silent, waiting to see if it was a singleton or one of a stick, then said to itself 'quite near enough for me, thank you' and began to prepare to leave with much feeling for hats and clicking of handbags and banging of seats tipping up, and then, just as though it was one person it changed its mind, sat down again and saw the film through. Only two people left.

In early March 1941, Orwell spoke to some friends, recently arrived in the capital, who told him they found Londoners 'very much changed, everyone is hysterical, talking in much louder tones, etc., etc.' He commented that 'if this is so, it is something that happens gradually and that one does not notice while in the middle of it, as with the growth of a child'. At this period, in fact, things were relatively calm in London. It was elsewhere in the United Kingdom, from Clydeside to Bristol, from Plymouth to Belfast, that the

bombs were falling thickest. But all that was to change in mid-April, on the nights of the 16th and the 19th, still known simply as 'The Wednesday' and 'The Saturday'.

General Lee, describing the first of these nights, wrote that

there was not much sleep to be had last night. London, particularly the West End, was bombed continuously until four o'clock this morning, when day began to break. And a good many of the bombs were very large ones ...

This was easily the worst attack that London has sustained at night. The only one that I can think of which would compare with it was the daylight attack on Dockland which initiated the Battle of London.

Just nine days earlier, on 7 April, Stephen Melville Woodcock had written in his diary that

the recent lull in raids on London is said to be due to German change of tactics. Disappointed with the results of raids on London, the *Luftwaffe* is now more interested in bombing our ports and aeroplane factories.

On the Thursday he was forced to admit that he had been premature in his judgment.

Return of blitz to London from 9.00 pm–4.00 am. There was continuous noise with scarcely a minute's interruption. Planes were lower and louder than usual, and we heard the zooming down low, presumably 'dive-bombing'. There was so much noise from gunfire that it was impossible to hear the whistles and explosions of many of the bombs, but at about 2 am the bedroom was filled with the acrid smell of explosives and burning ... it was a fairly light moonlit night, but nevertheless the Germans used 'chandelier' flames early on.

On the way to the office we passed damage by Barkers and much broken glass and Kensington High Street (west of Church Street) was closed. Piccadilly was closed and one could see a crater at the bottom of Hamilton Place. Victoria

Street was closed ... Nr the office, at 55 Broadway, Christchurch was gutted and still smoking and a fire-escape ladder and fire engine were lying in the road charred and broken ... The Strand is covered in glass between Fleet Street and Charing Cross. Charing Cross Station is burning still ... There isn't a single pane of glass in the New Adelphi building, the Little Theatre is burnt out ... In Leicester Square a fire was still burning next door to the Odeon Cinema, but close by there was a queue 100 yds long waiting to go into the Empire ... Jermyn Street and Duke Street have been badly damaged and fires were still pouring out smoke. South of the Ritz two old houses and the Overseas Club were gutted and smoking. The AFS men were getting snacks at the mobile canteens. The air was full of choking fire smells and the pavements dusty and covered in small pieces of glass. All along the Strand and Piccadilly the gutters were filled with glass which was gradually being removed in dust carts. The weather was fine and one saw office staff working at glassless windows and the pubs were open to the streets and doing a normal trade apparently. A particularly loud 'zooming' which Gwen and I heard about 11 pm appears to have been a bomber chased by a Spitfire. The bomber crashed in Camden Hill Road, one of its engines falling into a block of flats and the plane itself crashing into a wall after skimming the housetops. Fortunately its bombs had already dropped. The Spitfire was taking a chance of fouling the balloon barrage. Bits of the bomber's fuselage fabric have been picked up by wardens and seems to be made of three layers of stiff paper substance riveted together!

Years later, in his autobiography *Another Self*, James Lees-Milne was to write of that night and its aftermath. He had just that day been discharged from hospital where he had finally been diagnosed as suffering from a rare form of epilepsy; on arriving at his club he found a letter telling him that his old friend Robert Byron, from whom he had parted on bad terms some weeks earlier, had been drowned *en route* to Alexandria. With sadness in his heart, as he says, he went to dine with an old friend Peter Montgomery at the

Spanish Majorca, his first dinner out for a long time. The attack started while they were eating, one bomb shattering the front of the restaurant. Once outside they realised the safest thing to do would be to take refuge nearby.

We crept along walls, plunged across Regent Street and entered the Piccadilly Hotel where we drank until midnight. The raid getting worse we took a room on the fifth floor. There were nine floors in the hotel, and all the rooms on the ground floor were already taken. We half-undressed and quailed in our beds until 2 am. The bombs were hailing, swishing down on all sides so that sleep was out of the question. The explosions and the rattle of retaliatory gunfire were deafening. We dressed again and went downstairs. Peter left his khaki overcoat and I my Sam Browne belt in the bedroom. Downstairs we felt perfectly safe, for the Grill Room was two floors below street level. As we passed through the entrance hall we saw slices of thick plate glass strewn upon the carpets. The revolving doors had blown in.

Less than 20 minutes later the first bomb hit the hotel. The building shivered and a fine dry dust filled the air and made people sneeze. Men and women caught like us were sprawling as men and women sprawl at night times in railway carriages with their mouths wide open, on the floors and stairs. We stood, sat and wandered in the lower basement where, apart from an occasional thump and tremor, nothing indicated how the raid was proceeding. At intervals we climbed to street level to find out. Once I put my head out of doors. A gust of blast met me. I retreated. There was no point in courting death. Not long afterwards while we were below again, a second bomb fell on the hotel with a loud percussion. It was like a thunder clap above our heads. I was pitched off my chair. While the foundations rocked and swayed there was time to screw my body like a hedgehog into a protective ball against the masonry crumbling, rumbling down the marble staircase. Were we to be crushed, buried alive, underground? A cataract of boulders was arrested by a grand piano. A smashing, slashing of glass and wood followed in its wake. Nothing further. The lights went out.

Officious men's voices shouted, 'Keep calm!' Everyone kept calm. There was a stifling smell of cordite and the acrid stench of plaster and stale wallpaper. When torches were flashed on nothing was visible but blobs of light behind a fog of black, curling smoke. I feared I would choke and for a foolish second thought of poison gas. There was a rending cacophony of spluttering and coughing. Spitting.

Before the smell and dust subsided, a third bomb fell on the Piccadilly pavement just beside the wall against which we were crouching below. I was saying rather querulously, 'Peter, where are you?' because his companionship was at that moment very dear to me. He lit a torch and there he stood as sartorially elegant and serene as ever. Only one lock of hair drooped over an eyebrow; and his forehead was puckered because he does not care to be dishevelled. It is symptomatic of ill-breeding on somebody's part. The Germans. And now they were at it again. Crash! We were thrown by this fresh exhibition of outrageous manners clumsily against each other. This time Peter frowned without attempting to check himself. I said 'I have mislaid my gas mask', and Peter flashed his torch upon the ground through the whiskings and flickerings of the black dust. Then I laughed aloud. It did seem odd. My gas mask was floating upon a stream, borne beneath a plush sofa. The last bomb had hit a water main outside the hotel. Our ankles were immersed in a yellow slime. People were clambering upon gold, cane-seated chairs above the swirling stream, the women knotting their skirts about their middles. Men appeared with brooms. Someone opened a manhole and the noisy torrent — for it was that now — was directed into it.

So we paddled, frisked and waded knee deep from chair to chair, or hopped upon one, using another like a stilt, for as the torrent altered its course, there was the likelihood of being marooned on one chair and being unable to communicate with a shallower bottom save by swimming. And it was still early spring, in England.

At five o'clock the all-clear sounded. Peter — his tie was out of place — and I clambered through rubble, up broken flights of stairs, down semi-blocked corridors, over fallen girders, and through dislocated doorways to our bedroom. The second bomb had exploded in the suite next to ours. Our two beds were still recognisable, although mine was facing the wrong way, turned back to front and the iron chassis of the thing twisted like a whiting. The rest of the furniture and fittings, the cupboards, tables and window frames were not so recognisable. A cloth of lumpish grey was a shroud to the room. From under a hammock Peter disinterred his overcoat. He held it at arm's length and blew upon it. I did not recover my Sam Browne belt.

Piccadilly resembled a giant skeleton asleep upon an ice floe. The eye sockets of the houses looked reproachfully at the dawn. Like lids, torn blinds and curtains fluttered from every window. The brows of windows and portals were wrenched and plucked. On pavement and street a film of broken glass crunched under the feet like the jagged crystals of slush icicles. One had to take care that they did not clamber over the edge of one's shoes. The contents of shop windows were strewn over the pavements among the broken glass. Silk shirts and brocaded dressing-gowns fluttered upon area railings. The show case of a jeweller's window had sprinkled tray-loads of gold watches and bracelets as far as the curb of the street. I stooped to pick up a handful of diamonds and emeralds — and chuck them back into the shop before they got trodden on, or looted.

The sky had the gunmetal solidity of sky before a snow storm. Cinders showered upon our hair, faces and clothes. On all sides columns of smoke sprang from raging fires, the glint of whose flames could be seen above the rooftops, trembling upon chimney stacks and burnishing the dull surface of the sky. I was reminded of Pepys's description of the Great Fire of London in 1666, 'a most horrid malicious bloody flame, not like the fine flame of an ordinary fire'.

A cinder fell into the corner of Peter's eye and caused him pain. The eye smarted and watered. He was very good and followed me around. I wished to see all the damage there might be, to be saddened and maddened thereby. We could not walk up Piccadilly, because a stick of bombs having fallen from the Fifty Shilling Tailor's to St James's Church had penetrated a gas main. Tongues of flame were belching from craters in the road. We could not walk down Jermyn Street which was blocked by rubble from collapsed houses. Here I noticed the stripped, torn trunk of a man on the pavement. Further on I picked up what looked like the mottled, spread leaf of a plane tree. It was a detached hand with a signet ring on the little finger.

The Saturday raid two nights later was equally fierce. Both nights left over 1,000 dead, with a total of some 148,000 houses damaged or destroyed. But London was to face something even worse the following month, on 10 May. According to Cyril Demarne, the firemen

knew they were in for a bad night with the odds stacked against them, as hundreds of bombers maintained a shuttle service across the Channel, returning to their bases in northern France to refuel and bomb up for the return journey ... the raiders were able to choose their targets by the brilliant light of the moon and, later, by the glare of fires stretching across London from Dagenham to Hammersmith. Street mains were flowing only in the early stages; demand soon overran the supply as fresh fires were started; the flow became further depleted with the inevitable fracturing of trunk mains. Frustrated firemen who had laboured to bring their jets to bear on the blazing buildings, watched helplessly as the fire streams faltered and died. Their comrades meanwhile, sought emergency sources of water not already crowded out by pumps with suction hose set in. Fire boats lay 50 yards from the Thames banks, running their hose lines ashore over mud flats from what looked like a village stream, so low was the tide. But there were far more pumps seeking water than the fire boats could hope to supply and water officers directed crews to public swimming pools, canals and ponds. Some opportunist pump operators set their appliances into flooded bomb craters, even sewers, in an effort to make use of every drop of water available.

One of the firemen out that night was Jim Goldsmith who, at one point, was sent to Ludgate Hill to work

inside a building containing rolls of newsprint which were alight. We had jets on them to try to put out the flames, when the blocks holding the rolls in place decided to move. With flaming rolls coming at us, we decided it was time we moved and quick. Opposite the fire station was the *Evening News* offices ... during the night they used to deliver the next day's papers to the station for the men. We had returned to the station for more hose, fed up, dirty, soaking wet and still trying to stop the fires spreading, and what was the paper's headlines ... 'A RAID TOOK PLACE ON LONDON TONIGHT BUT BY THIS MORNING THE FLAMES WERE UNDER CONTROL'. How is that for faith?

Cecil King was out and about that night and in his diary entry for the next day describes how, were it not for the presence of fire-watchers, things might have been even worse.

Last night about 11 o'clock, off went the warning. Nothing very much happened for some time, so I supposed it was to be someone else's turn tonight. But gradually things warmed up. On my first visit to the *Mirror* office, there was a lot of AA fire over the East End, though very little near us. A number of incendiaries had been dropped to the west of us and, though they had not been put out, they didn't seem to be starting a fire.

However, shortly afterwards, I went up again to the roof and the fun was really starting. An incendiary had fallen through the roof of our old offices in Bream's Buildings, all wood partitions and loaded up with stocks of paper and string — very inflammable indeed. I led a party over the roofs from the main building and we threw up sandbags to a man who appeared on the roof above us. He put the sand on the flames and put them out. We then went inside the building and found the bomb on the floor burning fiercely. A fireman was covering it with bags of sand. Flames were breaking out in the lift shaft just by: the bomb was setting alight the boards of the ceiling below. We went down to the lower floor, forced open the lift door, and directed a stream from a stirrup pump on to the flames; meanwhile the flames were breaking out again on the floor above. Eventually they were both subdued. Elsewhere, some of the party were extinguishing a bomb which had fallen on the roof of Geraldine House proper.

I get rather muddled about the sequence of events in looking back, but about this time we saw another incendiary had fallen on the roof of a shop in Fetter Lane opposite the entrance to the office. I went over with one of the firemen to deal with it. We were contemplating the locked door when a watcher was sighted on the roof, who tackled it. I kept sending men back to our fire as I felt it might break out again. In due course it did, both on the roof and inside, but was soon put out. In the shop the watcher did not do his job properly, and before long immense clouds of thick black smoke were pouring out of the top storey and the place was well and truly alight. It spread both ways and eventually involved two other shops, the Moravian church, and a group of factories and printing works. The Germans overhead were in such large numbers that you could not distinguish the sound of individual planes ...

The roof watchers were splendid, paid no attention to bombs, but the editorial staff mostly cowered in a corner of the basement and were useless. Once the fires were well alight, the Germans started bombing them and the HE began to drop all around. I should estimate that on an average once a minute for five hours a bomb could be heard rushing or whistling through the air. Once when I was on the roof, one dropped fairly near, and one could see the flash and the column of dust from the explosion. Fires by this time were all round us — big ones and growing, especially a very bright one near the corner of Chancery Lane and Holborn.

Then a fire was observed on the roof of what used to be Wyman's building in Fetter Lane; it now belongs to Odhams. Evidently there were no roof watchers, and by the time the flames became visible from below the north-east corner was well alight. Unfortunately, there was a stiff north-east wind blowing. Very soon the whole building was burning fiercely and another fire was coming at us towards the Field building from the other side of Bream's Buildings. Bart [Harry Guy Bartholomew, *Daily Mirror* director] and Greenwell [photographer] turned up in AFS uniform and asked for (and received the promise of) ten pumps, as we were in the direct line. Another fire, on the roof of Charles and Read behind us, was put out.

As time went on and the fires in Fetter Lane and Rolls Buildings spread, it began to look pretty bad for us. I found Greenwell, who said the AFS had again confirmed their promise to send ten pumps. We had out all our own fire-fighting equipment, but by this time there was no water pressure. Eventually one pump arrived — not really for us, but to protect the [Public] Record Office. They set to work and pumped all the water in the 'dam' outside our office on to the flames. This helped, but was soon over. Then more water was got in from the Record Office, but most of this, too, was wasted on the shops in Fetter Lane, which were obviously past praying for. Then the Record Office water gave out. We scrounged around, found a small pipe in the yard which worked directly off the main and which still flowed, and Pyatt found one hydrant which still worked, though very slowly. These were directed into the 'dam' and slowly filled it up. When it was half full the AFS men had a drive at the side of the fire in Wyman's buildings nearest us, and partly because of this and partly because Birkbeck College between us and them was damaged by fire very early in the raids last autumn, so acting as a firebreak, we just got through. Mercifully also, at the critical moment, the wind changed.

Towards morning the smoke was such that you could not see it was full moon with no clouds; the air was full of flying sparks; every now and then there was the roar of a collapsing house. We had had our 'double red' warning on in the office for more than four hours. The lines from Paddington and Euston were blocked, King's Cross had had a direct hit, and most of the Southern Railway termini were closed. It was obvious that this was a really big raid, not just round us but on London generally.

Emily Eary was one of the many who crept out next morning to see what had been going on.

We'd been down the tube all night, but when we came out in the morning, to get out of the tube, we had to run through fires which were raging on both sides of the street. And there were hot falling embers, falling down on us. And my younger sister was quite a child then, and she remembers vividly running, terrified of the fires, not knowing when we got home, if home would still be there, and that was a very bad night.

But by then you see, we had got bunks down the tube, and we had a place that was sort of secure for us, that we knew that when we got down there, that was our number and when we got down there we were safe, we knew that whatever happened on top, whether there was raging fires or high explosive bombs, even in the morning when we came out through those terrible fires, we thought at least we can get back down the tube, and we'll know we'll be safe.

Those tucked up in the underground that night had been the lucky ones; for it had been the worst single raid of the war. The *Luftwaffe* had made over 500 sorties, causing well over 2,000 fires (including nine conflagrations involving over 100 pumps, and 20 major fires where between 30 and 100 were needed). Among the 1,436 dead was the Mayor of Bermondsey, killed on ARP duty, while the 1,800 serious casualties constituted a grim record for a single raid anywhere in Britain.

Four days later, on the Wednesday of that week, Moyra Macleod (then serving in the FANY) came up from the country to attend the English Speaking Union lunch. In her diary she wrote:

Poor old London! I went round a bit to see the damage and it was difficult on foot (cascades of broken glass tinkling down) and almost impossible in a car as there was a diversion at every corner and one landed up miles away from one's objective. North London did not seem to have suffered much but

Hans Place was a complete shambles and chaos, and Victoria Street sliced up — a half block of tall buildings swept away laying bare the mews behind. The little streets behind the Cavalry Club are grievously punished and Sunderland House — where our 'coming out' dance took place and we danced all that summer of Jubilee year — is gutted by fire. That grandiose, gilded ballroom with the burnished cherubs and the glowing ceiling is ravaged and open to the sky. We have seen the end of an era.

Saturday was certainly the worst blitz London has seen, the most ruthless and brutal and cynical. I hate Germans and hope we blow the whole bastard lot of them to pieces with their Berlin around their ears.

The outward face of Westminster was less terrible than I had expected. Big Ben was still striking, Richard Coeur de Lion holding aloft his crooked sword and Westminster Hall, though fire-blackened with a hole in the roof and probably a bad mess inside, still stands solid and inscrutable, with Cromwell keeping guard outside. The Abbey windows are out but that great mass, too, rises massive and challenging — the great quiet heart of London. The BBC has been hit again in several places. But life in London goes on.

And for Londoners, indeed for the people of the entire United Kingdom, life was soon to become considerably more peaceful. The *Luftwaffe* had been steadily losing planes (and, what was worse, pilots) in the course of raids over Britain. But many of these soon had to move eastwards, for on the 22 June 1941 Germany declared war on the Soviet Union.

Raids continued, it is true, but on a minor scale. As the Government pamphlet *Front Line* explained in 1942

In the latter months of 1941 ... targets were selected mainly for the propaganda value of being able to report raids to the German public without risking comparatively heavy losses to the slender bomber-force left in the West. All this lay (and lies) behind the frequent communiques announcing 'a solitary aircraft dropped bombs last night (or in daylight today) at some point on the coast of England (or Scotland)'.

Of course if a member of your family were killed, or if you suffered injury or were forced to leave your shattered house, it was little consolation to know that it was the result of a bomb dropped by 'a solitary aircraft'. But at least there was a chance for the people of London to tidy up and try to get things back to normal, as far as this could be possible in wartime.

The opening of *Westwood or The Gentle Powers*, a novel by Stella Gibbons, gives an accurate picture of what it was like in the capital during that period when no bombs fell.

London was beautiful that summer. In the poor streets the people made an open-air life for themselves as if they were living in a warmer climate. Old men sat on the fallen masonry and smoked their pipes and talked about the War, while the women stood patiently, in the shops or round the stalls selling large fresh vegetables, ceaselessly talking.

The ruins of the small, shapely houses in the older parts of the city were yellow, like the sunlit houses of Genoa; all shades of yellow; deep, and pale, or glowing with a strange transparency in the light. The fire-fighting people had made deep pools with walls round them in many of the streets, and here, in the heart of London, ducks came to live on these lakes that reflected the tall yellow ruins and the blue sky. Pink willow-herb grew over the white uneven ground covered with deserted, shattered houses whose windows were filled with torn black paper. On the outskirts of the city, out towards Edmonton or Tottenham in the North, and Sydenham in the South, there was a strange feeling in the air, heavy and sombre and thrilling, as if History were working visibly, before one's eyes. And the country was beginning to come back to London; back into those grimy villages linked by featureless roads from which it had never quite vanished, and which make up the largest city in the world. Weeds grew in the City itself; a hawk was seen hovering over the ruins of the Temple, and foxes raided the chicken roosts in the gardens of houses near Hampstead Heath. The shabby quietness of an old, decaying village hung in the streets, and it was a wonderful awe-inspiring thing to see and to feel. While the summer lasted, the beauty was stronger than the sadness because the sun blessed everything — the ruins, the tired faces of the people, the tall wild flowers and the dark stagnant water — and during those months of calm, London in ruin was beautiful as a city in a dream.

For other parts of the country it was not always so peaceful, as we have seen in Chapter 5. Nevertheless, as the table of the casualty figures for the UK as a whole shows, things had slackened off considerably.

Period	Deaths	Serious injuries
Last three months of 1940	22,000	28,000
1941	20,000	22,000
1942	3,230	4,150

This period of respite gave AA Command a chance to build up its strength and introduce more sophisticated weapons and instrumentation. It was fortunate that new radar-laid searchlights were in position by early 1943 since, on the night of Sunday 17 January, in retaliation for a heavy RAF raid on Berlin the night before, the first large-scale attack since that of 10 May 1941 was launched on London. The raiders were greeted, too, by a massive AA barrage, including the first use of the 1,000 mph Z battery rockets which, when fired in salvoes, sounded (according to Squadron Leader Bullers) 'like a hammer being pulled across a corrugated roof'.

The Germans, unhappy with the results of the raid, followed this up on the Wednesday with a surprise daylight attack, the biggest of its kind since 1940. A combination of equipment failure and miscalculation on the part of those tracking the invaders ensured that a number of FW 190 fighter-bombers, each carrying a single 1,100-lb HE bomb, managed to reach South-East London. Lewis Blake, in *Red Alert*, his study of the South-East London blitz, describes what happened in one part of Catford:

Rescue workers, police, soldiers and civilians clearing debris from the Sandhurst Road School disaster in Catford, south-east London in January 1943. In all, 44 were killed, including 38 children, and 67 were injured.

One Focke-Wulf roared up Sangley Road then Sandhurst Road, its machine guns and 20-mm cannons firing straight at pedestrians desperately seeking cover, or just too confused to know what to do. Six people died and 14 were injured in the street. It may have been the same plane which next circled Sandhurst Road School at 500 feet in preparation for releasing its bomb. Inside the school the sound of machine gun fire was the first intimation the staff had that there was something amiss. When they heard a plane flying overhead they began to usher children into the basement shelter. Some fortunate pupils had already left the building to take lunch at home.

Many witnesses saw the plane release its bomb directly on the school. The missile passed through the side of the building and came to rest on the ground floor. It was fused to explode in just under one minute, presumably to give the plane time to clear the danger spot. The short pause enabled about 30 children to scramble through ground floor windows and run for their lives across the playground. For those in the dining-room and in certain other parts of the premises there

292

was no chance to escape before the explosion overwhelmed them.

The whole centre of the four-storey building simply collapsed, killing 38 children and six teachers and seriously injuring over 60 children and a further seven teachers.

Hilda Carter, one of the firewomen quoted in Chapter 7, remembers the day all too well.

I was despatch rider following divisional officer, and we could even see the German pilots in their planes. Our balloons were down, and the Germans were firing at people walking in the streets, and they caught a gas holder at Sydenham gas works. The DO with fire appliances was sent there and I had to ring HQ to see if there was any more messages for the DO and then I received the message, 'Fire at Sandhurst Road School. Children buried under debris.' I had to climb the straight iron ladder right to the top of the gas holder to deliver message of same. The DO then gave station office on fire orders and we were to race on to the school. Pumps already on their way. I was frightened then. I remember saying 'How do I get down sir?' 'Same F — way you got up, Carter, but don't look down.'

There were 30 or 35 children buried. We were there all day and all night, passing bricks by brick with wardens, and we were bringing out young dead lovely children who were all dressed in their best because they were going to see 'Where the Rainbow Ends' I think, at Lewisham Hippodrome. And some teachers were killed, the parents and loved ones were roped off and I was still running messages in between. They grabbed me asking, 'Have you found my daughter so and so, or son?' I could give no answer, my heart was heavy and tears ... The Salvation Army were wonderful people, and climbed over bricks to get to us, without them we wouldn't have had a drink to wash the dust down our throats, they stayed with us over 24 hours, we wouldn't give up until we knew all bodies were recovered, and they were covered in dust in their caps and bonnets. We went to see them laid at rest at Hither Green Cemetery, bodies in little coffins, laid side by side, it makes me feel very bitter. Why young children? What an awful loss of life. We all cried who were there. I can understand how the children's loved ones grabbed me and punched into me for news of their children and you still never forget.

One police officer unearthed the body of his 13-year-old son. Charles Alford, home on leave from the AA, arrived at the scene in time to see his four-year-old daughter carried from the wreckage, then spent much of the rest of the night trying to dig for his other daughter, aged seven.

Reporting restrictions were lifted for once, giving widespread publicity to what was seen as a deliberate attack on innocent children. The *Kentish Mercury* wrote that

There have been few such incidents in this dreadful war which have aroused so much public sympathy, mingled with a sense of bitter anger against the fiendish onslaught of a barbarous foe, than the bombing of that large school ... and the destruction of thirty eight little children and six of their teachers.

Those who believed that such acts should not pass unavenged were soon to be satisfied. The new year saw a stepping up of the allied bombing of Germany, including the first daylight raids on Berlin just 11 days following the Catford disaster, on 31 January 1943. Throughout the year raids on Germany increased, both in number and ferocity. Over a 10-day period in late July–early August, more than 10,000 tons of bombs — including phosphorus incendiaries — were hurled at Hamburg, the RAF attacking at night and the USAF by day. In late November, following three nights of 1,000-bomber attacks, 'Bomber' Harris promised that Berlin would be attacked 'until the heart of Nazi Germany ceases to beat'. And on 20 January 1944 some 600 Lancasters and Halifaxes dropped over 2,300 lb of bombs on the German capital. It was the following night that the retaliation began.

This was the period known as the 'little blitz'. The worst nights were those of 21 and 29 January, with nine lesser ones following in February, culminating in three successive nights from the 22nd to the 24th. The Inspector-General of ARP reported that Londoners were 'more jittery', 'more helpless' than at any time in the war, and suffering from 'apathy' and 'war weariness'. Gwladys Cox caught the mood of the moment, as usual.

Houses blasted again with ceilings down and windows out and the coldest weather for two years. Fixing up our window-panes with stiffened muslin, now being used temporarily instead of glass. This waterproof muslin is nailed to the outside of the window-panes, each one of which has to be taken down and then put back. The muslin lets in the light, keeps out the rain and some of the draughts, and flaps in the wind like sails.

Homeless people are walking about with bags and bundles of clothes. A particularly poignant tragedy is that a man of the forces, who was to have been married on the day after the conflagration ... he had gone to stay with his father in West End Lane, and several members of the family had collected for a farewell party, which was actually in progress, when the bombs fell. They were all wiped out, and the bride, knowing nothing, waited, in vain, at the church the following day.

23 Feb 1944 — 2 am another heavy raid ... a dreadful experience, standing the whole time in an icy, pitch-dark hall ... the upstairs neighbours joined us — the old lady is beginning to look very tired and worn — and we all huddled together against the wall near the front door, startled by the occasional swoop of a bomb ... the all clear went, and so to bed, in our clothes — I have not undressed for a week. To the south east, the clouds are aglow with fires. There is much noise in West End Road, with demolition vans, etc., and a great hammering on all sides, windows being fitted up with the waterproof muslin.

Moyra Macleod, recently transferred from the FANY, was then at Greenwich for a fortnight's intensive training course before passing out as a WRNS officer. Her diary entry for 21 February reads:

Oh, the raids. When the siren goes at night we get up and put on sweater, slacks and greatcoat, clutch respirator, pillow, rug and torch, and go out to our 'fire stations' in the corridor (which is supposed to be reinforced). Here we stay till the all clear. We had a raid (quite heavy) Sunday night, when the Treasury was hit and burnt out; two raids on Monday; a very heavy one on Tuesday; one on Wednesday; and an early, sharp one on Friday. Tuesday at Greenwich was the noisiest. It was like some diabolical symphony, or (an airy dive into mythology made by a tired mind after midnight) like being in the thunder palace of Jove. Beginning with a growling thunder, the guns closed in around us, rising in crescendo until the house shook — reverberating crash after crash with the drone of the bombers overhead. Then dying away again, shade by shade, into the insistent thunder. It was an inspiring and tremendous barrage.

On one of the later nights an unpleasant whistle came over and we waited for the crash, but it was the empty shell of one of our new rocket cases. A fire-watcher brought it in to show us; it fell on the lawn outside. Moral, don't wander about in the barrage.

On Tuesday night we were all very quiet. I think we had been pretty scared and were thankful to be alive, though we appeared very nonchalant and full of OLQ (officer-like qualities!) and one girl even fell asleep and snored. Two nights, fires made an ugly glow in the sky after the raids were over — a fearful, terrible sight.

But sights like this were to become rarer over London, and on 18 March 1944 the *Luftwaffe* sent their last bombers to the capital. It made no sense for the Germans to continue such attacks. The allied ground and air forces had become so efficient that some 60 per cent of German planes were failing to get through. Planes could be replaced, but crew losses on this scale were unacceptable.

And besides, the new weapons of revenge, the ones that needed no pilots, were nearly ready for launching.

9.
THE WEAPONS OF REVENGE

The silence between the engine stopping and the explosion was as if everyone was holding their breath. The horses would stop and keep their feet still. The bakers and milkmen would stop their rumbling carts. What little traffic there was would sometimes stop, just waiting. During this period, whether the sirens had sounded or not, no one took much notice about sheltering — after all it was fate where a doodlebug ran out of fuel. We ignored the V2s even more; there was no warning, just a bang and you were either here or not.

Mr K. Cushen, 13 years old at the time

I notice that apart from the widespread complaint that the German pilotless planes 'seem so unnatural' (a bomb dropped by a live airman is quite natural, apparently), some journalists are denouncing them as barbarous, inhuman, and an 'indiscriminate attack on civilians'.

After what we have been doing to the Germans over the past two years, this seems a bit thick, but it is the normal human response to every new weapon. Poison gas, the machine-gun, the submarine, gunpowder, and even the crossbow were similarly denounced in their day. Every weapon seems unfair until you have adopted it yourself. But I would not deny that the pilotless plane, flying bomb, or whatever its correct name may be, is an exceptionally unpleasant thing, because, unlike most other projectiles, it gives you time to think. What is your first reaction when you hear that droning, zooming noise? Inevitably, it is a hope that the noise won't stop. You want to hear the bomb pass safely overhead and die away into the distance before the engine cuts out. In other words, you are hoping that it will fall on somebody else.

George Orwell, writing in Tribune, 30 June 1944

THE V1

Vergeltungswaffen they were called, weapons of revenge; revenge for the relentless bombing of German cities to which Orwell was referring, and a final attempt to wrest the war back from the Allies, now closing in from the west as well as the south and east. They eventually became known as V weapons, from the initial letter of the German name, but the public bestowed on the first of them oddly affectionate nicknames — bumble bomb, buzz bomb, doodlebug.

The V1s started arriving in the early hours of 13 June 1944, launched from sites in the Pas de Calais just a week after the Allies had landed in Normandy farther along the French coast. Harold Nicolson noted in his diary the following morning, 'There have been mysterious rocket planes falling in Kent, the thing is very hush at the moment.' To most people, maybe, but intelligence sources had revealed as far back as December 1943 that such weapons were in preparation, and many of those who needed to know had already been briefed.

These included RAF personnel involved in Operation Crossbow, a series of concentrated attacks on the launching sites and storage areas, among whom was Ken Dorman. He was told about them in the March and believes that he probably saw the very first pass overhead.

The land south of the Thames was very liberally sprayed with ack-ack units complete with searchlights and one of their functions was to assist any of our aircraft that appeared to be lost. This they did by lighting the searchlight in a vertical position as near as possible to the 'lost' aircraft, waggling the beam about 15 degrees to either side in the same vertical plane and then coming down to a horizontal position indicating the track that the pilot should follow. Any pilot so doing would either find a landing strip at the end of the beam or an intersection with another beam from a different ack-ack crew who would have gone through the same procedure as the first before gently lowering their beam to the required horizontal direction. And so on, until the distressed aircraft had been safely guided to a suitable landing strip.

After an op in the early hours of 13 June we were debriefed and went for 'supper' or 'breakfast', depending on how you look at these things. We were at Gravesend in tents, and on the way home from the mess tent, together with my Canadian pilot, I noticed a plane flying at about 2,000 ft with a light showing from under the fuselage. He was flying at about 150 mph and at first I took no other notice than to comment that the pilot couldn't have realised that he had left a light on somewhere. Then the searchlights started; each following the same procedure, but as the plane took no notice, the searchlight crews waggled their beams faster and faster. Bert and I realised at this moment that it was a V1 and couldn't respond to the energetic but clearly frustrated searchlight crews. Crew after crew persevered with devotion that caused us to burst out laughing I'm afraid ... Eventually the engine cut and I believe fell near the south bank of the Thames at Dartford. Like others I saw many bombs after that. They tended to fly faster; up to 250 mph.

Those whose job it was to identify and track all enemy aircraft also had to know about them. Hazel Williams, a plotter at RAF Tangmere, reports that the first person to receive a message about one of the new machines was expected to shout 'Diver, Diver, Diver' (the code-name for the pilotless planes).

One of our girls was plotting on RDF South (covering the area south of our ops table area), Suddenly she gave a startled look, faced the controller and said, 'Oh sir, I've got one of those Diver things!' completely forgetting that she was to shout it out three times. And so the first of the hundreds of V1s was plotted.

Finally it was necessary for some ARP personnel to be fore-warned. Stephen Woodcock's diary entry for 15 June reads:

About 2 in the morning a plane passed very low over the post making a great deal of noise. It considerably startled us in the warden's room as we had not heard a German plane so low before. Those in the porch said it was an extraordinary sight; in the low misty clouds it showed a bright glow at the tail. Searchlights were covering it and AA shells were bursting above it but it was too low for the guns to hit it. Trickett soon afterwards burst in to say he was sure it was a jet-propelled plane. These ... had been expected by wardens since the 4 May when a confidential description was issued: a small jet-propelled monoplane of 18 feet wingspan and 25 feet long, the forward end consisting of a bomb of 1 ton weight of blast type.

But for most people the VIs came as a complete surprise. Beryl Mullins says that

the first night they came over we didn't know that they were unmanned. Mother and I stood looking through one of the windows that still had glass in it at one of these things with flames gushing from the back of it and anti-aircraft all round it. 'Oh God,' said Mum, 'it's someone's son.'

And Brenda Rhodes, on ambulance duty that same night, remembers her colleague calling out, 'Look at this poor sod, his plane's alight and he'll come down' before the engine cut out and they heard the crash.

The reasons for concealing the existence of such weapons from the public are explained by Mr D. Silverman, then a Government censor at the Ministry of Information. This policy had been decided upon

firstly, so as not to inform the Germans that they had landed in any particular area, but more important it was a matter of public morale. A flying bomb might destroy a whole street and the people had no warning, you could not take shelter otherwise you would live in your shelter day and night. And to prevent this knowledge seeping through the country, even to comparatively safer areas, would have been devastating to the morale of the nation.

Even the Reverend Markham had not been informed.

Although I was supposed to be briefed with all the secret information about German weapons likely to be used on us, the V1s and V2s as they were called arrived unannounced on London as far as we wardens were concerned ... I take my hat off to the tight security that surrounded the possibility of flying bombs and rockets. Certainly the nerve of many people left in London would have been severely strained, if they had heard rumours of what the Home Office knew might happen.

It took three days, until the 16th, for Herbert Morrison to put an end to what rumours had been flying around since the arrival of the first V1s. 'When the engine of the pilotless aircraft stops and the light at the end of the machine is seen to go out,' he warned, 'it may mean that the explosion will soon follow, perhaps in five or 15 seconds.' That same day, as Cecil King reports, the V1s started arriving in London.

The great event of the day is the first full-dress pilotless-plane attack on London. We had just turned out our bedside reading lights at 11.30 when off went the warning, followed almost immediately by the roar of a plane apparently diving on Lincoln's Inn. However, it flew over, was then fired at, and eventually came down with a crash in Kentish Town. This was rapidly followed by two others, which were being fired at before they came within earshot of us.

Admiral Thomson, the Chief Censor, [said] this afternoon that in all, 104 of these planes arrived in this country last night and this morning. They seem to have fallen thickest in south-east London, but there are reports of 'incidents' in Sussex, in Windsor and in St Albans ... The Government at the moment is in two minds whether to keep on the present warning system or whether or not to shoot at the planes.

And next day he noted that

the pilotless planes are becoming tedious. We had three hours of them last night and several alerts this afternoon. I went to

ALLIED INVASION STARTING...

But while your divisions are fighting and dying on the coast of northern France the Germans are striking back at England with their

V NUMBER 1

Large parts of London and southern England have already been devastated or set ablaze. The conflagration can be seen for more than 150. miles. British officials had to admit that nothing can be done about that monstrous new weapon

V NUMBER 1

You soldiers know best what it means for your forces fighting in France when behind them their supply bases in England are being systematically smashed up.
Churchill may say it makes no difference to England's war effort. You know better. Perhaps you will now understand why the Germans are not laying so much stress on this secondary front in Italy.

But this doesn't mean that **YOU** are safe.

CHANCES ARE THAT IT WILL STILL GET YOU

AI - 077 - 6 - 44

V I propaganda pamphlet dropped over Britain by German planes.

How the allies are going to win the war!

What good are all your planes, warships and tanks against that new German weapon

V NUMBER 1

Are you still convinced that you are winning?

Your armchair strategists have always claimed that the new dreadful weapon is an invention of German "propaganda". But out of a clear sky it struck.

Since June 16th, London and southern England are being continuously blasted day and night by those mysterious flying meteors.

The entire British press was immediately muzzled by rigid censorship. What a nice job your politicians do have now in hiding the truth about the disastrous effect of

V NUMBER 1

BUT **YOU** will learn the truth just the same. You will also find out that Germany has just begun to play one of her trump cards.

How about V Number 2 to V Number X

AI - 079-6-44

Kentish Town to see the damage done by one of the first. It is quite considerable. It is curious that they have been saved up until now and have apparently not been used against our invasion ports.

He also referred to the way that the German propaganda machine was 'working flat out on the subject', a point taken up by Harold Nicolson in his diary entry for the 19th.

They are putting out stories of panic, of the evacuation of London, of vast explosions, of a pall hanging over the city which prevents the *Luftwaffe* from taking photographs. I see no signs of all this. My train arrives on time, there are buses running as usual, and I can see no difference in the streets.

The civilian population of Germany needed something to cheer them up. But to claim, as one German newspaper did, that 'for nearly 30 hours Southern England has been shaking as if in the grip of an earthquake' was rather an exaggeration. The main reaction in England was to say, 'Oh God here we go again. Let's hope it lands on someone else.'
During the rest of June about 100 V1s a day were launched, about half of them reaching their principal target, Greater London. Most of those which failed to get through were brought down over Kent or Sussex, which soon became known as 'Doodlebug Alley'. For those living under the flight-path the sight of V1s became a part of everyday life. Geoffrey Dormer, a Kent schoolboy at the time, remembers that on the very first day

it seemed they were coming over every five minutes until about eight in the morning, some cutting out and going down to explode. The black smoke goes up with a shape like a mushroom. The clouds were lit up by the flames and some were moving at a terrific rate. At school the next morning, some of the teachers appeared to be just as weary as we were with a sleepless night. I felt absolute shock — now there was something being launched at London for which we could not find an answer. Close to, the V1 looked just like a dagger and the flame extended far behind the plane — the flame white, not red. Once I saw a V1 going across the sky being chased by a Spitfire which never caught up with it — so the speed it could go was quite tremendous.

According to Roger Bowler, from West Wickham,

It wasn't long before days were punctuated by dives into the Morrison shelter as soon as the characteristic note of the V1 was heard. Our dog heard these long before we did and would rush up the garden barking madly. You knew it had passed over because everything in the house rattled at that point, presumably with the direct shock waves from the jet exhaust.

Many of them failed to pass over, of course, some landing at RAF Keston where Joyce Moore was then stationed.

I remember coming off duty one night with another Waaf and walking along the road to our billet, a distance of about half a mile I suppose. We had our tin hats on because we had received a red alert. I looked up and saw these brilliant flaming swords. They were literally queueing up above our heads — insidious things, quiet and sneaky. I hated them much more than bombs. I shuddered at the thought of the loss of life, pain and damage they would inflict — no one was about and everywhere was quiet, so we were surprised to suddenly come across a little old lady standing at her garden gate and shaking her fist at us crying, 'You're in the Air Force, why don't you get up there and do something about those things, instead of walking around here in those tin hats?' Of course we tried to placate her and explain that we were not all air crew in the RAF and that we were trying to do our little bit on the ground, in order to free more men for flying duties. I'm afraid the poor old darling was too scared to accept any explanation but we did manage to persuade her to go indoors.

The flight path converged on South London, and Beryl Mullins and her mother, while walking with their dog in Eltham Park,

would sometimes stand and look out over the skies of Kent and watch the 'doodlebugs' explode on the barrage balloons or see the Spitfires fly alongside them, tip their wings a trifle and the things would fall to the ground.

Mr R. Murphy from Whitechapel, out hop-picking in Kent, would often watch the fighters taking off to intercept the VIs.

Looking towards London we could see the start of the barrage balloon defence around London and the fighters would chase the V1s almost up to the balloons before turning away and leaving it to the guns to claim as many as possible before they reached London.

For the people of London the VIs rapidly became a familiar part of everyday life. On 23 June Cecil King noted that they had been arriving non-stop from 2 to 7 pm.

The men on the *Mirror* roof saw 16 robots come down over London in 12 minutes. Morrison made a speech in the House today rather making light of the little brutes, but I don't think the general public shares this opinion. Not only do we have long alerts at night, but continual ones in the daytime as well. Most of my office staff would prefer a straightforward blitz, even if the casualties were larger.

Since the bombs might arrive at any time, day or night, Londoners could never relax, a feeling summed up by Giles in a cartoon which showed people going about their business, each with a hugely enlarged ear permanently poised. George Beardmore wrote in his diary of 2 July:

Normal life is quite literally paralysed ... Housewives run to the shops and run back to hang round their homes and duck at almost any noise overhead. Such children as go to school are said to spend their time in the shelters, in which lessons of a sort have been organised. At the office, which is representative of most, I imagine, an unspoken trepidation is always present. Our ears are forever cocked for *that* drone.

Mrs Fisher, then working in an aircraft factory near Elstree, reports that on some days they

were having 'Take cover' warnings as many as 16 times in a nine-hour shift. Production fell well below what we were used to turn out. We had an emergency shop-steward's meeting to ask management to call a factory meeting. We asked the workers if they would be willing to work through the alerts if there was a look-out on the roof. At the sound of a klaxon everyone would race to the nearest shelter all down the middle of the factory and also underground ones; no one was more than a minute from cover. No one HAD to stay working if they were afraid. As the days went on, fewer and fewer people felt they must take cover and production went up to an even higher level than before the bombs. Our section had a sweepstake on how many times the siren would sound in the day. I think 16 times was the highest score; one of the canteen ladies thought we were dreadfully wicked to make a game out of it.

School life, too, was disrupted. Michael Borrow remembers that

the flying bombs caused havoc with the exams. Although the rest of the school went to the shelters, those of us taking exams had to sit it out. We were allowed to get on the floor under desks when a bomb came near but we were not allowed to talk to one another! Luckily we escaped only with glass and plaster coming in from one particular bomb.

Though the arrival of a flying bomb could prove a blessing, as John Cusdin recalls.

We were taking our school certificates in the school gymnasium. We could not hear the V1s approaching as the building, typical of those days, was built partially below ground with windows high up above the wall bars.

Towards the end of our history papers, probably within the last 10 or 15 minutes, suddenly there was an almighty explosion, and all the windows caved in. We all dived under our desks which were showered with glass. The sticky tape applied to the windows helped to minimise the size of the fragments. Within seconds the master who was supposed to be up on the roof to give us warning if a V-weapon approached, looked in at the door to see if we were all right.

In fact what had happened was that a V1 had landed in the school fields, and as it was lunch time and all the rest of the school had been sent home we were the only remaining pupils, so he had left his post.

In those days we did not have ball point pens — they were being used by fighter pilots to write on a pad on their knees, but had not appeared in civvy street. We used fountain pens or pens with nibs. In exams everybody had a bottle of ink in case your pen ran out. In the blast many had got blown over and spilt, and one boy had his paper completely soaked in ink. Not a word was visible! The investigator had to send in a full report on the incident, and due account had to be taken of the occurrence. The boy whose paper was obliterated had to be marked on his previous class work, and I think everybody was given at least a credit standard ... we were very lucky to be blasted through to such good results!

Children might have been pleased by such incidents, even exhilarated. But few adults were. By mid-July Cecil King was noting that

more and more people are leaving London and no one can say morale is high. When the internal warning went in the office a couple of weeks ago, most people took no notice, but now there is a general scuttle for shelter.

Odette Lesley, indeed, remembers 'feeling disgusted at

seeing grown men avidly pushing women and children aside to flee down the underground stations during daylight raids of doodlebugs'. But not everyone reacted in this way. As Squadron Leader Bullers puts it,

the feeling of personal helplessness against the arrival of the missiles very often became one of indifference with a measure of bravado — if the siren sounded while you were in the cinema, you stayed to see the film. If you heard a doodlebug you had one ear for the film, one ear for the motor. It was only when the motor stopped that you got down between the seats and willed it to go away. After the explosion you sat up and watched the film again.

Perhaps the best example of nonchalance in the face of the V I is that of Edith Sitwell during a poetry reading at the Churchill Club in the autumn of 1944. According to John Lehmann.

As Edith got up to read, and began with her poem about the air-raids in 1940, *Still Falls the Rain*, the warning whistle was sounded in the club. She had, I believe, never experienced a doodlebug raid before; but she seemed quite unperturbed. As she reached the passage

> Still falls the Rain
> Still falls the blood from the Starved Man's wounded Side
> He bears in His Heart all wounds—

the rattle grew to ominous proportions, and it was impossible not to think that the monstrous engine of destruction was poised directly overhead. Edith merely lifted her eyes to the ceiling for a moment, and, giving her voice a little more volume to counter the racket in the sky, read on. It was a magnificent performance, worthy of a British Admiral coolly dictating orders from the bridge in the middle of a fierce naval engagement. She held the whole audience in the grip of her discipline, the moral of her unspoken asseveration that poetry was more important than all the terrors that Hitler could launch against us. Not a soul moved, and at the end, when the doodlebug had exploded far away, the applause was dea ening.

It needed even greater courage to keep calm when personally affected, however, Grace Walton, a VAD nurse, had married a young Spitfire pilot in 1942. Their baby was born in March 1944 and when the VIs arrived she used to tuck him up in bed with her and pray.

One day my sister, myself and the baby were just about to go into the entrance of the flats when we heard the drone, and then when it stopped, we fell into the porchway of an old house and after the explosion picked ourselves up unhurt except for some minor cuts, but found the back of this house had gone and our flats almost demolished ... a few minutes earlier we would have been in there. We ran back to my mother's house — I left her with the baby, grabbed a gasmask and helmet and a large bag to go back and salvage. But as I was about to step on to the trolleybus, my husband was getting ready to get off the same trolleybus. I thought he was on ops over France and Belgium, but he had got a 48-hour pass and had a bottle of Vat 69 whisky under one arm and a Jerry helmet under the other. We just stared at one another on the step of the bus.

'What are YOU doing here? I thought you were overseas?'

'Where are YOU going?'

'Do make up your minds, are you getting on or off?'

So we both went together to where the flats were and they were carrying out the wounded. We drank the bottle of Vat 69, picked up a few bits of our house, watched the first set of barrage balloons go up and went quietly away hand in hand.

The wardens now found their roles changing, as we were told by Elizabeth Jane Howard, the novelist. She spent most of 1944 in London, sharing her grandparents' St John's Wood house with her young child, her cousin Audrey and a variety of friends. Since she often spent whole nights broadcasting on the BBC overseas services, she volunteered to be a warden, a job which could fit in with her rather irregular hours.

By then it made little sense to go out on patrol. As it was impossible to predict where and when the rockets might fall, she would stay at home waiting for a call from the post to go to wherever she was needed.

On this occasion we'd heard it cut out so we knew it must have landed not too far away. In fact it was in Mortimer Crescent, just round the corner from us. When we arrived quite a lot of people were already assembled there and someone from the post told me there was a very old lady living on the top floor who hadn't come down and I was to go up and get her.

Houses are rather like big ships. They might seem to be in a very bad way, but then there are bits of them that are quite untouched. From the outside of the house it was difficult to believe there was a staircase inside at all. It looked as though the bomb had fallen into the middle of it; roof caved in, windows out, bits of wall falling off. The staircase was intact, though they'd warned me it was no longer safe. I went pounding up it, to get it over with, and found the old lady in

Firemen helping to salvage furniture after a VI incident at Petherton Road, Canonbury, London N4.

her room in severe shock. I managed to talk her downstairs, moving rather more carefully. The whole place looked as though it was going to crumble any minute.

And at the bottom she turned around, this bulky old woman, and ran upstairs like a young girl. That's the sort of thing people could do when they were in shock. There was nothing for it but to go up after her, cursing and feeling very frightened. When I got to the top floor I found her with a photograph in her hand, of her son; and we came down again. Then I realised she'd been hit; her clothes were torn and she was bleeding. So I asked the head warden, as we lived so close, if I could take her home, look after her, give her a cup of tea. It was just a rather nasty cut on her shoulder, so we cleaned it up, talked to her for an hour or so, then they came and took her away.

This new type of war meant that anybody could be first to arrive at an incident. Off-duty firewoman Kathy Clayden was on her way to see her mother-in-law when she heard the sound of a VI.

The engine stopped and I could see it coming towards me. For a second I was rooted to the spot, then I dived into an alley. The bomb came down. I have never heard such a noise, the earth really moved and my ears were blocked. The dust was so thick I thought I had gone blind. The part of the wall where I was remained intact, but the rest was blown down. When I turned the corner to see if my mother-in-law was all right there was only half a house left. I was making my way quickly across the road when I heard a plaintive cry from a little old lady who was sitting on the kerb. I was going to ignore her pleas of 'Help me, please help me!' so that I could get to my mother-in-law, but I couldn't. She had been blown from the upstairs flat through the windows and blood was soaking her clothes. She was cut from one ear, under the chin to the other ear. I held the cut together and the blood was seeping through my fingers. It seemed ages that I was sitting with her. Luckily the fire appliance turned up and I called out to Bill and Len for a dressing. I heard afterwards that the dear old lady lived through her ordeal ... My mother-in-law, together with an aunt, had gone under the stairs which remained standing. Her first words to me were 'I can't find my stays.' Apparently she had been doing some exercises for a broken arm and she'd left them off. I said 'Never mind your stays, let's get you out of here!' But she refused to leave without them, so one of the firemen dug amongst the debris and found them under her pillow. I remember him waving them in the air with the long laces hanging, shouting 'I've got 'em.' I thought how amazing to lose your house and possessions and all she wanted was her corsets!

Michael Borrow, then a schoolboy, wrote the following account based on his wartime diaries.

25 June 1944 — We had had no warning since the all clear that morning, after a raid lasting from midnight on Saturday, but the sirens went again at 21.20 that evening. I was helping my father, who was an invalid, out of the front door on the way to the surface shelter in the side garden, when we heard the racket of a flying bomb motor, and saw it low down heading for us. It cut out and started to dive. We crouched down on to the doorstep as it exploded in Mount View about 400 metres away.

After the tiles, glass and dust had settled, I got my father into the shelter, jumped on my bike and got round to the site of the incident within six minutes or so of it landing. It had exploded in the back garden of the house on the corner of Mornington Road where a friend lived.

The area was absolutely still, no movement, nobody around and the roads completely carpeted with green leaves and blasted debris and earth and the cloying smell — which I still think of as a 'green smell' — from fallen leaves.

I found the first victim in the road, a man who was still breathing and I went on to the next, a woman in a summer dress, obviously dead. I noticed the 'greeny bronze' tinge of her body. People then began to arrive. Marion Neave, a girl of my own age, a St John Ambulance cadet, had cycled over from the other side of Chingford and immediately went into a nearby house and came out with blankets with which we covered the man and the woman. We then went over to a car. We saw that the driver was slumped over the wheel and as the vehicle was so blasted and shattered we assumed that he must be dead.

Marion went back to tend the man in the road, and I went off to search in the rubble of what had been the front room for my friend. Before long a rescue team arrived and I told them about the family that I thought was buried there and left the scene, after helping for a spell, feeling I could do no more. My mother reminded me that I had exams to do the next morning, so I went to bed in the shelter that night because the warning went again at 23.15 hrs.

Five days later Cecil King, though not the first on the scene, arrived at the Aldwych before the dust from a V1 had settled.

The whole area was carpeted with broken glass and bits of lamp standard. The bomb ... cut off its engine some distance away and came in on a silent glide. It fell on the roof of the Air Ministry, then into the road, where it went off, completely wrecking two buses, blasting the Air Ministry and the income tax part of Bush House, killing a horse, causing two fires, and so on ... I thought the casualties low, with a few cuts from flying glass and one Waaf being carried off on a stretcher. The reporter we sent down, however, said he saw about 40 corpses lined up — most of them killed in the street (it was about 2.15 pm), but some of them in the Air Ministry, particularly the ground floor. I ran from Lincoln's Inn, and yet by the time I arrived the fire brigade and ambulances were there, bleeding girls in ragged trousers were being got down from the first floor of Bush House, a trouserless man was taking refuge in the Air Ministry, the Waaf was being pushed into her ambulance, and others with slight cuts were being helped away.

The woman in the greengrocer's made the best comment: 'Hitler'll get hisself disliked if he goes on like this!'

Removing casualties to the Clearing Station after the VI incident at the Aldwych on 30 June 1944.

The stories of those who survived direct hits are particularly graphic. Here are three, starting with that of Kathleen Mannerings from Kent who was only four years old when it happened.

One afternoon I was standing at the back door of the cottage when I called my mother to 'come and see a plane on fire'. I was suddenly grabbed by the arm along with my six-month-old baby brother and we were pushed under my Mum's iron double bed. I remember crying that I wanted my bike — apparently my pride and joy — the next thing I knew we were walking amongst brick rubble and running water. The cottage had totally collapsed ... Next we were put into an ambulance because Mum had a nasty cut on her leg. At the hospital a nurse tried to feed me bread and milk which I hate to this very day. We were then taken to stay with the local policeman. The next day Mum took us to see the remains of the cottage where all that could be seen was the big range under which our cat had been found alive! My Mum says I saved our lives as she had not heard the doodlebug ... Eventually we were rehoused in a wooden bungalow opposite the original cottage. After this experience I remember crying every time the warning sirens went off and for years I had dreams of being chased by German soldiers in uniform wearing those distinctive helmets.

Len Milford was a Welsh Guardsman training at Sandown Racecourse in Esher before being posted to his battalion.

Our quarters were the horse stables — cleaned out and whitewashed, with three double-tiered bunks installed and straw mattresses added — one box each for our private kit! Up above the quarters was a small copse where we used to practise digging trenches. We did not know what a favour we were doing for ourselves because when the doodlebugs started to arrive, we were running for these trenches all the time ... at night all you could see was hundreds of pairs of white trunks running like mad.

In June, 1944, we were to hold our sports day at Imber Court some two miles from camp. A new intake of young officers had just arrived fresh from Sandhurst. There were a lot of American servicemen with us. The weather was beautiful and the sports got off to its usual style ... I was in the grandstand watching and waiting my turn to compete, when we heard the sound ... suddenly the engine stopped and we all looked up and saw this thing right above us and we were all aware at once that it was meant for us. We immediately started to run. I, for some reason, ran to the centre of the field. I had nowhere to go except to throw myself on to the floor as it exploded. Next thing I remember was that I laid there in pain not knowing what had happened. I could move around, so I realised I was OK. But when I looked around it was carnage everywhere, bodies minus flesh, dead bodies, able bodies like myself who were able to walk, the uninjured desperately trying to help those, some past it, who were critically injured. I remember my CSM (Woolly Bear) just lying there, a cigarette in his mouth, so badly injured that I was surprised that he would, did live. A squaddie of mine, Gibbs, who had some knowledge of first aid, rushed from one to another with first aid from our field packs, working like three men, never stopping. The CSM pushed aside help so that others might be saved. I have thought later that he did not expect to recover at the time ... when I had time to think it over, people around the explosion and those further away than myself were either dead or seriously injured — it was as though the force of the blast blew, lifted over and then levelled out. I was one of the lucky ones.

My injuries were minor, dislocated arm and shoulder and shock. I was taken in an ambulance to Chertsey Hospital, and when I heard a voice from another ward shouting 'That nurse there, pull your chin in, put your shoulders back and swing your arms' I knew then that our CSM was very much alive.

Val Ranken was 14 when the family house in Balham was hit. He wrote the story down in 1946, with the details still quite fresh in his mind.

On the morning of 27 July 1944, I decided to overhaul my bicycle while my mother was visiting my aunt at Euston. I had on my oldest shirt and a pair of old flannel trousers covered in bicycle oil, French chalk, rubber solution and the like. When the air-raid siren sounded at 4 pm I was in the front room, but when I heard the V1's engine cut right overhead, I rushed to the Morrison in the second bedroom, my Kerry Blue terrier at my heels. By the fireplace Mum had stood some inch-thick planks to give some protection against blast and flying glass. As I dived into the Morrison, the flying bomb hit the front corner of the house, 40 feet away. As I came to I heard my puppy whining. He usually waited until I was in the Morrison, then followed — but there hadn't been time. In the dark I could feel only rubble covering him, but I couldn't move my legs. I wasn't in pain, but a large block of bricks — probably from the chimney — had bounced into the Morrison and dropped between my legs, pinning my trouser-legs to the floor. I hacked at the trousers with my Scout knife until I was free to move. I dug with my hands and freed my puppy. I could see through the dust cloud that the blast had ripped the planks to shreds. I clambered up and up, when suddenly the ground gave way beneath me and I landed almost on top of the Civil Defence worker. I had fallen over the edge of the next door neighbour's house — only now this was only a few feet above the pile of rubble that had once been a double-fronted house.

I remember, the day after, going to the rest centre in Balham and being given some clothing, sent from America, from a long line of tables piled high with clothes. Normally, one pair of trousers was given to the 'bombed out'; I was given two pairs, the lady was horrified at the sight of those I was wearing! I also received a couple of coats and a jacket. (Whenever I wore these clothes I always felt a bit odd — the style and cut were just different from ours.)

My puppy, with one flank all singed brown by the blast, had been handed over to the PDSA — but it died from shock and effects of the blast in a day or two. We had to go to Wandsworth Town Hall and produce our identity cards to obtain a special permit to buy an alarm clock. We hunted around for the best part of a week before we eventually found

Val Ranken, taken a few days after the V1 incident at his house in Fontenoy Road, Balham, on 27 July 1944 at 4.20 pm.

one in a little shop in Westminster on the opposite side of the road to Big Ben.

We slept in the deep shelter at Clapham South every night for the next two or three months, then we had temporary use of another maisonette in the same square in Bedford Hill. The window frames at the back had been blown in, and the ceilings brought down by the same doodle-bug, but we worked hard and soon had it temporarily repaired and a home made with bits and pieces salvaged from our old home, to make it look nice for Dad when he returned. But he didn't return. He died in India on active service, 23 Oct 1944. To lose her home and husband within the space of three months was almost too much for my Mum to bear.

South London, where Val lived, was now taking the brunt of things. William Downing was part of a Pioneer Corps unit, billeted at Purley, whose job was to patch up the affected houses, a mammoth task when up to 20,000 were being damaged a day.

Bombs were dropping all around us. Croydon had had 170 flying bombs, and there was one big disaster when a V1 dropped on Woolworth's at Streatham and killed 200. There was no warning and the shop was full — also a Woolworth's at Catford was hit with loss of life. We had our truck and we went each day to where a V1 dropped — we put tiles back on the roof, black-out up to the windows, putting ceilings back, plasterboard up, windows in — we were supervised by the engineers, the damage was terrific. We were kept busy going out on Sundays working, but we were allowed one day a week off — all leave was stopped.

By the end of August nearly 9,000 V1s had been launched from ground sites, all but a handful directed at London. But during July the Germans adopted a new strategy. John Teale, then in the Royal Engineers, remembers the night he experienced it at first hand.

I was heading back to barracks in Halifax when I suddenly

thought I was having a nightmare. Either that was a doodlebug I was hearing or one of my mates had the weirdest one-lunger motor bike I ever heard. Oh oh, it was the former. Apparently it had been brought under the belly of a Heinkel and let go over Yorkshire. It went down west of Halifax. It really put the wind up me though. Now there was no such thing as a safe haven apparently.

There were two reasons for the introduction of air-launched VIs; to start with, the ground-sites were rapidly being overrun as the Allies moved eastwards through France; in addition, the use of specially modified Heinkels and Junkers greatly extended the range of the weapons, while making the direction of approach less predictable. The main burden of defence against the new type of attack fell, once more, on Anti-Aircraft Command, and it is perhaps the moment to give them credit for their role in the fight against the robot planes.

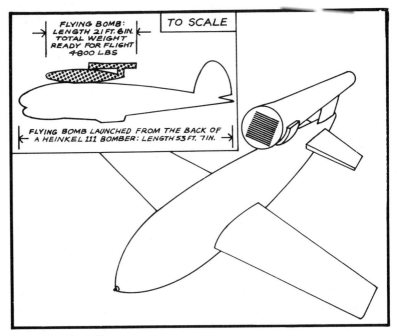

An air-launched VI.

General Frederick Pile, Commander-in-Chief of AA Command, had been warned in late 1943 that the Germans might soon have the capability of launching pilotless aircraft against Britain, possibly at the rate of 200 an hour. The army and RAF promptly worked out a plan for the protection of London based on three main lines of defence: firstly, planes from Fighter Command, with searchlight support at night; the second line would be formed by AA batteries south of the North Downs; finally, the balloon barrage would be intensified. In practice, when the VIs arrived, it proved difficult for the services to act in a coordinated manner. On one occasion Balloon Command bagged an area where AA Command had planned to site their 40-mm Bofors guns. And fighters, whose speed barely exceeded that of the VIs, often had to break off the chase just before making the kill in order not to be fired on by their own side.

By the end of June there were 376 heavy and 576 40-mm guns forming a belt stretching from Maidstone to East Grinstead, with a further 560 light guns on the coast, manned by the RAF Regiment. But the success rate was very low at that time, between 9 and 13 per cent. There was a series of problems concerning the siting of radar, and intelligence sources had been inaccurate in predicting the height at which the pilotless planes would be flying. At this period, as General Pile explained,

the bomb, a very small target, flew at a high speed and at a height which was most difficult of all to deal with; it was just too high for effective light anti-aircraft fire and too low for easy engagement by the heavy guns.

Nor were the fighter planes particularly successful at preventing the VIs from getting through. When they did so it was in a pretty dramatic way, however, and the RAF managed to have the details in the papers the following day. That the army was losing the PR war is clear, both from contemporary reports and from the accounts we have received from people looking back 50 years: civilians and service personnel alike mention having seen or read about fighter planes shooting the buzz-bombs down or sending them off-course with a nonchalant flip of the wing; few (if not in the army) praise the role of the ack-ack.

On 13 July questions were asked in the House of Commons about the inefficiency of the AA. People wanted to know, moreover, why there were no London-based guns firing (in spite of the fact that a downed VI was just as dangerous as one landing in the normal manner). But doubts about the role of the guns soon became a thing of the past. There were two reasons for this. Firstly, the entire AA belt moved down to the south coast (except for a number of units sent to give protection against any VIs coming up the Thames Estuary). There were now four lines of defence: fighters over the Channel; the AA firing 10,000 yards out to sea; more fighters behind the guns; then the balloons. This, in General Pile's words,

would give the fighters plenty of room for interception over the Channel and plenty of room for interception behind the guns, where they would be acting as wicket-keepers, with the balloons away in the distance as long-stops.

The problems of separating spheres of action were thus greatly reduced. But even more impressive was the ever increasing efficiency of the gunners. They had finally received the new American SCR 584 radar system Pile had been asking for since February and this, in conjunction with the new BTL predictor, practically eliminated the possibility of human error in gun laying. At about the same time supplies of new 'proximity fuse' shells began to arrive. These, as their name implies, exploded when close to the target. True, they were triggered by the odd bird, even the occasional cloud, but at least few VIs escaped them. And as the crews became used to the new equipment their rate of destroying those targets entering the gunbelt mounted steeply, practically on a daily basis. The figures for the five weeks following the move south are 17 per cent, 24 per cent, 27 per cent, 40 per cent and 55 per cent; by the end of August it had reached 74 per cent and on one day that month only four out of 96 VIs reached Greater London.

This very success rate posed a danger for those within the vicinity of the gun-sites. Mr E.J. Hamlen, a former RA officer, was off-duty one day

watching the lads popping off at a V1, when they 'winged' it, it turned over in a loop and hurtled straight for us. I knew there was a slit-trench some 40 yards away and I always said I broke the Olympic record in making that trench. As I slid into it feet first, the thing exploded, we were bombarded with clods of earth and sundry rubbish. A deal of material damage was caused, but, thank Heaven, we had no casualties and were back in action within the hour.

The gunners, exhilarated by their high success rate, could take this kind of thing in their stride; those living near the gun-sites were less delighted. In an early (and literal) application of the 'not in my backyard' principle the people of the South Coast were often angry at the fact that their days and nights were shattered by the noise of guns which, when accurately fired, would bring crashing down on them VIs safely heading towards London. The people of Hastings were particularly vocal in expressing their annoyance. 'Their hostility was palpable', we were told by Evelyn Hambley, then an officer with a mixed AA regiment.

Some local dignitaries asked us not to fire at night because of the disturbance it caused; and the fact that we were trying to save Londoners' lives meant little to them. They were not alone in suffering from exhaustion, but at least we got our priorities right and continued the work required of us.

The people of the South Coast did not have to endure their discomfort and danger much longer, however. With the allied forces capturing the launch-sites in the Pas De Calais, the final VI from France arrived on I September. Attacks from elsewhere continued for a while, but on a much diminished scale and spread over a wider area. The danger now came from a new and more deadly source; for on 8

September, from a site in still-occupied Holland, the first V2 rocket sped towards London.

THE V2

People are complaining of the sudden unexpected wallop with which these things go off. 'It wouldn't be so bad if you got a bit of warning' is the usual formula. There is even a tendency to talk nostalgically of the days of the V1, the good old doodlebug did at least give you time to get under the table, etc., etc. Whereas, in fact, when the doodle-bugs were actually dropping, the usual subject of complaint was the uncomfortable waiting period before they went off. Some people are never satisfied.

George Orwell, 1 December 1944

The rockets, like the flying bombs, had been expected. General Pile, in fact, knew of the V2 threat before hearing of the VI, while Harold Nicolson had a rather gloomy conversation on 21 June 1944 with Florence Horsbrugh, Parliamentary Secretary at the Ministry of Health, who told him

that there is no doubt that Hitler's secret weapon, unless we can control it soon, will make heavy inroads on our nerves. People are unable to sleep, and the continuity of the bombing is very trying. What is more distressing is that other, and perhaps more serious, secret weapons are about to be launched. I fear we are in for a bad two months.

The Government, as usual, tried to keep the truth from the people as long as possible. George Beardmore, as a warden, had been briefed at a meeting in early August when his area controller

enlarged on the kind of incident we might expect in the future from rocket-bombs, of which he had been forewarned by Whitehall. He envisaged 45 acres of devastation.

But he was able to note in his diary, 12 days after the first landed in West London, that there was still

no word yet from any source about the mysterious bangs we have been hearing, not preceded by the familiar droning in the sky. The first of the explosions [was] followed by a rumour that it was a Home Guard arms-dump blowing up. Also a rumour that a plane had crashed with its bomb-load.

Several people report hearing the explosions on that first day. Cecil King, who had noted on 1 August that they were promised the rocket 'at almost any minute', was sitting at an open window in the Royal Institution when there was a loud explosion.

It sounded as if one of the Hyde Park guns had gone off. There was no follow-up: most people thought it was a clap of thunder. However I looked into the office in the evening and learned that it was indeed V2. There had been two explosions caused apparently by rocket shells, one in Epping and one at Chiswick. The former did no damage; the latter destroyed six houses, seriously damaged 50, and killed four people. There was little blast, but the explosion, unlike those of a V1, made a crater 15 feet deep and 50 feet across. Any mention of the explosion is rigidly censored, and so far we have had no others.

This must have been the Chiswick rocket. Michael Borrow, further east, heard the other one.

Keith Foster and I were leaning on our bicycles on the high ground by the Royal Forest Hotel looking out over Epping Forest, when we heard a loud explosion and saw a column of smoke rising over the trees in the direction of Epping town. We agreed we were hearing and seeing something quite different — particularly the secondary roar afterwards. This sounded strange to our well-tuned ears and we took it for granted it was a new toy that was being used against us.

Many people record having been told that the Chiswick explosion was due to a gas main going up, but as Hilda Mason says, 'Of course the truth will out. After all, with all those "gas mains" explosions there wouldn't be much gas left!' In fact the 'gas' stories became a bit of a sick joke. Trixie Duke reports that Ilford was badly hit by V2s.

At 12 noon most days the centre of the town was empty as so many went off at that time of day. It was eerie — no public, only public services. We would shrug our shoulders and say 'another gasometer has gone up'. We lost the cinema, theatre, station and many, many homes.

The V1s had followed a low, shallow trajectory, passing over the coast at about 250 mph, increasing to a maximum of 400 mph. Their distinctive noise betrayed their presence, and the ensuing silence warned people of danger. There was often time to take cover, to run or even stroll away from them. The rockets, by contrast, gave no warning. They travelled at above 3,500 mph (five times the speed of sound), climbed to over 300,000 feet, then landed almost vertically. In Squadron Leader Bullers' words:

As the weapons arrived unannounced there was only one rule: if you heard the explosion you were probably still alive — in deep shock maybe, if it went off near you, but still alive. People had to continue with their daily life, when without warning there would be an explosion, flying glass if you were unlucky to be near enough, and perhaps a crater as big as a bowling green capable of swallowing a house.

You might just, at the top of their trajectory, see a double puff of vapour as they re-entered the atmosphere, but this was only a matter of seconds before impact. No weapons then in existence could harm them. As Hilda Mason confirms, there was nothing that the ack-ack batteries could do.

The only defence against the V2s was to find out where they came from and destroy the base. We played a very small part

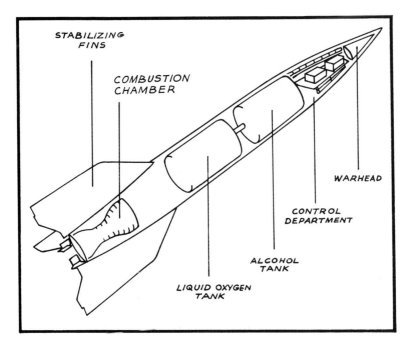

STABILIZING
FINS

COMBUSTION
CHAMBER

WARHEAD

CONTROL
DEPARTMENT

ALCOHOL
TANK

LIQUID OXYGEN
TANK

The V2.

in this by helping to track their flights. They were very fast, but if our radar and other instruments could 'place' them just for 20 seconds then, by marrying up reports from those units taking part, a little indication could be gained of the direction from which they had come.

Many of the V2s were destroyed on the ground or in storage by Allied bombers, which meant that the Germans could send over no more than half a dozen a day. This was fortunate indeed since, had they been arriving at the same rate as the V1s, the damage would have been unbearable. Those that did land on built-up areas caused people, animals, cars, buses, buildings, simply to vanish. Empty coffins were buried since there was nothing left to put in them.

The worst V2 incident took place at New Cross, in South London, on 25 November. It was a Saturday, which meant that the shops were crowded with people, including June Gaida.

I was going shopping for my mother, and suddenly there was a blinding flash of light, and a roaring, rushing sound and I was lifted off my feet, and all around me was this terrible noise, this din, beating against my eardrums. I fell to the ground. I curled myself up into a ball to protect myself and I tried to scream, but I couldn't because there was no air. When I picked myself up after the noise had faded a bit, I was coated in brick dust and splinters of glass, and things were still falling out of the sky, then there were bricks and bits of masonry, bits of things and bits of people. I walked towards Woolworth's. I remember seeing a horse's head laying in the gutter, and further on there was a pramhood all twisted and bent and a little baby's hand, still in its woolly sleeve. Outside the pub there was a bus that had just been concertinaed, people were just sitting inside, rows and rows of people covered in dust and they were all dead. When I looked towards where Woolworth's had been, it was just a huge empty open space.

Charlie Draper went there to help clean up.

The damage, oh it was vast. There were nearly 200 people killed and roads were blocked off for about 200–300 yards each way. I think it was about 12 shops that disappeared, including the whole of Woolworth's shop.

[People] were upset and cracking up and saying oh this is the sixth time this has happened you know, I don't think I'll ever start again, I've had enough. But when you was on the sites, when you see the damage the rocket done, they was digging people out, oh for days after and finding bodies on the roofs all way round the area, within half a mile they were still finding bodies, two or three days after the incident.

It was a time of something approaching despair, with the feeling of impending victory overshadowed by the daily tragedies. Those fighting in Europe were, in one soldier's

words, 'more worried about their relatives back home than the Huns at the front'. Those dealing with the aftermath of the bombs were more tired than ever before. For Brenda Rhodes, still driving her ambulance to pick up the shattered bodies, there was

little time now to think of going to concerts and theatres and dances. We were busy all the time — staying on duty as long as was needed, falling asleep standing up. Meals taken between rushing about on duty and sleeping. For this period of the war seemed to everyone to be the worst.

George Beardmore felt the same, as his diary entry for 28 January 1945 confirms.

We arc — all of us, at the office, in the shops, and at home — weary of the war and its effects. Intense cold has arrived (my feet at this moment are resting on a hot-water bottle and the panes are frosted over) with snow, ice, hail and sudden clashes of thunder that go to make the illusion that we are on the Russian front. The V2 rockets also help the illusion. Four mornings in succession they have woken us up — not bangs so much as prodigious muffled explosions which resound in all quarters at once, reverberating for about ten seconds.

But the home front was not to suffer much longer. As the first signs of spring came to Britain the last twitchings of aggression from Germany gradually became stilled. On 4 March the *Luftwaffe* made a final, futile raid; on 27 March the last V2 landed in Kent, followed, on the 29th, by the last of the VIs. The sirens, in Angus Calder's words, 'had lost their occupation'.

The tally of casualties, since the sirens had first sounded in September 1939, is fairly easy to establish. The bombers and air-launched VIs caused about 52,000 deaths and 63,000 serious injuries. The ground-launched VIs, the V2s and long-range guns based on the French coast were responsible for a further 8,500 and 23,000 respectively. The chances of being killed by attack from the air were about 1 in 800 for citizens of the United Kingdom generally, 1 in 160 for Londoners.

But while we are pondering these sad figures we should perhaps add a few more to the list: worldwide dead, 55 million; Soviet troops dead, 13½ million; Soviet civilians, nearly 8 million; Chinese civilians, 10 million; Polish civilians, over 5 million; German civilians, nearly 4 million, including perhaps 100,000 — who knows — in Dresden alone on the night of 14 February 1945.

We have not cited these statistics to diminish the importance of the suffering endured by the civilian population of the United Kingdom but to underline the extent to which others — allies and enemies alike — shared that suffering. And at this time, some 50 years after the events described and recalled in this book, it is perhaps appropriate to reaffirm our determination that it should never happen again.

We started with a poem of grim foreboding, looking ahead to the call of the 'evil sirens' and the arrival of the 'impartial bombs'. Let us end on a note of reconciliation, using words spoken in German from the Kreuzkirche in Dresden during the service linking that city with Coventry on the fiftieth anniversary of the outbreak of war between the two countries.

All that kills abundant living,
Let it from the earth be banned:
Pride of status, race or schooling,
Dogmas that obscure our plan.
In our common quest for justice
May we hallow life's brief span.

Coventry, spring 1944. Looking down into the roofless shell of the blitzed Cathedral from the west tower. Debris has been cleared from the central nave and a cross made of charred roof beams, roughly bound together, stands on the site of the high altar.

GLOSSARY AND ABBREVIATIONS

AA Anti-Aircraft (also known as 'Ack Ack'). Many AA batteries were 'mixed', with women responsible for the 'gun-laying' (i.e. the aiming) and men for the actual firing. Batteries were composed either of 'Heavy' guns, mainly 3.7 inch and 4.5 inch, or 'Light' guns, notably the 40mm Bofors. Extra heavy 5.25 twin naval guns were also used at times, and multi-barrelled rockets were later added. (*See also* 'searchlights', also operated by AA Command.)

AFS Auxiliary Fire Service (became part of the National Fire Service in 1941).

Alert The 'Alert' warned that a raid was imminent, and was indicated by a siren making a rising and falling wail for two minutes.

All clear The 'All clear' was a steady two-minute blast on a siren which signified the end of a raid. (It was originally to be called the 'Raiders Passing' signal, but everyone took to calling it the 'All clear', despite the fact that this term was meant to indicate that all the gas had been cleared following a gas attack.)

Anderson shelters Shelters half-buried in private gardens. Excellent protection against blast, though not against a direct hit.

ARP Air Raid Precautions.

ATS Auxiliary Territorial Service. The women's equivalent of the army. Women in the auxiliary forces were at first confined to support roles (clerks, cooks etc.) but eventually took on anything from operating and mending radar equipment to field work behind enemy lines. (*See also* WRNS, FANY and WAAF.)

Baedeker raids These were the raids on beautiful towns and cities of little or no strategic importance. The name came from the well-known 'Baedeker' guide books.

Barrage balloons Huge balloons tethered to steel cables and put into the sky when raiders were expected, forcing the bombers to fly high in the hope that accurate bombing would be impossible. Sometimes known as 'blimps'.

Battle of Britain The period in the summer of 1940 when the German Air Force was trying to inflict maximum damage in preparation for the invasion of Britain.

BD Bomb Disposal.

Blast People, unless safely sheltered, were more likely to be injured or killed by blast — the powerful wind generated by an explosion — than by the explosion itself.

Blitz From the German word *Blitzkrieg*, which literally meant 'lightning war'. By this they meant a quick decisive attack in which bombers and fighter-bombers would cow the population so that the ground forces would have an easy victory.

Bofors guns *See* AA.

Bombs See separate entries for butterfly bombs, delayed action bombs, HE, and incendiaries.

Bombers The main German bombers were various models of Heinkel (HE), Junkers (Ju) and Dornier (Do). (The main escorting fighter plane was the Messerschmitt (Me) 109 or 110). Focke Wulf 190's were later introduced as fighter-bombers. (Note that German bombers could be distinguished by the sound of their unsynchronised engines — a ploy to make radar detection less easy.)

Butterfly bombs Small, innocent-looking, anti-personnel bombs, which exploded when stepped on or handled.

CD Civil defence (i.e. the wardens, fire service etc.).

Delayed action bombs Bombs set to go off at a pre-selected time after being dropped.

Diver Code-name for the operation against the VI.

FANY First Aid Nursing Yeomanry. An organisation of women volunteers formed early this century. During World War II, they specialised in two areas: motor transport and Special Operations.

FAP First Aid Post.

Fighters The main RAF fighter aircraft were the Spitfire and the Hurricane; the main German fighter was the Messerschmitt.

Flak Anti-aircraft fire.

Flares These were dropped at the start of a raid to provide bright lighting for the next bombers to aim by.

FW Focke Wulf (*see* bombers).

Gas masks Issued to everyone (even babies) because of the fear of attack by poison gas. Sometimes referred to as respirators.

HE High explosive. HE bombs were dropped once the incendiaries had caused enough fires to light up the target well.

Home Guard Originally called the Local Defence Volunteers, this was an organisation of people (mainly men) who were too old or otherwise unfitted for the services yet who wished to do their best in the event of an enemy invasion.

Incendiaries Bombs dropped at the start of a raid in order to start up a series of fires so that later waves of bombers could easily see the target area. Later ones were often fitted with explosive charges intended to harm those dealing with them. Incendiaries were normally dropped in containers of various sizes, known as bread baskets.

Incident An incident was anything which required the intervention of the civil defence. The word 'occurrence' was sometimes used in the same sense.

Land mines Similar to sea mines, these were dropped by

parachute. Not only were they silent, but they landed so gently that the blast was not partially absorbed by impact with the ground, as was the case with HE bombs. AKA 'parachute bombs'.

LCC London County Council.

LFB London Fire Brigade.

Luftwaffe German Air Force (literally 'air weapon').

Mass observation An organisation set up before the war to report, through observation rather than direct questioning, what people were saying and how they were acting. MO's reports are an invaluable source of information about, for example, the immediate reactions of people to the blitz.

Morrison shelters Cage-like shelters erected inside the home. Available from 1941 and named after Herbert Morrison, the Minister for Home Security.

NAAFI Navy, Army & Air Force Institutes. Operated canteens for the forces at home and abroad.

NCO Non-commissioned officer.

NFS National Fire Service (*see* AFS).

Parachute bombs *See* land mines.

RA Royal Artillery.

Radar Radar — originally 'Radio-location' — was first used on ground sites to spot approaching aircraft (and ships). Airborne radar was a later development. AA Command used it increasingly both to help with gun-laying and with searchlights.

RAF Royal Air Force (divided into various 'Commands', including Fighter and Bomber Commands).

RASC Royal Army Service Corps.

Refuges General term for public shelters.

Rest centres Centres where people bombed out of their homes were directed to.

Sealion Operation Sealion (*SeeLöwe*) was the code-name for the planned German invasion of Britain.

Searchlights Powerful lights intended to illuminate (and possibly dazzle) enemy planes. They also provided homer beams to show friendly planes, when damaged, the way to the nearest landing site.

Shrapnel The popular name for splinters of metal from exploded bombs or — more commonly — AA shells.

SOE Special Operations Executive.

Starfish sites Decoy sites situated near major target areas. Highly combustible materials would be set alight at the start of a raid to lure the bombers away from the real target.

Stick A stick of bombs was a number dropping in quick succession.

Stirrup pump Simple pump found in many homes. Adequate for putting out minor fires.

Strafing Machine-gunning people on the ground from the air (from German *strafen* — to punish).

Tip-and-run raids Raids involving few aircraft (often just one), aimed at sapping civilian morale while providing the German press with evidence that attacks were continuing on Britain at a time when much of the *Luftwaffe* was in action on the Eastern Front.

UXB Unexploded bomb.

V weapons From the German *Vergeltungswaffen*: revenge or retaliation weapons. The VI, a pilotless bomb, was launched either from a ground site or from a plane. The V2 was a rocket travelling at five times the speed of sound.

VAD Voluntary Aid Detachment (nursing).

WAAF Women's Auxiliary Air Force.

WRNS Women's Royal Naval Service, members of which were familiarly known as 'wrens'.

WVS Women's Voluntary Service.

FURTHER READING

The two best general books on the Home Front are *The People's War* by Angus Calder (Jonathan Cape, 1969; Granada, 1971) and *How We Lived Then* by Norman Longmate (Hutchinson, 1971; Arrow, 1973). Calder relies mainly on printed sources, Longmate on a great number of informants from the general public. Both contain extensive bibliographies. (Longmate has also written two books not consulted by us, *The Bombers* and *The Doodlebugs*.)

Books dealing more specifically with the blitz include *London at War* by Joanna Mack and Steve Humphries (Sidgwick & Jackson, 1985); *Blitz on Britain* by Alfred Price (Ian Allan, 1977); *Living Through the Blitz* by Tom Harrisson (Collins, 1976). And for those who want to know where every single bomb and V weapon fell (or so it seems), there is the mammoth work *The Blitz Then and Now* edited by Winston Ramsey and published in three volumes (Battle of Britain Prints International, 1987, 1988, 1990).

For literary life during the war see Chapter 8 of Calder's book and *Under Siege: Literary Life in London 1939-1945* by Robert Hewison (Weidenfeld & Nicolson, 1977; Methuen, 1988). Two books by Andrew Sinclair also sound interesting: *War Like a Wasp: The Lost Decade of the Forties* and *The War Decade: An Anthology of the 1940s* (both Hamish Hamilton, 1989).

Two specialised accounts we have found of particular interest are *Firemen at War* by Neil Wallington (David & Charles, 1981) and *Ack-Ack* by General Sir Frederick Pile (George G. Harrap, 1949).

Less easy to obtain are various HMSO pamphlets produced during the war, notably *Front Line 1940–1941* (1942) and *Roof Over Britain: The Official Story of the A.A. Defences 1939-1942* (1943).

It is also worth looking out for the very large number of books or pamphlets dealing with specific towns or areas, many dating from the war, with titles such as *Bombs on Belfast*, *Coventry Under Fire*, *Bristol Under Blitz*, etc.

And most of the books from which we quote extracts will be worth reading in full.

More books from Optima

Women in Wartime by Jane Waller and
Michael Vaughan-Rees
ISBN 0 356 12887 3
Price (UK only) £9.95

'... a fascinating look at the unsung heroes of the Second
World War.'

Woman's Journal

'A fascinating book ... makes nostalgic and enlightening
reading.'

Woman's Weekly

'A fascinating anthology ...'

Sue Arnold in *The Observer*

The unsung heroines of the Second World War were the
women who were left behind. Isolated from the action,
fearful for the lives of their menfolk and hopeful for a future
at peace, they adapted well to a rapidly changing world.

This book provides a full commentary on home life during
those wartime years. Drawing on an unrivalled collection of
contemporary women's magazines, the authors have
extracted features, fashion tips, morale-boosting stories,
mottoes and recipes to present a panoramic view of
women's shifting roles.

Emotional reactions, the practicalities of working and
maintaining a home, relationships with Allied troops and, of
course, love, leisure and fashion are all included, together
with advertisements and readers' letters from the war years.
As never before, the portrait that emerges of women in
wartime is one of immense courage, good humour and
ingenuity.

All Optima books are available at your bookshop or news-agent, or can be ordered from the following address:

Optima, Cash Sales Department,
PO Box 11, Falmouth, Cornwall TR10 9EN

Please send cheque or postal order (no currency), and allow 60p for postage and packing for the first book, plus 25p for the second book and 15p for each additional book ordered up to a maximum charge of £1.90 in the U.K.

Customers in Eire and BFPO please allow 60p for the first book, 25p for the second book plus 15p per copy for the next 7 books, thereafter 9p per book.

Overseas customers please allow £1.25 for postage and packing for the first book and 28p per copy for each additional book.